I Did It OTWAY

Regrets, I've Had a Few!

KLG Press

Published in 2010 by Karen Lawrence Glass
Copyright © 2010 John Otway

Printed in the UK by **CPI William Clowes, Beccles NR34 7TL**

Edited by Nick Creasy
Art Direction, design and editing by John Haxby
Picture research by Karen Lawrence
Every effort has been made to trace the copyright holders
of the photographs in this book but one or two were
unreachable. We would be grateful if the photographers
concerned would contact us.

ISBN 978-0-9564343-1-9

AUTHOR'S NOTE

It is over a year since I posted the first draft of this book to Nick Creasy and I have been religiously doing the corrections he has sent me since then, to turn this into a piece of readable English.

Meanwhile John Haxby, my designer, and Karen Lawrence, my publisher, have spent a similar period going through the many thousands of pictures of myself I have collected over the past twenty years (one of the major problems they had was that I kept finding more).

It cannot have been easy for any of them – they deserve my thanks.

John Otway, March 2010

This book is a journey.
I would like to dedicate it to the roadies
who safely did all the miles, especially
Jon Padget, Brian Blunnie and Bill Masterson.

PROLOGUE

Ever since he was nine, John Otway has believed he was a
star. It began at playtime, when a crowd of school children
gathered to watch and laugh at Otway sing Lonnie Donegan
songs; it was reinforced considerably four years later when an
even larger crowd of over one hundred congregated at one end
of the Grange County Secondary School playground to witness
him drink a bottle of ink in one.

Because he was an unusual child, he was bullied and
picked on. However, the word Otway would always prefer to
'unusual' was 'gifted', and the more bullied and picked on, the
more gifted he believed he was. By the age of fourteen the
mental and physical evidence that John was gifted/unusual
was overwhelming and John knew fundamentally that he was
destined to be a huge star.

The foundations of that belief are so strong that they have
only been shaken twice in his whole life. And on each of these
occasions he has written a book.

Otway was not a good musician. He could, and still can,
hammer out a few chords. His voice has never, even by his
most avid fan, been described as melodic – he was not talented
in this way. On the plus side he had always been particularly
uncoordinated, and although it might not be instantly obvious
that this was a positive, it made him look funny when he tried
to do something on stage. It was his main natural resource
and over time he would learn to use it beautifully. The early
John Otway shows could divide an audience between those who
were fascinated by someone who was prepared to do anything
however dangerous or stupid to keep their attention, and those
who just thought "what a prat".

It is quite possible that John Otway would have remained
a local Aylesbury eccentric had he not teamed up with the

remarkably talented musician Wild Willy Barrett. Two elements combined to make the John Otway and Wild Willy Barrett duo successful in 1977. Firstly John had, over the years, become a reasonably adept lyricist and together they managed to put together a fair number of songs; secondly 1977 was the big year of punk rock and for a very, very short period the shocking, dangerous and ridiculous things Otway did on stage were cool. In the autumn of that year Otway was able to do a shocking, dangerous and ridiculous thing in front of millions of people on BBC2's *The Old Grey Whistle Test*. Whilst leaping on top of Willy's amplifier his foot had slipped and a fair percentage of the population of the United Kingdom watched as he landed astride the very hard piece of musical equipment. It was excruciatingly painful and it was excruciatingly funny and the results were almost instantaneous. Sales of the Otway and Barrett single, *Cor Baby, That's Really Free*, soared and shortly afterwards they were in the charts and on *Top Of The Pops*.

More success was possible, but the Otway/Barrett partnership was unstable. Otway had used the opportunity offered by that first hit to release a solo follow-up, *Geneve*. Unfortunately this was a romantic six-minute orchestral ballad, written for a girl he fancied, which as Willy pointed out "would not appeal to the punks who had liked *Cor Baby, That's Really Free*". *Geneve* was the first of many flops to come. Otway then released the solo album *All Balls And No Willy*, which did not help the strained relationship and the pair went their separate ways.

Over the next ten years Otway struggled desperately to have another hit, refusing to believe that *Really Free* was his fifteen minutes of fame. For most of that time he was able to support himself doing gigs, as his live shows were still quite popular. But the decline from the days of his punk hit were as relentless as the rise of his overdraft.

As another route to stardom, he tried to get into acting with feature parts in some TV commercials and bit parts in a couple of TV series. Enough to keep him with a major acting agency but nothing so far to fulfill his destiny.

In 1987, in order to address the mountain of money he and his wife owed the bank, John had spotted an opportunity to cash in on the booming property market. They sold their flat and along with Chris France and his girlfriend bought a big house in Portnall Road, North West London with a view to converting it into two flats.

Chris and John had been friends since they were both in their teens. Chris had helped John many times over the years, had a natural business ability and had also gone into the music industry as a publisher and record company manager. His career at this point was in the ascendency and he could see the profit that could be made from converting the house. After they had moved in, it was agreed that the builders would finish Chris' flat first and then Otway's. Just when Chris' flat was complete and the roof had been removed to do the conversion on John's building site flat, the four received a visit from the council. "You haven't read your lease," they were told. "Not only are you not allowed to convert this property, you don't even own the roof you have removed." All work had to be halted with immediate effect.

Otway tried to budget. He fired the music agency that booked his live work to save the commission they charged and gave Peter Bullick, his roadie, the job. Within a short period Peter's inexperience as an agent became apparent, when they played to an audience of three people and Otway did not have enough money from the door takings to pay either Peter or his guitarist Ronnie Caryl.

John's wife had had enough and left him for good.

By the end of 1987, with his home, career and love life in tatters, Otway was in despair. At his local pub, a writer friend of his told John how popular music-related books were at the time and that publishers were "crying out for them".

"What about an Otway one?" John suggested.

"One with all your cock-ups and disasters would sell millions," he said laughing.

And Otway saw his opportunity. The current situation could now be viewed not as a disaster but as a bloody good story, a part of *Otway – the rock and roll legend,* and he instinctively knew what he had to do.

CHAPTER 1

It is 2005, a Jumbo Jet emblazoned with the words OTWAY WORLD TOUR taxis towards Terminal 5 at Heathrow Airport. In the departure lounge John Otway, his band, a feature film crew, several members of the press and 400 fans are heading for a checkout desk clearly marked OTWAY AIRLINES.

Many of these travellers are wearing rather neat tour jackets with a list of dates printed in an easily readable font – so readable in fact that from a considerable distance one can easily make out that the venues on this particular tour include The Sydney Opera House, Carnegie Hall and The Royal Albert Hall.

"That's how I want the next book to start," Otway explained to Richard Cotton, a friend who had worked with him on many projects over the years. "The last book finishes with me down and out, and when people start this one they will know within the first page that some pretty exciting things must have happened in order for me to rise phoenix-like from the ashes of the roofless flat in Portnall Road to do something no Rock Star has ever done before. Book One was *Rock & Roll's Greatest Failure*, Book Two is its *Greatest Success!*"

Otway was getting into his stride and talking faster. "It's like a mathematical equation. If it's elegant you can say it in a few simple sentences and it has that right tasty feel about it, you know it's correct. Let's do it, I feel the hand of Rock and Roll destiny upon me. Come on let's make history."

It was December 2003 and Otway was demonstrating an unorthodox approach to the sequel to his autobiography. Whereas most people write about what they have done in their lives, John believed he could decide what he wanted his history to be in advance and then go and live it. Why? Well he'd just had a bit of success and it had gone to his head.

How do you describe a failure? A possible definition could be someone who under-achieves. However, a *great* failure could be someone who succeeds and then screws up in the most spectacular fashion. In order to make one's fall from grace as spectacular as possible, it is not sufficient to just fall from a great height, it helps if you dig a hole for yourself too, especially if there is deep poo at the bottom waiting for you.

The last book finds Otway completing the hole and being in said 'poo'. This book is about how our hero gets out of that poo, out of that hole and climbs way up, way out of his depth, so far that he is almost unrecognisable as a star in the cosmos. But, being Otway he goes one step too far, and destiny becomes a force equivalent to gravity upon our star. He plummets from the dizzy heights past us mere mortals with our feet on the ground, back into the deep hole and the poo that we found him in at the start of this book. This is the story of that journey.

It starts with John penning his autobiography in 1988. "I remember Otway writing his book," recalls Chris France. "He'd just been through the mangle a bit and writing that book helped him come to terms with how crap he was. He had often thought that others were to blame when things went pear shaped, but he started to look at things a bit more objectively once he got into writing that.

"He showed it to me as he was progressing with it, and he enjoyed reading the libellous bits about me out loud. I laughed along too; I mean it never occurred to me that it would get published. For God's sake I'd been to Grammar School and have read the occasional book in my time. Otway failed his 11-plus, failed his English O-level twice and read the occasional comic if it had pictures as well as words. The problem was that John was an enigma, I don't mean that he was mysterious, but simply that he was like one of the code machines the Germans used during the war that changed straightforward text into something bloody difficult to read. But the cathartic experience was doing wonders for him and really seemed to cheer him up."

Those days Otway was to be seen permanently attached to a black folder that was slowly but surely filling up with the words that he would use to portray his life. The order in which he wrote down these words explains why he needed those three attempts to pass his O-level English and the order of the letters within these words explains why he regularly lost at Scrabble. In fact a few years earlier it would have been impossible for someone like John to complete a book. That he could now was due to recent advances in technology.

Alan Sugar had just launched an affordable Amstrad Word Processor that made computer technology available to the masses. Just as the first computers were built to crack the German Enigma codes, this amazing machine came complete with a deciphering program – a spellchecker. Back then this was cutting edge stuff, and it is unlikely the Otway autobiography would have got very far without one.

Back in Portnall Road John would type in all the stuff he had scrawled into his folder that day, and for the first time since he had moved there you could hear a joyous noise coming from John's room: the sound of Otway laughing at his own jokes.

A mistake many people made when encountering our star furiously scribbling away in the bar of the Warrington pub in Maida Vale was to ask what he was writing. If they were lucky they would be given the most recent few chapters hot from the Amstrad Dot Matrix Printer, if they were unfortunate they would be given the whole book to date – not to take away, but to read immediately whilst the author studied them intently.

Otway's talent as a writer was similar to his other talents like his guitar playing, singing and acting: it was not the ability that provided the entertainment, it was the enthusiasm that he put into them. Most people would be wary about showing off their first attempts at English prose to professional authors of distinction – not Otway. His enthusiasm and pride in the work he was doing grew as these learned people laughed out loud as they read his book. "If I can amuse people like that," Otway said, "I must be onto something." And if you looked at things the way John did, he had a point.

Between the winter of '87 and the summer of '88 there was a change in Otway's fortunes. Writing the book was part of this improvement, but more importantly love had re-entered his life. He had started to go out with Karen Lawrence, and by the summer the couple were in that period of new romance when even a hit-less boyfriend with a roofless flat and a big overdraft was attractive. It didn't matter that much, as Karen was independent, her career as a glass artist was taking-off, she owned a flat with a roof and had a non-existent overdraft. And, John's attempts to impress the new love of his life were about to be given a boost.

John had done an audition for a TV part. He hadn't given it much thought afterwards – he had met the director and chatted amiably, but because he was not asked to read anything or stand in front of a camera or give any indication of his ability, Otway just assumed he was the wrong age or shape. But two weeks later a phone call from his agent informed him that he had landed himself with a role as a regular character in a major new TV series. The next day a large package containing six scripts of *Forever Green* were couriered to Portnall Road. These confirmed that the main characters Jack and Harriet were to be played by John Alderton and Pauline Collins, and amongst the other characters were two decorators Stanley and Martyn, to be played by Brian Coburn and John Otway.

It was very exciting, and when the shooting schedule arrived it became apparent that John and Brian would be required on set pretty much every day.

And so it was that on the 4th July 1988 John arrived on location at Kings Farm, Tunley, near Cirencester. It had been chosen because it was a truly delightful little piece of rural west country England and in July that year it was beautiful. John arrived and was taken to the caravan he was sharing with his co-star Brian.

Brian Coburn, unlike Otway, was a very experienced actor, with a great many film and TV credits. He had a major role in the film of *Fiddler on the Roof*, and had worked with Roger Moore in *Octopussy*, and Woody Allen in *Love and Death*. And he was now working with John Otway in *Forever Green*.

"Good grief! What's all that you're carrying?" Brian asked when they first met.

"These are the scripts for this TV thing we're doing," replied John.

"You don't need to carry the whole 60 pages per episode around with you, just go through the script and take out the relevant pages. Here, pass it over. You see this episode, we've just got one short scene, and you've only got the words 'Morning Mrs. Boult.' Just carry this one sheet around with you if you think you might need to rehearse your line."

John could not understand why they were needed every day if they just had one short scene in that episode.

"We're what's known as weather cover – we're kept hanging around here all week in case it rains. All our scenes are interiors, so if it rains everyone can keep working. It's not too bad though, they pay us for hanging about."

Then it was off to make-up.

"Ah I see you dye your hair infrequently," smiled the make up lady measuring the length of John's grey roots. "Which dye do you use?"

"I think it's a L'Oreal, or something like that."

"Which one?"

"Brown."

"I'm pretty sure they do more than one brown please try to remember."

"Is it important?"

"Well it's not going to help with continuity, is it? Could you find out what colour you've put on your head so we can keep you the same all summer?" she asked.

Otway promised he'd find out and went to look around. With the sun shining and not a cloud in sight, he was unlikely to be doing any work that day.

This was the start of a great day. The catering was sublime, and he was getting paid to wander around and chat to the other stars. And when there was none of that to do he sat in the sun and worked on his book.

"What's that you're writing?" asked Pauline Collins with inevitable results. After the routine grilling she admitted to enjoying the bit about the ink drinking.

Unbelievably it was to get even better. After the day's 'work' John's driver took him back to the hotel. The Fleece in Cirencester was a wonderful hotel in comparison to the accommodation on a typical Otway tour. John picked up his key and headed upstairs. To his amazement he had been given the most luxurious room in the place. It was huge with a stunning view and a rather elegant four poster bed. It turned out that the rooms were swapped around each week and that first week John had struck lucky.

John wasted no time in calling Karen, "Hi, two things. Firstly, can you remember the name of the dye I used last time I did my hair? And secondly is there any chance of you taking a couple of days off to join me down here? You just can't imagine how great this is."

Then it was down to the bar. The routine that would last the whole of that shoot was that everyone who was working on the programme would sit around a large table and take turns in buying a bottle of champagne. Those who had a big scene the next day would head off to bed early to learn their lines. This never applied to John as his scenes were all small, so he was able to enjoy fully those long evenings chatting about life in the TV and film industries. He was where he'd always wanted to be. "If the parts just get bigger, I'm quite happy to settle for this sort of life," he thought.

The next day Karen was able to arrange to visit some galleries in the West Country and take some of her work, so was able to join John in the Fleece. She also arranged some holidays too so she could enjoy the location and the evenings at the hotel as well. The difference between being broke in the building site in London and the life in the Fleece in Cirencester was vast. The expenses John was being paid covered the cost of being away, and the wages he was being paid for his weather cover job eased his finances sufficiently to put a smile on both John's and Karen's faces.

The acting went well too. The first week's "Morning, Mrs. Boult," was in the can in a couple of takes and the following week's line "I think the head gasket's broken," was captured perfectly first time.

John had one other big opportunity to impress his new girlfriend as Peter Bullick had managed to book Otway to play the main stage at Reading Festival. He was booked for the opening spot on the Sunday morning. This was the biggest audience John had played to in years. It was a decade since he had last played Reading Festival and he felt he could make just as much impact as he had then. "You're going to enjoy watching me play a big crowd," John told Karen.

When they arrived at the festival the big news was that on the Saturday night Meatloaf had been bottled off the stage. "I've got a plan," said Otway. "Let's finish with *Down The Road* and we can do a *Meatloaf Down the Road* at the end. Peter if you can start throwing a few bottles at me and get the rest of the crew on the stage to do the same thing, maybe the audience will join in and it'll be hilarious."

Otway could be extremely entertaining and he was that day. The audience were still coming on to the site when he took the stage but by the time his set was coming to an end there were a fair few thousand up on their feet cheering the end of each number. John has always been fortunate with the musicians he has worked with and Ronnie Caryl, his guitarist at the time, was one whose great rough raunchy rock and roll style of playing and natural sense of theatre worked well in a duo.

Their finale was the aforementioned *Down The Road,* with Otway at his most theatrical. "I want to hear Boris Becker down the road," he sang. Ronnie grabbed his microphone from its stand then swung it round faster and faster giving it the momentum necessary to reach the other side of the stage before letting it go. Otway swiftly turned his guitar over and thwack, he batted the flying piece of equipment straight back to Ronnie, who jumped up, caught the microphone and yelled "love fifteen" into it.

"I want to hear Eddie the Eagle down the road," yelled Otway, who grabbed two microphone stands and climbed up the scaffolding at the side of the stage, then leapt using the stands as ski poles.

The audience was loving it. "I want to hear Meatloaf down the road," he sang. On cue Peter threw a bottle at John, followed by the rest of the crew on the stage. The audience took only moments to remember what they had been doing to the headline act the previous night and within seconds were joining in the fun.

"I've never ever known anything like that before," remembers Otway now. "All the other times I'd been bottled off the audience were relatively small and it was more annoying than scary. This was bloody frightening! You could see these quart bottles flying towards you and somehow from their trajectory you could tell that they were full of liquid and heavy enough to take your head off. Within about thirty seconds there were so many of them coming we just legged it off the stage. But the cheer that went up and the sound of the applause was deafening. Boy was I happy."

"Good, wasn't it?" John said to Karen as they all headed to hospitality backstage at the festival. Jack Barry the promoter sent over a couple of bottles of champagne and an hour later a little drunk but very happy Otway was driven from the site back home.

A couple of hours later a desperate Jack Barry was searching the hospitality area clutching two thousand pounds in cash looking for John and Ronnie to go back on. It turned out that Otway had started a trend. Two more acts had been bottled off and Jack needed someone on stage who could keep the show going. This is a good example of behaviour that seems to form a repeating pattern in Otway's career – what seemed like a good idea to John, and appeared to work very well from his perspective, was not in fact a very good idea at all.

If you put 'Reading Festival 1988' into Google you come up with quotes like:– *In 1988, the festival hit its lowest point with the likes of Meatloaf and Bonnie Tyler being bottled off the stage. The festival was declared a disaster and its future was under threat.*

It's true that it was Meatloaf who started the bottling on Saturday night. But it's also true that had the audience not been encouraged to start bottling first thing on Sunday, Jack Barry might not have had to give up the festival the following year, and might have even given Otway another go on the Main Stage.

The summer was coming to an end and John had finished his book. With some of the money from *Forever Green*, John and Karen took a romantic holiday in Turkey before starting the autumn gig schedule.

Most people are a bit short of money in December, therefore Chris France was not in the least surprised when Otway told Chris that he needed to speak to him alone with some urgency.

"I think it might be an idea if you got yourself a drink, I've already got one," suggested John. "No I'm fine I think I can handle this without fortification," replied Chris. "Go on then, what is it and how much do you reckon it'll cost me?"

"I don't need money, I just wanted to tell you I'm going to be a dad," beamed Otway.

"In that case I'll get myself a drink."

CHAPTER 2

As choices go, the choice was both simple and one that John was not allowed to make: where shall the couple's new child be brought up? John lived in a building site in North West London, Karen had a two bedroomed garden flat in South West London. And so John moved out of Portnall Road. The problems, the building work and the legalities would take a further four years to sort out and when the arithmetic was eventually worked out, it was pretty obvious by the length of the number after the minus sign that the Otway Property Development Scheme was not a profitable one.

Amy Otway was born in June 1989. Having a family tends to have a fundamental effect on us all, and the effect was benign upon Otway. He felt that while the child was growing up he could not take the sort of risks that he had been taking and his work should, if at all possible, support his family. Ideas and plans that had a possibility of bankruptcy and financial ruin were best avoided during this period.

Even John was realistic enough to recognise that there was not going to be a bidding war for the publishing rights to his book. It was, after all, an autobiography of an act that had one small hit that got to number 27 over ten years before. Whilst writing the book, Otway had just thought that if no publishers were interested he'd simply publish it himself. The concept of vanity publishing did not concern him as he had already done vanity records, vanity films and didn't the vanity go all the way back to his school days when he won his own vanity talent contest? But vanity publishing would be costly and would not fit with the new 'responsible breadwinning Otway' that John was determined to become.

So however unlikely it was going to be, a proper publisher was the only option if he was going to be a successful author. The first problem to solve was the 'howls of derision' the grammar attracted. Andy Wood, who had arranged a sponsorship deal with Shure for John, was given a photocopy of the book and suggested that his friend Nick Creasy could help. Nick's work involved making computer manuals entertaining and comprehensible to the masses. Andy thought he might be a good bet to sort out the Otway autobiography. John was very precious though and very concerned that if the unconventional use of language was changed then the humour might be lost. In fact Nick had to argue with Otway that he should be allowed to work for several hours a week on John's book for nothing, and a deal was struck only after it was agreed that the author did the actual corrections himself.

And so, every week Nick would send John a few chapters in the mail with the corrections to be done. Throughout the long process they would argue over what was funny and what was good English. In time John accepted that you could have an exclamation mark or a full stop – but not both together – and Nick realised that by saying 'by mutual disagreement they disagreed to split up', the application of appalling grammar conjured up an image of two people who were not in harmony, something that would not have occurred to him before.

Many publishers do not welcome unsolicited manuscripts and no-one had solicited John's. Nevertheless the book was photo-statted many times and the new grammatically-improved edition was sent to anyone in the *Writers' and Artists' Yearbook* who might be interested in his life story. Otway felt that he had a funny, interesting piece of work that came from an unusual angle for a rock'n'roll biography, and further believed that if a publisher actually read it then they would undoubtedly accept it.

The rejections came as regularly as John sent out books. One thing that surprised him was how many publishers suggested rival publishers as good places to send a copy. "Not our kind of book – have you thought of trying our main competition?" they would write whilst turning the book down themselves.

It was Maurice Bacon, Otway's old manager, who finally solved the problem. Maurice had been given a copy and thought it was "A darned good read." During one of the many phone conversations that Maurice had with John in an attempt to recoup some of the money he was owed, the subject of what was going to happen to the star's memoirs came up.

"Do you want me to have a go at getting a deal?"

Although John was a bit concerned that this might involve giving away a percentage of the fortune he would eventually make out of his writings, it did mean Maurice would not be asking him for money during the time he was receiving the rejection letters. And, as he was out of ideas himself, he was pleased with any help he could get.

Book publishers generally have an idea of what there is demand for, and commission authors to write books to fill that demand. Now this is where the crux of the problem was, a publisher needed to be found who felt that there was a demand for a 70,000 word autobiography on John Otway. However, there are a group of people whose opinions publishers listen to and take very seriously indeed. These are wholesalers. And there are a group of people whose opinions wholesalers listen to and take very seriously indeed. These are the booksellers.

Maurice got Peter Beaumont, his mate in his local bookshop to read Otway's story and he got David Clarke, a wholesaler at Pipeline Books, to read it too. David was charmed by John's story and, whilst being pressed to stock some other titles, he persuaded his mate Frank Warren of Omnibus Press to take a serious look at it.

So the next phone call John received from Maurice was most welcome. It was to arrange a meeting at the Crown And Two Chairman in Soho with Frank Warren and Chris Charlesworth from Omnibus Press to discuss a publishing agreement.

CHAPTER
3

Omnibus specialise in music-related books. If you had looked through the catalogue of releases at the time of their meeting with John and Maurice, you would have been hard pushed to find a title whose subject matter had sold less than a million records.

"Your book is going to be different from the other books we publish," Chris Charlesworth told John. The idea Chris had was to market *Cor Baby, That's Really Me!*, the title John had in mind for his book, as 'Rock and Roll's Greatest Failure'. "Instead of the usual flashes on the front that say 'International Best Seller', etc, yours can have flashes like 'Bad Records' and 'Rank Incompetence'."

It wasn't exactly what John had in mind; in John's mind he was a star. The self-effacing humour in his writing he felt was the ability of a confident person being strong enough to accept their mistakes. But he was not about to jeopardise his chance to become a published author. So 'Rock and Roll's Greatest Failure' it was.

"Deep down I genuinely felt that I was going to be a famous rock star. I thought about it for a short while and figured that if the journey included a brief period as rock's great failure, then the subsequent success would look all the more impressive."

Throughout that meeting John warmed to the idea and, after a few pints of fine ale, had embraced the concept entirely. He now looked like, sounded like and was indistinguishable from the great failure that was his new image. Success would have to wait, failure would have to come first.

By the end of the night they had worked out a deal. It would be five months before the book launch, time for our star to get used to his new role. John was to find this a refreshing change; his life had been spent trying to persuade people how great he was, now he had to do the opposite and it was a darned sight easier.

It was still a bit of a shock when John was given the first copy of his book. Subtlety had gone out of the window. It was bright yellow, and, as well as the flashes on the front, the text on the back read:

Time was when John Otway looked forward to platinum albums, stadium gigs and a squad of bodyguards to see him safely aboard his private jet. Unfortunately it didn't happen that way. A series of dreadful career decisions, financial blunders and bad records has left Otway down but not out. This is the story in his own words.

- *Almost rejected Pete Townshend as his producer*
- *Has never repaid a record company advance in his life*
- *Once put on a benefit concert for his own record company after they had cancelled his contract*
- *Signed himself to the mighty Warner Brothers label simply by pressing his own records with the WB logo in the middle and*
- *Broke up with Paula Yates telling her it was the last chance she'd get to go out with a rock star.*

Cor Baby, That's Really Me! is *John Otway's hilarious yet moving account of his insane assault on the music industry, a tale of blind ambition and rank incompetence, and a salutary lesson for aspiring musicians on how not to achieve greatness.*

Maurice Bacon spotted an opportunity too. John hadn't had anything released on the new CD format yet – all his previous releases were on vinyl. A compilation of tracks that made up the Otway story could also be called *Cor Baby, That's Really Me!*, and use similar artwork to the book. Because of the nature of the book the words 'Best Of' were deemed inappropriate and Maurice felt that the 'Bad Records' flash was probably best left off the front of the CD as he didn't think it would encourage sales. The liner notes though did give some idea of why the tracks belong to the book, such as: *Turning Point – John now starts doing for Stiff Records what he did to Polydor; In Dreams – John tried to turn this song into a 1977 punk classic, sadly this is 1982; Green Green Grass Of Home – Not as big a hit for John as it was for Tom.*

John used the five months before publication to put together his promotion. He started getting dates together for a UK book tour and managed to get 32 to fit into 30 days. "Didn't authors do signings in book shops?" – he could do them during the day as he was travelling around. And after a great deal of research it was decided that The ICA next to Buckingham Palace was a pretty good place to hold a book reading event. Omnibus provided flyers, posters, worked on the press and media resulting in a pretty good response. John attracted more attention than he had in years.

The reviews for the autobiography were very encouraging with almost everyone approving of the lessons to be learnt from the way John had lived his life. Otway had developed his interview technique too. "I was always able to take a promising situation and turn it to my disadvantage," he would say when asked why he was such a failure. And if it was radio, he would add "Here's my CD. Play any of the 22 tracks apart from The Hit and it's self evident."

There were features in the Daily Express and the Independent, on Radio One, Radio Four plus lots of local TV and radio. If anyone who had been under the impression that John Otway was a successful pop star, this blitz of publicity had left them re-educated and in no doubt that he was anything but.

Murray Davies wrote articles for the Daily Mirror – John met him midday at the Chelsea Potter in King's Road for an interview. Otway was by now a dab hand at explaining what a disaster area he was, good at pointing out his weak spots and where he was most vulnerable. He was also funny with it, and over a few drinks positively charmed the Fleet Street hack into doing a feature.

"WHAT A PRAT I AM" ran the headline in one of the best-selling national newspapers in the United Kingdom. A whole page of tabloid on Otway. He was over the moon.

Karen was not as delighted as John. "When Amy goes to school, do you really want everyone asking her if her dad is a prat?" John could obviously see her point, and of course would not want to embarrass his family, but he was torn. All his life had been a struggle for stardom, and although this prat thing wasn't in the game plan, he had managed to create something that people found funny and entertaining.

It was a strange area full of paradoxes. There are very many who would say "Never call yourself a failure". These are the same people who would say "People should laugh with you not at you". By writing the book in the third person John had got these people to be comfortable with laughing at someone who was calling himself a failure, because within a couple of pages they had forgotten that is what they were doing.

He also discovered that he actually got some respect. When he turned up to a book shop to sign his autobiography he noticed that the shop managers and sales assistants afforded a reverence to authors that rock stars never achieved. At the shops they did not want the authors to sing a few numbers or somersault between the fiction and non-fiction, they welcomed them politely and offered them a glass of water at the small table they had prepared for them. "Here's a pen," said the pleasant manageress of Dillons Bookstore, Kingsbury Square, Aylesbury, where John did his first signing. "You'd be amazed how many authors turn up to these things without one."

This being Otway's home town and the location of much of his story there was actually a queue waiting for him. The last author to sign books on that table was Bill Oddie. It transpired that Bill had only signed two bird spotting books on his visit, so from this point on John referred to a unit of two books as an Oddie. And in Aylesbury he clocked up a cracking fifteen Oddies.

As with all of the projects Otway undertook, the book project did not achieve what he imagined would happen – millions of sales and a first class ticket to celebrity and stardom. But it was a turning point. Since *Really Free* had been in the charts, and despite huge efforts (or maybe because of them), he had seen his career slowly but surely decline. There was now a definite perceptible change. The new CD was selling spectacularly well for a John Otway recording, Omnibus' failure was selling as many books as any of their successes and the book tour saw audience numbers increase substantially. There was now a spring in John's step as he walked across the stage for the applause. "I'm not going to be able to hang on to this failure tag for long now," he thought.

Having had one successful book the natural thing to do would be to write another. The problem was that Otway was only passionate about one subject, and that was himself. He figured quite rightly that, on past experience, it would probably be about twenty years before he had lived another book's-worth of life so another route back to stardom would have to be found.

CHAPTER
4

Things were changing in the Otway world. His guitarist Ronnie Caryl got a leading role in the West End musical *Good Rockin' Tonight* and would shortly go on to work with an even more successful rock star – Phil Collins. Peter Bullick gave up his roadie/managing job to start a very successful CD manufacturing business. So why not try something that had worked in the past, something tried and often tested before – the devil he knew?

Thanks to lack of trust and bloody-mindedness, John and Willy had not played a live show together in years, and as each year passed the interest in an Otway and Barrett reunion grew.

"Especially after the book came out," says Chris France. "All the fans had read the Otway version of how impossible Willy had been to work with, so a properly promoted one-off show at somewhere like The Rainbow or Hammersmith Odeon would have probably sold out. They could have made thousands for just one night's work if they had done it sensibly."

Willy had a new manager, Kevin Parker, who Willy felt could possibly mediate between them and make the event possible. After a great deal of tough negotiation it was agreed between the parties that before attempting anything major they would try it out at a small low-key folk venue, The Weavers Arms in Islington. "If it doesn't work out and is a disaster, who's to know?" was the general feeling.

A few days before the date of the gig, John had a call from The Jonathan Ross TV show asking if he was available to do a short spot. "Could he do *Headbutts* and a short interview?" It was a stupid question, of course he could do *Headbutts* and a short interview. Ever since he had shot to fame after the painful leap astride Willy's amplifier on *The Old Grey Whistle Test* back in 1977, John had realised the power of live television and had kept his eye open for another opportunity to shoot back to fame again. Here was another chance to hurt himself in front of millions of people and recruit another army of fans.

Unfortunately things didn't quite work that way. What Otway had done on the *Whistle Test* was a brave attempt at something spectacular that went wrong, he had hurt himself and it was funny. Otway banging his head and hurting himself on purpose was not very funny at all. And when he didn't get the reaction he wanted for the first bang of the head he made it worse by trying even harder for the second bang and ending up with blood trickling down his forehead.

"Is there any chance of an Otway/Barrett reunion?" Jonathan Ross asked a bleeding dazed Otway in the interview after the performance.

"Yes, in fact we're doing the Weavers Arms in Islington on Saturday," Otway replied.

The results of the Jonathan Ross show were two-fold. Firstly John's mum was not happy. She had never liked the song *Headbutts*, and didn't like it when Willy banged her son's head hard against the microphone to make him say "Ow!" so imagine how cross she was with him when he was doing it to himself almost twice as hard as Willy did. "I remember, she really told me off about that," says John. The other result was the turn out for the low-key Otway and Barrett reunion in North London: the queue for the one-hundred-capacity venue snaked up Newington Green Road for as far as the eye could see, a line of people that could fill a theatre the size of the Rainbow or Hammersmith Odeon.

One of the people on the guest list was Paul Clerehugh, a successful restaurateur who'd booked Otway to play about three weeks later. He was as impressed as everyone else at the size of the queue. "Would Willy be interested in doing The Crooked Billet with you?" he asked John.

"You can ask him, but I doubt it, this is our only gig in seven years," Otway replied. But to John's surprise, Kevin and Willy agreed to do the show on the condition that Willy did not get paid a penny less than the two hundred pounds flat fee that Paul had agreed with Otway.

What Paul failed to tell the duo was that the day before the proposed show, The Crooked Billet was due to host the reception for a big Henley-on-Thames society wedding. So instead of playing to fifty people in the back room, the performance could be held in a vast marquee, which covered the field at the back of the restaurant and Paul (who was very good at this) took a fraction of a millisecond to work out that the show could now be re-promoted as the big reunion. If the tables were removed and the small stage moved from the back room into the corner of the marquee, a much larger number of standing people could be squeezed into that vast space. The number is of such magnitude that even today, when it is multiplied by the number of pounds that Paul was charging for the tickets, John hates the idea of trying to envisage its size.

The sell-out gig at the hundred-seater Weavers Arms and the four hundred quid gig at The Crooked Billet were deemed to have been such a successful re-union that John and Willy agreed to do a whole tour later that year.

The Otway/Barrett Tour was exactly what one could imagine. Because of the earlier two shows, the excitement of the re-union was already over so the audience turn out was reasonable but not spectacular, and the tour started and ended with the underlying deep overtones of mistrust and suspicion you would expect.

As with previous tours those on the road split naturally into two camps that didn't talk to each other, didn't travel together and turned one-upmanship on stage into an art form.

It wasn't all bad though, as both John and Willy were well aware that this could make for a hilariously funny show. Audiences can smell as well as hear discord – it is just more entertaining than watching two people who get on well together, especially as it was topped off with Wild Willy viciously banging the Otway forehead in the song *Headbutts*.

Years ago the Otway camp would have consisted of at least six people but John, the new prudent family man, was now on his own. So to even things up a bit John was donated Richard Cotton to be in his camp, look after him and drive him around. Willy's manager had hired him to help on the tour, but within a few days Willy's camp was not talking to Richard as they thought he was now on John's side and Otway wasn't talking to him either because he thought he was a spy.

"For someone in their teens around Aylesbury during the punk revolution of the late '70s John Otway and Wild Willy Barrett had a near mythical status. The idea that a star-struck music-obsessed bloke like me would one day tour manage an Otway/Barrett re-union tour would have been beyond my wildest dreams. Much later – when I ended up doing just that – it turned out to be one of my worst nightmares," Cotton said later.

The relations between John and Cotton thawed eventually. There were similarities between the two: both had already made and lost their first fortune and they were both headstrong and passionate and dived straight into the deep end with any idea that captured their imagination.

"He'll learn," said Willy, "and it will end in tears."

Willy was right, but the lesson took many years to learn – so Richard Cotton now stays with us until the finale of this book, and the tears that it ends in.

CHAPTER 5

Other collaborations were more harmonious than the Otway/Barrett partnership and would ultimately be more rewarding. For a three week run at Edinburgh Festival John teamed up with poet Attila the Stockbroker. A shared love of real ale enabled the unlikely pair to put together a potpourri of songs, poems and prose for a show they called *Headbutts and Halibuts*.

The height of the show's humour can be judged by the quality of its climax. *The Glue Medley* was a piece about glue sniffing, created by using the simple device of swapping the word 'you' in popular songs for the word 'glue' in such a way that you got things like *She Loves Glue Yeh, Yeh, Yeh* and *I Can't Stop Loving Glue*. John and Attila discovered that it could be enhanced further by using the simple device of drinking several pints of bitter. By just imbibing a certain amount of alcohol the pair realised it was possible to extended their creation from the elementary *I Can't Live, If Living Is Without Glue*, and *I Got Glue Babe*, to the more surreal *Come On Come On Let's Stick Together* and *Tonight I Sellotape My Glove To You*.

Eventually the medley would include Mud's wonderful ode to this teen habit, *Then She Walked In Looking Like Araldite*, and the genius:

> *Pritt Stick on your collar*
> *Told a tale on you*
> *Pritt Stick on your collar*
> *Told me you sniffed glue.*

From the reaction to their Edinburgh show both of them felt it would be worthwhile coming back the following year and spent the next twelve months composing an original piece *Cheryl, A Rock Opera*. When they returned to perform it they brought with them producer, arranger and musician Richard Holgarth.

"As we were up at the festival for three weeks, I thought we might as well book a studio and record it during the day as well as perform it in the evening," says John.

Attila was living in Harlow at the time and was closely involved with an enthusiastic team of talent that had created a venue called The Square. It contained a recording studio, video editing suite and a 150 capacity room with one of the best sound and light systems in the country. It attracted the coolest touring bands and nurtured all those with creative aspirations in the locality. Almost every new band on the path to stardom had played there (embryonic Oasis and Blur as well as Coldplay and Pulp).

Richard Holgarth was one of the engineers there and had done the sound for many of these acts – he had also played a major role in building up the studio and had produced many CDs for the local Harlow acts including several for Attila. He had what Otway lacked, he was a naturally gifted musician, producer and sound engineer, possessed a rock star's head of hair – and women loved him. He also knew what an act needed to sound like if it was going to make an impact in the 1990s, and how to make that sound.

A couple of weeks after a successful festival run with the theatrical *Cheryl, the Rock Opera* in Edinburgh, Richard Holgarth handed over the recorded version. It was a musical epic with passages of rock, classical and rap backing Attila and Otway's saga of heartache and political wisdom.

As well as being responsible for the production and arrangements Richard had played nearly all the guitar and keyboard parts. Otway loved it and felt he had now found someone who had the talent to get him to where he really wanted to be.

The following year Attila secured them a couple of spots at Glastonbury Festival: one on the Saturday to perform *Cheryl* augmented with Richard Holgarth and other assorted Harlow musicians, and one on the Sunday to do their own material. Since Richard was there with his guitar, John got him up to back him on things like *Really Free* and *Beware of The Flowers*, which he knew, as well as things like *Body Talk* and *Down the Road*, which he didn't. For years afterwards John would enjoy telling the audience about their first gig as a duo. "We managed a ten minute rehearsal in the backstage bar before going on. I remember saying, 'This is *Body Talk*. I put these drum pads in my pockets and hit myself and you just play along. It's in E'."

Which is exactly why that first gig could have been their last. Richard had reservations about becoming part of the deliberately anarchic Otway show, which at times only made a cursory nod towards music, but he eventually decided that there were enough challenging elements in it for him to give it a go. "At the end of the day the show was funny," he says.

The Otway/Holgarth duo show soon developed into something unrecognisable from their first Glastonbury appearance, with a format that would do about a thousand shows over the next fifteen years and serve them both well. Not only was Holgarth's cutting guitar giving the show a musical edge, he was also in possession of a good sense of comedy timing.

The old song *Down the Road* was replaced with the Osmonds' song *Crazy Horses* for the piece of ridiculous fun to end the show. It started with John surprising Richard Holgarth by telling the audience that his partner had a special talent. "He's really good at making animal noises" he told them, and so:

"Crazy horses" sang John, and Richard Holgarth would make the appropriate sound.

After a few shows, when Richard Holgarth had become comfortable with, and some would say good at, the crazy horse noise, John would add an extra bit to the end:

"Crazy chickens" sang John, and Richard Holgarth became comfortable with the concept that there could be other creatures that he might have to do.

"Crazy Portuguese man of war" sang John, and Richard Holgarth discovered that some crazy creatures were easier to do than others.

Further challenges were provided by *"Crazy paving"*, *"Crazy golf"* and the unimaginative, but effective, "He does do requests, is there any animal any member of the audience wants Richard Holgarth to do?"

There was usually a stepladder on the stage which John used for a dramatic effect earlier in the show. When there was, Otway would often choose lemmings as his final animal. One night, at the Tower Arts Centre in Winchester, Richard Holgarth was presented with a very tall ladder, and so took the sensible precaution of climbing half-way up for the usual seven foot drop to the stage. John immediately turned to the audience, "Hands up those who think lemmings dive suicidally to their death from the top of a very high cliff, and hands up those who believe lemmings think it's safer to do suicide from half-way up."

This might appear to be bullying, and of course it was, and very funny it was too. Here we had this talented musician who had been delighting the audience for an hour with his playing being made to make animal noises and jump off very high ladders.

Sometimes John would just invent stories about his guitarist. It started one night just before they played Bachman Turner

Overdrive's *You Ain't Seen Nothing Yet*, when John told the audience "Richard Holgarth is a very good heavy metal guitarist."

Before long it was "Richard Holgarth's great love is heavy metal guitar playing. I know it is, he's got Marshall Amplifier wallpaper in his bedroom, this girl told me." And soon John was announcing that Richard Holgarth had his own heavy metal band. Holgarth knew that any denial would give these things credibility, so he just smiled and let John get on with it.

Then one night John turned to Holgarth and asked: "What's the name of your band, then?" Holgarth, without blinking, replied: "Weevil", but it's got a hyphen so it's: "We-evil." It might have been quick, bright, witty and funny, but it was a mistake. Now Holgarth had given the band John had invented for him a name, so at every subsequent gig they did, and as we know there were a hell of a lot of them, John would tell the audience all about We-evil. The audience believed him, there was no reason why they shouldn't, and to this day Richard Holgarth gets asked about how his band We-evil are doing.

Everyone had been delighted with the way the recording of *Cheryl, A Rock Opera* had gone: Maurice had agreed to release it on CD and the combination of the Otway and Attila fan bases had bought enough copies for it not to have made a loss. So another CD – *Under the Covers and Over the Top* – was put in the pipeline.

John had always peppered his show with an odd mix of cover versions, such as The Sweet's *Blockbuster* (where humour was extracted by carefully enunciating the lyrics), *I Will Survive* (sung with an accent that made it sound surprisingly like a Bob Dylan song) and *You Ain't Seen Nothing Yet*, which sounded most amusing when John's singing was accompanied by Attila doing a German translation. It was a good idea to record them. Even if the CD did not do well in the shops, it would be a good merchandising item for those that enjoyed these songs at the shows.

Before Richard Holgarth it would not have been possible to do something like this, but as Richard was one of the main sound engineers at The Square, he had access to the down-time at the studio. He was able to record without running up crippling bills. He could play most of the necessary instruments and could call on the cream of Harlow talent for anything he couldn't manage himself. Recording a CD was now not only possible it also made sense – so much sense that John was able to persuade Chris France to invest in the new record label 'John Otway Records' to release it.

John had not given up on the idea of another hit record and getting back on *Top Of The Pops*, and a single had been picked for release from both of the last albums: a part of *Cheryl* from the *Rock Opera* and *Two Little Boys* from *Under the Covers and Over The Top*. John's idea that some major Radio 1 DJ might love one of them and suddenly start playing it regularly was like buying a particularly expensive lottery ticket. The simple fact was that Otway was now approaching forty, his last hit was thirteen years ago and even though he was now more known as rock's great failure he could not let go of the belief that he was still going to become a huge star.

"If he had just released the two CDs and sold them to fans he would have made a bit of a profit on them," says Chris. "But any profit got swallowed up by releasing singles in a futile attempt to get in the charts."

One weapon that Otway and Holgarth felt would help in the battle was getting a good band together. John had done a show with a band for his 40th birthday and it went down a storm. Everyone had been impressed with how much he looked and sounded like a star with the powerhouse of a rhythm section behind him. "You really ought to do more shows like that," Karen said to him on their way home together.

"You know some good players, could you put a band together for me?" John asked Richard Holgarth when he spoke to him the next day.

CHAPTER
6

John spent a considerable amount of time explaining to Richard Holgarth exactly what he wanted his new band to be like. Richard Holgarth completely ignored him and spent a considerable amount of time getting John a new band that he knew the sort of audiences that went to The Square would like and the sort of band the musicians he wanted to use would enjoy playing in.

John had been at pains to point out that he wanted an almost cabaret style band that could play arts centres and theatres and support the comedy direction that his show was going in. This was 1993, the time of the emergence of alternative comedy, so John had a point but Richard Holgarth was having none of it.

"For a rock star he was his own worst enemy," says Richard Holgarth. "He was forty and losing his hair, so what does he do? He starts smoking a pipe and asking me to put a cheesy pop band together. I couldn't do anything about his age, his bald patch or his consumption of St. Bruno ready rubbed tobacco but I could get him a band that rocked and kicked ass."

Not only did they rock and kick ass, they looked good and were considerably younger than their front man. The new Otway band, the *crème-de-la-crème* of the Harlow music scene, was about to add an element of excitement and glamour that an Otway show had not had for years.

John had wanted a keyboard player, but Richard Holgarth felt that keyboards had a tendency to smooth out the edges of a guitar based band, so Richard had simply been unable to find a suitable one in Harlow for the band's first rehearsal.

Otway was convinced that this was going to be the start of something very important and booked his friend, cameraman David Painter to film the band getting together. So John arrived at The Square sucking on his pipe followed by a film crew to start work.

They started with what John called The Hit: *Cor Baby, That's Really Free!* The band had worked out the parts from the record and it sounded remarkably like the Hit that it was. Next they played what John called the B-side of The Hit: *Beware of the Flowers*, and John started getting excited. When they eventually moved on to the flops, (i.e all the other songs John had recorded) some of them even sounded like hits, and John got even more excited. After the rehearsal, to mark this significant moment in his history he did his piece to camera and said something like, "Today we have turned a key, and started the engine of a juggernaut."

If the new Otway band were to tour, they would need a roadie. Roadies are the unsung heroes of any rock and roll story: they work the hardest and have the unenviable task of taking the star home at the end of the night. It takes a special sort of person to be able to cope with this.

Otway loved being on stage: when it was going well he would be pumped up with adrenalin and throwing himself around the stage amusing the audience; when it wasn't going well he would be pumped up with adrenalin and throwing himself around the stage desperately trying to win them over. As he had now been doing it for years most of the time he was triumphant, so came off grinning and celebrating with a large whisky and a few pints. It was only on very rare occasions that John would leave the venue before the manager had closed the bar to him. Usually the roadie had packed the gear into the car by this point and was waiting. On the way home the subject would be exclusively Otway and usually a complete analysis of the show he had just done.

"I'd prefer to have had a miserable person in the car," remembers one roadie who lasted a mere two shows. "I'd just watched the whole show and on the way back the car would be full of pipe smoke and John's voice, going over the whole thing again, song by song, intro by intro, headbutt by headbutt"

If roadies for a solo or duo show were hard come by and short-lived, band roadies were almost impossible to find. They were the first to start as they drove around picking up the musicians and their gear one by one and then after the show they would have to drop them off before being allowed to go home themselves.

Richard Cotton was naïve enough to assume that because of the way the Otway/Barrett tour had ended he would never hear from Otway again. John was wise enough to realise because Richard Cotton had lasted to the end of the tour, his card was well and truly marked and it would not be long before he got the phone call.

Otway had spotted Cotton's special talent: unlike most people who had driven him he enjoyed John's enthusiasm after shows and would often join in.

"He was great," says Otway. "It was like having an extra bonus audience on the way home. He actually encouraged me."

And strange as it may seem, when Cotton got the call asking him if he fancied being the roadie for the new Otway band he was delighted.

"I just couldn't believe my luck," says John. "The day after I asked him he was calling me back to say that he had blagged a stunning van deal from a local firm, agreed the itinerary with the band and been in touch with the venues to organise get-in times for the sound-checks and to double-check the fees."

"When John told me about the band, it didn't make sense," says Cotton. "He'd complained enough about how hard it was to make a living when he had to split the gig money with Willy and here he was paying four musicians, so I tried to help him out by getting a good deal on the transport and making sure he had fixed up the deals and contracts properly."

The first John Otway Big Band gig was on 27th January 1993 at the Concorde in Brighton, and it was immediately obvious that Richard Holgarth had got the musical equation right. The band were very tight and all very, very good players, but on Otway's strictest orders none of them was allowed to take it seriously. "If the audience see we're having a laugh they'll join in," seemed to be his motto. So, that's what they did from that first gig: they piled into the bar and had a few pints, then wandered on stage and had a ball.

"I had been in bands before who had a drinking rule like 'only two pints before you go on to do the show'," says Murray the guitarist. "So on that first show I asked Otway about his drinking rule. He replied that he tries to get in at least three and, as I was obviously heading to the bar, could I get him a pint of bitter."

John enjoyed having some great players with him and they enjoyed the freedom and fun of working alongside him. Most of all though they absolutely loved the reaction that the new show was getting. John had fallen on his feet – he had got a band that worked superbly with him, and in Cotton had found someone as passionately driven as himself and almost as enthusiastic about the Otway Band as he was.

It did not take long for the excitement of Otway's new band show to build. Maurice Bacon and Chris France checked out the new five piece and were pleasantly stunned by it and the new positive atmosphere provided a force that would accelerate John's career quite dramatically. Richard Cotton realised that with some focus and strategy they could build on that force and produce results.

"All over the country, you've got small groups of people who come and see you. And all the people who remember you from The Hit in 1977 might be tempted to get interested again if you could give them all something to focus on," he told John. "We could get some serious press and even get you back on telly, but the media are not going to do a feature on a pub rock act just because they are doing some shows. They need something to hang a story on."

CHAPTER 7

It only took three band shows before the two of them had cooked up the next big project for John's career. During the many hours John had talked about himself Cotton had sussed that in his career he must have done almost 2,000 shows, so he asked Otway to check his diary. Because Otway felt that it might at some point be historically important, he had kept a record in his diary of every performance he had ever done, and sure enough he was able to confirm that Cotton's arithmetic was accurate. At the present gigging rate, the 2,000th show would happen sometime towards the end of the year.

Cotton knew that a lot could be done with a focus on this idea. They had about ten months to plan it and promote it, so he set about writing a press release.

John Otway. 2000 gigs – and counting.
2000 gigs...
That's one hell of a lot. Imagine spending a whole year of your life in the back of a Transit van just getting to the show. To put the mileage into perspective, try driving around the world twenty-five times. Then, when you've arrived, think how many beers you'd sink killing the tedious hours between the soundcheck and the show in the bar you're stuck in and multiply it by 2000. Probably enough to fill a swimming pool, right?

John Otway really has been there, seen it, done it. Of course there are no prizes for being an expert on motorway service station food, BUT how many people can say they know what it's like to headline at the Reading Festival, tour the USA or play a gig with The Clash or Squeeze as support?

At the end of the day the most endearing thing about Otway the man is the plain fact that it's not the money or the trappings, it is still, quite simply 'being up there' that he loves. Asked recently in an interview what luxury item he would take with him to his desert island Otway replied "an audience".

Otway's 2000th gig will be one luxurious desert island.

One of John's first constructive ideas was: "Wouldn't it be great if we had an audience of 2,000 for the gig?" At the time he would play to 150 fans on a good night so both of them felt that the target was nigh-on impossible but agreed to see how close they could get to it.

With the financial restrictions John placed upon himself and with Cotton not having the funds to pay for a big Otway show, the pair of them went looking for a promoter. John realised that promoting a major Otway show was a potential big loss maker and like all acts he hated shows where the organisers put him on and then incurred a big debt. However, there was one promoter Otway was quite comfortable seeing lose a small fortune.

"I'll give Paul Clerehugh a call and see if he's up for doing it," John told Cotton.

Paul Clerehugh was a fan and his fondness for Otway had increased considerably after the big marquee sell-out show at his small restaurant. He liked the Gig 2000 concept and also fancied his hand at promoting a sizeable London show. He promised John that he would have a look at some possibilities and get back to him.

It ended up being a choice between the Hackney Empire and the London Astoria. Because of its location in the West End of London and the deal he was offered, the Astoria was agreed to: on Friday November 12th 1993 John Otway would walk onto a stage for the 2,000th time in his long career.

Otway and Cotton set about booking the exact number of dates required for the Gig 2000 tour and sussing-out whether it was possible to print all 2000 dates on the T-shirt for the tour. After John had typed in all the gigs he had done and popped it on a floppy disc, Cotton set about designing the Gig 2000 T-shirt – he had become adept at computer graphics and owned an Apple Mac. He discovered that it was indeed possible to fit all the gigs on a T-shirt: they would be in very small type, but definitely legible. The new up-beat Gig 2000 T-shirt could take over from the current one, *John Otway The Hitless Years 1977–1993*.

John was very impressed with all the things Cotton could do with his new Apple Mac and an idea occurred to him. Back in his home town twenty years previously, his career had been helped considerably by a local music newspaper *The Aylesbury Roxette* – put together by Pete Frame the editor of *Zigzag*. It occurred to John that it might be possible to do a Gig 2000 paper. Whereas the *Roxette* had been a labour of love for Pete Frame and his team of helpers, with the new technology Cotton would be able to put a paper together himself. Unlike the *Roxette*, which featured all the local acts, this paper would concentrate on just one – read about Otway on pages 1,2,3,4,5,6,7 and 8. Soon John was on the phone asking as many people as possible to write about him for his newspaper.

Whether thinking about pressing his CDs, ordering T-shirts or getting publicity photos, he would always estimate the amount he needed and more than double it. This is what he did when he worked out the print run for his newspaper.

"Anyone would know that a print run of 10,000 copies was enough. Unfortunately it cost only a few hundred pounds more to get 20,000, and as that number had a two and several zeros in it he felt that it would be unlucky to get the smaller quantity for Gig 2000," explains Richard Cotton. "The thing was that nobody apart from Otway had thought about where we were going to store them all, and John was thinking that they all could be stored at my house. Most people don't think about how much room 20,000 newspapers take up but Jeanette, my girlfriend, thought about it a great deal when they moved in with us. Especially when you bear in mind what was on the front page."

The front page was a series of photos showing John apparently swallowing a Shure microphone. John thought that putting the picture on the cover would impress his sponsors and sales of these microphones would be increased because it could be made to look as if he could stuff one whole into his mouth, but it is highly likely that Jeanette has been put off them for life.

For Paul Clerehugh the gig was important. He felt that Otway had underachieved: he rarely did a bad gig and yet he rarely did a big gig. He felt that there were a lot of people like himself who would like, just for once, to see the man strutting around a big stage with a great light and sound system doing exactly what he had craved for all his life, being a big rock star. He did a lot to make the show special: the first few hundred tickets were sold with free after show party tickets and all the advance sales came with a John Otway bootleg cassette of out-takes and demos.

That year's Glastonbury removed anyone's doubts about whether the band was capable of rising to the big occasion, and the way that the 5,000 strong audience reacted at the end of the show remains one of bass player Seymour's top five memories.

And come the autumn the 2000th gig bandwagon began its roll onto the countdown to the big gig itself. Cotton-designed Gig 2,000 stickers started appearing on every piece of correspondence, and at every gig more and more fans came up to the band saying "See you at the Astoria." It started to get terribly exciting.

Tickets for the after show party and bootleg cassette went on sale and after a couple of weeks it became apparent that Paul Clerehugh was not about to lose the fortune that John thought he might, but was in danger of discovering a fortune John did not realise was there.

Once advance sales hit one thousand, it was pretty obvious that this was going to be the biggest Otway gig since the late 70s.

Otway, Paul and Cotton met regularly at John's new local, The Park Tavern, where the promotional strategy was hammered out. Cotton would print out minutes of these meetings, so it is now possible to look at them and realise that the success of the forthcoming gig was aided greatly by the methodical and practical approach that now supported the Otway dreams.

Richard Cotton spotted an opportunity to make his first steps into the music business proper and reckoned that the show should be recorded. There was not a live CD in John's catalogue, the production costs would be low and so it should be a good and profitable debut record for a new label. With this in mind he booked one of the finest mobile recording studios in London to record the event.

During the Park Tavern meetings the three put some thought into getting press and what could make the actual show special.

Paul and Richard did well with the press, organising coverage in Viz Magazine, The Daily Express and The Independent. Johnny Walker had John on his Radio 1 show, which was a huge coup. "We've invited loads of big special guests, like Sting, and none have got back to us to say they can't make it, which is promising," John told the millions of listeners to the show. Johnny was a fan and would be a huge help to Otway's career. Not only was he going to come but when he heard that the show was going to be recorded, he asked if John and Richard Holgarth could come back to the studio the day after the performance with a tape of the show.

John's list of what could make the show extra special included a set of bagpipes, a Sinclair C5 and Wild Willy Barrett. "He will never agree to do it if I ask him," said John, so Paul offered to see if he could persuade Willy to do a couple of numbers and then join Otway for a song. If the listing in the programme read 8:50pm Wild Willy Barrett (if he turns up), that covered them for whatever Willy decided to do and it would also add to the drama of the evening.

Richard Cotton's girlfriend, Jeanette, was managing director of a firm that installed sprinkler systems into industrial units. On units with particularly high ceilings, they used hydraulic platforms to raise the fitters high enough to put in the pipe work. "They are quite compact," Cotton told Otway, "I reckon we could get one on the Astoria stage, if you think it would be any use."

To make the band version of *Racing Cars* more interesting, drummer Adam Batterbee lent John his skateboard. From his position directly behind John when performing, he realised that Otway's combination of a good sense of balance and lack of co-ordination should make the skateboarding front man a highly entertaining spectacle. And in that run up to the Astoria, highly entertaining it had been.

The Fleece and Firkin in Bristol, one of Otway's regular pub gigs, has one of the longest bars in the UK, which runs the whole length of the side of the pub. Otway had successfully skateboarded from one end to the other at breakneck speed with just one scoot. The velocity was actually slow, it was just the fact that he was moving at all that made it breakneck.

If John got into difficulties on the skateboard, he would use his safety first rule, i.e. his safety first. However fast he managed to scoot, if he felt out of control he would just step off the board and let it take its own course. This wasn't too bad for Richard Holgarth as John's favoured method of skateboarding was from stage left to stage right, but it did leave Murray and Seymour in a rather perilous position on the other side of the stage and they became quite adept at leaping out of the way. It must be pointed out that the band had now reached the level of proficiency that this could be done without missing a beat.

"I remember this gig at the Wedgewood Rooms in Portsmouth," Murray says. "Otway had already cheesed off the sound crew by hammering the dents out of his microphone before they had a chance to turn it off and then, during the show, half the PA went dead. At the end of the night the engineers discovered a skateboard embedded deep within the electrical circuit of the main power amplifier."

It was probably at this gig that Otway met Eric Hayto, a real skateboarder, a local champion who had actually won skateboarding contests and medals at skateboarding. He was approximately the same height and build as John.

"I've got a great idea," John said when they met. "Why don't you be my double at the Astoria gig?"

CHAPTER 8

On November 12th 1993, John Otway broke the house record for the largest audience at the London Astoria – over the 2000 he and Cotton had dreamt of and, more unbelievably there were ticket touts.

Promoters and artists usually have a loathing for ticket touts, but Paul Clerehugh was not surprised or displeased. In fact he was very pleased, unable to throw any light on where they might have got the last few tickets that they were selling at a premium. For John the touts had a novelty value. He could not remember having them before and he was ecstatic. "We've got ticket touts, bloody hell ticket touts," he would tell anyone who would listen.

Venue Manager Chris Alexander had never seen anything like it in the Astoria before.

"I think it's fair to say that at that time John was one of the smallest acts we had headlining. When Paul Clerehugh told me it was going well I took it to mean that they had covered the hiring costs and he was about to start making a bit of a profit. It would never have occurred to me that John Otway would break the house record.

"The other thing that was surprising was that even though we had the biggest crowd we had ever had, as soon as the first act went on the bars were empty. At big shows, you always have a number of people who take a break from the music and spend at least part of the evening at the bar. But that night when the show was on they were empty."

Backstage John was full of nervous energy, smoking his pipe and trying to get the drones working on the set of bagpipes that had been hired for him.

"You know that really horrid sound that you can make with these things," he said to the band. "Wouldn't it be great if we started our set with that."

Whether he was right or not we shall never know. Blow as hard as he might he couldn't get a sound out of the instrument horrid or otherwise.

The Gits were the first act on fronted by Steve Frost, instantly recognisable from countless television appearances, a regular part on The Young Ones TV series as a policeman, and famous for saying the words "I bet he drinks Carling Black Label," on a television advertisement at the time. He was a great help to Otway, a friend who was prepared to be a special guest when people like Sting would not. His band were fun too. They did a short set and went down superbly well. So far, so brilliant.

Next up Murray Torkildsen was the Otway band's rhythm guitarist, and was also an accomplished singer-songwriter. John was a fan of his material and Richard Cotton was interested in getting him to record for his new label, so a spot at the Astoria was a good opportunity for a bit more exposure. He was as great as everyone thought he would be and the expectation grew.

If Otway was right, and he might well have been considering the excitement in the room, then everybody was desperate to know if Wild Willy was going to turn up. The question was answered as Willy took the stage with harmonica player Errol Lynton for his ten minute set before the three-minute one-song reunion *Louisa On A Horse*. A great first half.

A short interval then the multi-track tape machine in the mobile studio parked outside the stage door was turned on and the John Otway Big Band took the stage. They opened up with a punked-up version of Roy Orbison's *In Dreams*. Listening now to the live album of that show, you can tell by the speed that everything was played how much adrenalin was flowing in the veins of everyone on stage.

Next up was *House Of the Rising Sun*. From as far back as John can remember, members of the audience had heckled his version. He would start singing:

"Well there is,"
"What?" they would yell.
"A house," sang Otway.
"Where?" they would call back.
Otway: *"In New Orleans."*
Audience: *"What's it called?"*
Otway: *"They call it The Rising Sun."*
Audience: *"What's it been?"*
Otway: *"It's been the ruin of many a poor boy."*
Audience: *"How do you know?"*
Otway: *"Well God, I know."*
Audience: *"Who's a prat?"*
Otway: *"I'm one."* ... etc.

Years ago there would have been only one or two people yelling the lines. By Gig 2000 the majority of the audience knew about it and joined in. The sound of 2000 people yelling "who's a prat?" at him was one of John's favourite moments of the night – and there were quite a few of those.

As Richard Holgarth began the first solo in *Racing Cars*, Otway disappeared off the stage, only to re-appear a few moments later at the wheel of a Sinclair C5. When he had stage-tested the vehicle before the show, he had discovered a design fault – the turning circle was too large to do a u-turn on the Astoria stage, so the choreography had been worked out: the band would step back so that Otway could go backwards and forwards several times without running over a musician. There was something poignant about Otway at the wheel of Clive Sinclair's great dream and the audience loved it, but they hadn't seen it all. As Richard Holgarth began the second solo, Otway popped on a baseball cap and signalled to the crew at the side of the stage to set up a huge semi circular ramp.

"You could really feel the excitement build at that point," says Murray. "Loads of people in the audience had caught one of the gigs leading up to that show and had seen how dangerous and out of control he was on that skateboard. Suddenly the audience sensed danger as they knew Otway loved showing-off and tonight he had more reason to show off than ever. Was he going to kill himself?"

Otway placed the skateboard stage left in front of the soloing Holgarth. He did his usual scoot and skidded towards the hastily retreating Seymour and Murray. Apparently, unable to separate himself from the board, he disappeared into the wings, but instead of the expected crash he was back on stage within seconds travelling much, much faster than he'd ever been seen travelling before, heading straight for the ramp.

2,000 people at John's 2000th gig held their breath as they watched him fly up the ramp so fast his body became parallel with the stage. This horizontal body revolved a complete 180 degrees, then flew back down the ramp and back into the wings. The place went wild, and Holgarth's solos were forgotten… though if anyone who had not been at the show, listened to the song on the live CD today, they would marvel at the standing ovation that followed them.

Towards the end of the show was the ballad *Best Dream* which was possibly the romantic song that worked most successfully with the band as it avoided the wimpiness of a lot of his other slower numbers. Smoke covered the back of the stage as the song began with a duet between John's voice and Murray's rhythm guitar – then Seymour's bass and Adam's drums came in as the song built towards the chorus. Following which Otway stepped back as Richard Holgarth moved centre stage for one of the loveliest solos of the night.

More smoke filled the stage and for the first line of the repeat chorus, the star could not be seen. Then suddenly, there he is, rising, being lifted above the billowing smoke, picked out by the follow-spot as he ascended above the band. He is, for just a short time, a true rock star.

Then the moment was gone as most of the audience recognise that what was hoisting him to the heavens was the sort of lift that fitters use to put fire sprinkling pipe systems into industrial units with very high ceilings – and he is John Otway again.

Then it was *Cheryl's Going Home* with the somersaults and the leaping off the ladder, a great roar demanding two encores, the last of which was *Geneve*, before a beaming Otway headed for the after show party.

It was one of the triumphs of John's career. In less than a year the Band, Richard Cotton, Paul Clerehugh and Eric the skateboard double had taken Otway from a pub gig in Brighton to a sell-out show at the London Astoria.

Richard Holgarth did not get much sleep after the biggest gig to date. He had to be in the studio bright and early to mix two tracks from the night's gig for the Johnny Walker show on Radio One. Johnny had been to the show and loved it. The radio listeners who had been told just a few days earlier how good the show was going to be could now be told how good it actually had been. And Richard Holgarth was able to provide the audio evidence.

CHAPTER
9

During the Gig 2000 campaign John, Paul and Cotton had to work out what to do with gig 2001, which John saw as a potential problem. "It could split the audience since people might think that the concept of *2001 A Space Otway* is as exciting as Gig 2000 itself. Let's do something as far away as possible, like Sydney, then if that turns out to be impractical we could do somewhere closer, maybe Mexico City or New York. Let's agree to make it a foreign city, and see how far it's possible to go."

Eventually, as Gig 2000 got closer, John complained to Paul Clerehugh that nothing had been organised for this other significant gig. Paul was in complete agreement in that whatever 2001 was going to be, it should not take away from the main event in punters, money or time. Eventually he came back with what he described as the perfect solution: Le Dyke, Dunkerque, France. "Bloody simple," he said. "I'll sell a coach load of tickets and we can all get the ferry over the channel the weekend after the Astoria."

So the weekend after the Astoria gig a coach containing the band and a load of Otway fans did the crossing from Folkestone to France.

That evening's gig at Le Dyke was the most drunken gig the band had ever done. On the way over Richard Holgarth had been able to play the mixes of the concert on the coach; after the long build up to the concert and a solid week in the studio he was able to let his hair down. So the small crowd in France discovered that he could play the guitar almost as well horizontally as he could vertically, a talent that he demonstrated several times during the evening.

A lot of acts tend to separate themselves from the fans and their audience, but Otway never had, often heading straight for the bar after the first set and spending the whole interval chatting to the audience. To interpret this as professionalism or going the extra mile is to misunderstand the man: he simply loved the attention.

A lot of acts would not enjoy being stuck on a coach with the audience on the way to a gig, playing to them in the evening and then being stuck with them on the way home the following day – but John was more than happy. He could even be seen holding court in the bar on the ferry both on the way over and the way back.

Richard Holgarth felt equally at ease, he had an easy going manner with the fans and was not averse to the praise he was receiving either. Whether it was by luck or design the band members he had chosen complimented this style.

The Otway Band, with Gig 2000, had blurred the line between being on and off stage. All aspects of John's career had started to be part of the entertainment and something that the fans could be a part of. Not only could they discuss current plans and progress with the band in the bar, the new regular newsletters kept everyone involved with how things were going. With Dunkerque came the concept that the fans could also go on tour with the band. Too close for comfort for a lot of acts, cosy for the Otway Band and crew. It was a trip they all thoroughly enjoyed.

It was an instant hit for the fans too, and became a regular event for the next 12 years. The year after the first one, two coaches and a double-decker, or as Otway preferred to call it a 'convoy', crossed the Channel for a Saturday night gig in down-town Dunkerque and a Sunday lunchtime cabaret show in a beach bar.

The Saturday show would be a straightforward band gig, but the Sunday show was an improvised mix of music, comedy and general mayhem. For the climax of his show, the Star changed into a pair of swimming trunks and headed to the Channel for a swim. It was bitterly cold and towards the end of November. To the astonishment of the locals going for a brisk walk, a lanky Englishman wearing a swimming costume walked out of a beach bar followed by two hundred people who stood on the shore clapping and cheering as he thrashed about in the freezing Channel for a few minutes.

Word spread around the town, and in future years, a few curious French people would come to the gigs to watch this strange Englishman. It was, however, a localized phenomenon and did not significantly increase Otway's profile internationally.

Keen to capitalize on the success of Gig 2000, Otway and Cotton started work on the next project. Ever since Holgarth had produced *Cheryl, A Rock Opera* and *Under the Covers*, Holgarth had been using the down-time at The Square to record an album of new material that he and Otway had, for the past two and a half years, been writing together.

Employing the same successful formula they had used for the last big event, another nationwide tour, newspaper and Astoria show went into the promotion of the first album of new songs by the artist John Otway in thirteen years, *Premature Adulation*.

Richard Cotton, with his ambition to make his mark in the music business, was more than happy to release the album on his label and try and get the record into the album charts. But John, who had lost money on so many records in the past, was more interested in selling directly to the fans, either at gigs or by mail order through his newsletter. Furthermore, there was no obvious single on the album. So although the new album was very popular with the fan base, who turned out in large numbers to see the *Premature Adulation* launch at the Astoria (about two thirds as many as Gig 2000), the rest of the population was largely unaware of its release.

Soon, the paths of Otway and Cotton started to go in different directions. Cotton was young and ambitious and quickly discovered that Otway could only take him so far towards his goals in the music business. His attempt to get John booked on the main stage of Glastonbury failed when, having managed to get promoter Michael Eavis on the phone, he discovered that Michael was not sure what 'Otway' was. Also the joy of roadying for Otway had lost its appeal within a short period of time.

John had always encouraged his roadie to be a part of the show, one of his favourite tricks being to throw his guitar across the stage for the roadie to catch. This was always highly entertaining to watch because no-one could work out the trajectory of the instrument until it had left John's hands. Fortunately the laws of physics dictate that if there is no force other than gravity acting upon a musical instrument thrown stage left to stage right, then it forms a predictable arc and Cotton became adept at performing a catch with no resulting damage to himself or the guitar. However, if the gig was, for instance, being filmed for a video and the star was more interested in looking good than the safety of his roadie or equipment, there was a way of providing an additional force on the flying instrument. On one such occasion Otway stood on the lead of the guitar shortly after it had left his hands, thus applying another force to the instrument when the wire became taut: this force made the trajectory very unpredictable indeed. It is only by studying the video afterwards that one can see how John managed to get the headstock of the guitar to make the necessary contact with the Cotton head, and do what eventually became known as 'Hospitalizing the Roadie'.

As well as the long drives and the hospitalization, there were other things about Otway that Cotton found annoying. One of the arguments they had was over London gigs. "You can't keep doing all these London shows," Cotton told Otway.

Because he did not sell records in quantity, have regular character roles in TV series, and had no other form of income, live work was how John made a living. As a job, this work meant that he would often be away from home and family a couple of days a week. The days when there were London gigs were his favourite, as he would not need to leave for work until 5pm, and would often be back home by midnight. Therefore a quick glance in John's diary would reveal a couple of local shows per month.

"You need to move your career up a notch and just do the one big occasional London show," Cotton advised.

John did not listen, and the Half Moon in Putney, the Weavers Arms in Islington, and many another pub rock gigs in the capital would host an Otway show on a very regular basis.

"It's the reason the audience was smaller at the *Premature Adulation* launch than it was at Gig 2000," Cotton persisted.

"He would not shut up about it," says John. And so in order to answer the question as to whether one could or could not do all these shows, Otway booked the 'London Pub Crawl' tour: twenty gigs within a month, all within the M25.

In order to make it fun, Otway gave out cards to people who came to the shows which were stamped at each gig. Those who collected fifteen gig stamps were awarded a rare Otway record, and those with a fully-stamped card could join Otway and Holgarth at the end-of-tour curry. It was fun, and John had more time at home. But after that, Cotton felt it was definitely worth looking for other acts to work with, acts that were younger and had the simple but effective combination of good records, good shows, good looks and who would listen to him.

After completing his apprenticeship with Otway, his rise in the music business was nothing short of meteoric: under his guidance, the Candyskins had a hit record (and not too many London gigs) and he signed the UK-based act Stretch Princess to a seven-figure recording deal with a major American label. He packed his bags and rented a smart flat in Greenwich Village and moved to New York.

Following Richard Cotton's decision to allow someone else to drive Otway and Holgarth around, a replacement had to be found. Adam, the band's drummer, was roped in, but only lasted a few gigs – yet even in that short time Otway managed to earn him a trip to hospital for four stitches above his right eye. It was a while before the next permanent roadie arrived, in the form of Brian Blunnie, a man who could probably be summed up in one word: hard. "You wouldn't want to mess with him," would be the comment most of the residents of Harlow who knew him, or even just met him briefly, would be likely to use. But mess with him was what Otway did. Even though Brian's hair and beard gave him a striking resemblance to a Star Wars character, few would have been comfortable with yelling 'Wookiee' to him in front of a couple of hundred people. Maybe it was the fact that he could have so easily 'decked' the star that he couldn't be bothered, or more probably it was that he had a similar sense of humour.

"Brian always wanted to join in with our show, but he hasn't really got any talent," John would tell the audience. "So I spent ages wondering how we could include him. Eventually we came up with an idea – Brian can bang two bits of wood together! So we allowed him to do it, and all the way home in the van he was so excited about his performance he kept saying: 'How was I?'." At which point the Wookiee was invited centre stage.

Brian the Roadie became very popular with the fans, and for a while contributed to such an extent that the Otway/Holgarth show pretty much became a trio. Brian even made his own two bits of wood, hinged together so they would make a bigger bang. One day, driving the band to a Crooked Billet show, he came up with an addition of his own: headbutting the breeze block. This is the strongest indication we have that Brian and Otway's sense of humour were indeed very similar.

The expression 'Hospitalizing the Roadie' was first used after a gig in Exeter Arts Centre in 1996, and only later used retrospectively to describe the visits to the A&E department by Richard Cotton and Adam Batterbee. "Richard Holgarth had been complaining all day about his sprained ankle," says John, "and I could tell he was looking for a way to get out of doing 'The Lemming', so I thought Brian would enjoy doing it for a change. I reckoned that after banging the bits of wood and splitting the breeze-blocks in half with his head, leaping from the ladder wouldn't prove too difficult. So I thought the look of agony and the rolling around on the floor after the landing were a piece of theatre. It was only after the audience had left and he still looked in pain, and we had to help pack the gear up, that we realised that he might have hurt himself."

In fact, Brian had caught his ankle on the edge of the stage on his way down and was convinced it was more than just bruised. "I think I'd better go to the hospital" he said. "We were thinking of having a curry," John told him. "If we do the hospital first and then the curry, the restaurant might be closed. But if we do the curry first the hospital will still be open afterwards. Tell you what, as you've hurt your foot, I'll buy your starter.'"

"It's too late, no starters, only mains," the waiter told the trio when they arrived at the Indian restaurant.

"It's not your day, is it?" John said to Brian – and it wasn't. A couple of hours later, a doctor in the emergency department of Exeter General Hospital was carefully studying an x-ray of the ankle that had come into contact with the Exeter Arts Centre stage, and identified five fractures in that area of Brian's foot. "You won't be leaving here for a while," he told him. If the doctor had thought that Brian was going to stay and have his foot sorted out, the doctor thought wrong. "We've got a gig tomorrow, and I'm discharging myself," he announced.

The next day it was discovered that the only way Brian was going to be able to take John and Richard Holgarth to Bournemouth for the gig, take Otway home, take Holgarth home, and then take himself to Harlow hospital, was if his ballooning foot was surrounded by icepacks and encased in a child's semi-inflated rubber ring. "I thought it best under the circumstances to leave 'Lemmings' out of that night's show." says John.

For the next three months, Brian's left leg from the knee down was encased in plaster, and Brian had to roadie on crutches. "It always got a laugh when John knocked the microphone stand over and there was this 'clunk-clunk' as Brian came on stage to set it up again, especially when John did it a few times in succession," remembers Richard Holgarth. "He was a bloody good roadie. We all missed him – me, John and the fans – when he finally packed it in and moved to Birmingham."

CHAPTER 10

Forever Green was to be the last major acting role Otway would have. It was Adam, John's drummer, who finally got the message across.

"Yeah, but of course you can't act," he laughed during a conversation, as if he was stating an obvious truth that anyone with even the slightest knowledge of John was aware of. And in fact he was stating an obvious truth that anyone with even the slightest knowledge of John was aware of. Barring, of course, John himself. Adam to this day swears that he thought Otway must have known he was a crap actor, and didn't mean for it to come as a shock when he said it. "I mean there was enough evidence about," he points out.

But John was shocked at what Adam had said, and when he checked the videos of his various roles he discovered that his only successes had been in *Supergran and the Chronic Crooner* and a spectacularly unsuccessful rock star in an Irn Bru commercial, where the leading man had an uncanny resemblance to Otway himself. So the calls from Frazer and Dunlop, his acting agent, became fewer and fewer.

But as well as the acting work, John had made up an audio tape to try and get some voice-over work. When directors cast these artistes, they normally prefer not to audition them in person as this can affect their choice. In this way, Otway had previously been picked to be the voice of a little Playdough man in a McDonald's commercial. In the summer of 1995, John's agents phoned to say that he had been chosen to do the new Weetabix ad.

"I thought it was a voice-over job," says John. "But when I arrived, I discovered that someone – the director, the client, or someone in the agency – must have been a bit of an Otway fan, as they wanted me to sing *Delilah*. I was over the moon. The words 'Hit Record' came instantly to mind, as loads of people have hits off the back of TV ads. This was going to be a big campaign and I was the new voice of Weetabix."

When TV commercials are made, the voice is often one of the last things to be done and the adverts are often aired a short time after the recording, which was the case with Weetabix' *Delilah*. Conversely, singles are usually recorded a considerable time before release, so John had precious little time to get his hit sorted.

Richard Holgarth was put on hold and the VHS machine set to record all the commercial breaks from the day the advert was expected to be on. As soon as he had a video, copies were made. Holgarth summoned the band to the studio and John went to visit Chris France, whose label had recently had a big chart success with The Ambassadors of Funk, and so in Otway's opinion was the best person to ensure a big chart success with *Delilah*. However, John's old schoolmate realised that whilst trendy Levi's and Coca Cola commercials could secure big hits, Otway singing 'I felt the spoon in my hand and she laughed no more,' was unlikely to. "It was very frustrating. There I was singing my potential hit record on TV several times a day, and no-one would release it," says John.

Eventually Maurice Bacon bowed to the pressure, he agreed to give it a go and endured the inevitable loss of money on an Otway single. The release coincided with the final week of the Weetabix *Delilah* campaign, so for one week, *Delilah* reached the number 186 spot in Music Week's chart – John's highest position for several years. As Otway would point out at all his subsequent shows, it was his band's first taste of the charts.

There was another Astoria gig that year, for which John had a special guitar built. Although John is actually left-handed, he had always played a right-handed guitar because the first instrument he learnt to play was the violin (check out any orchestra, and you won't see any left-handed violin players). However, he had discovered that with a little practice he could manage a few chords the other way round. So he built an instrument out of two guitars with the two necks pointing in opposite directions, *The Ambidextrous*. The first attempt at creating this guitar produced an instrument over five foot from head to head, but as there were no strings crossing the middle, there was no reason why the two halves could not be hinged together and folded for transport. It was then a small mental leap for Otway to realise that if instead of a catch to hold the guitar open, something elastic "like a hoover belt" was used, the guitars could be made to 'flap', and would look quite fascinating. The prototype worked well, and Gordon Smith Guitars agreed to build a proper version with one left- and one right-handed guitar, with a hoover belt and the same serial number embossed upon each headstock.

Paul Clerehugh had not been allowed to do any of the Astoria shows after Gig 2000, in case he made another killing, so John promoted this show directly with the venue manager Chris Alexander. Chris had suggested that another popular act should be added to the bill and booked Wilko Johnson, which was a great choice as both acts enjoyed each other's playing and company, and there was a considerable crossover with their respective fans.

Even with Wilko and *The Ambidextrous*, this was now the third big London show and, with Otway's insistence of playing the capital around twenty times per year (forty in the case of '98), the impact was not the same as Gig 2000. Audience numbers reflected this, and the balcony was closed for the 1,000 fans who showed up, still a huge number for an Otway gig, but not the spectacle or the huge success the first show had been.

There was evidence however, that Otway was thinking ahead to something bigger. Although not promoting the concert, Paul Clerehugh was putting up posters around the Astoria that read 'John Otway plays the Royal Albert Hall'.

John felt he needed to be seen doing more and more spectacular things on the route to stardom. As soon as one big goal had been achieved, it was ticked off, and an even bigger one was chosen. This technique was essentially like pyramid selling, and would eventually lead to his downfall. John had never worked out exactly what stardom was, and if he had he would have probably chosen something other than a narrow uphill path that had no summit, just big drops on both sides. Nevertheless, it was a fun path to watch Otway climb, and considering his lack of innate talent, fascinating to watch just how far up that path he was able to go. And there were big successes on the way. Gig 2000 was one of them, and this could be another, even though John's passion to go a bit off the rails left him far too close to one of the edges of that path for even his own comfort.

CHAPTER 11

After the first big Astoria show, John Otway and Paul Clerehugh had met occasionally for a few beers. Both of them knew what they wanted to do next: The Royal Albert Hall would work if they could get just twice as many people as they had for their unbelievably successful Gig 2000. After a few beers, John would say "If we stuff The Royal Albert Hall, no-one will be able to call me 'Rock and Roll's Greatest Failure' ever again."

Paul was tempted – he had done very well out of Otway and the idea of making his favourite star a successful one had strong appeal. But it would be over ten times more costly in terms of time, effort and money. "I think the deposit on the Astoria was around £500, whereas it was more like £10,000 for the Royal Albert Hall," recalls Paul. And that was just the deposit. By the time Paul had put together a budget that included PA, lights, marketing and so on, the total figure was pretty scary, and the responsible family star unable to put a stake into the gamble. But the beers at their meetings eventually paid off. "Put some teaser posters up at the Astoria and see what the reaction is with the fans," said Otway. And as he predicted, it was good.

"Wow, are you really planning to do The Albert Hall?" they asked Otway.

"I will if Paul Clerehugh will do it. He's over there, go and ask him," Otway replied.

Nobody can remember when John and Paul finally decided to go for it, but it was probably in a pub a couple of weeks after Paul had put up the poster at John's half-sell-out Astoria show. John and Paul booked the downstairs room of a pub to invite all the fans who were interested in the project to a meeting to discuss the Albert Hall gig.

"That was my idea," says John. "I had quite definite ideas about what I wanted and I didn't think I'd get many of them past

Paul, no matter how many beers we'd had. But I thought that if I put them to the fans in front of him, he'd get a bit carried away with enthusiasm and succumb."

Two of these ideas were very important to John. Firstly he wanted to make the point that he could fill the Albert Hall on his own merit, so, unlike Gig 2000, there would be no special anniversary, nor would any other artists appearing that night be advertised as anything other than special guests. And secondly he wanted a symphony orchestra.

As soon as he realised he could possibly get The Royal Albert Hall, he really, *really* wanted a symphony orchestra. A lot of bands play there, and a lot of them augment their show with a few strings or maybe a bit of brass, but Otway wanted to do it as someone like Frank Sinatra had, and pose around the stage "with a bloody great orchestra behind me".

It would obviously be prohibitively expensive to use something like The Royal Philharmonic or the BBC Symphony Orchestra: the simple arithmetic of multiplying the Musician's Union minimum rate by the number of members of a full orchestra would appear to make any symphony orchestra out of reach. But John had an idea that he was about to put to the meeting. In his school days he had been a member of the Aylesbury Youth Orchestra and had, for a very short time, even been the leader. If they still existed, he told Paul and the group of fifty fans listening to his ideas, maybe they would be prepared to do it. If he used any old Youth Orchestra, people would probably say it was because he couldn't afford a grown-up one (which was of course true). But this was perfect, he even had his introduction worked out.

"I'd like to introduce my first band, they've been through a few line-up changes since I was one of them. Please welcome the Aylesbury Youth Orchestra."

Richard Holgarth wanted the much simpler addition of a few strings and brass players to work with the band, which would be a far easier and more achievable objective than a whole orchestra. "It's dead easy to do, it'll make the band sound great, and I even know some brilliant players," he announced to a brick wall that had already made up its mind.

Other things were discussed and planned that night. Wilko Johnson would be asked to do something with Otway, as would his old friend Attila. There would be another newspaper and the question would again be posed: "Willy or Won't he?" John came away from the meeting with pretty much all he wanted. It was going to be simply 'John Otway at The Royal Albert Hall', and he had permission to find out about the Aylesbury Youth Orchestra and, if they still existed, invite them to do the show.

A couple of months later, John met with Hugh Malloy, their conductor.

"I was both nervous and excited about that meeting," recalls John. "It was the sort of thing I dreamt of when I was in the Orchestra myself – one day I'm going to play The Royal Albert Hall and I'll come back and invite this lot to back me. It was one of the lovely, magnanimous, benign things one could do when one became a rock star, and here I was doing just that."

John's enthusiasm was infectious, and Hugh was prepared to ask the orchestra if they would like to do it. However, the orchestra was programmed around the school year. A considerable number of the students in it were in their final year of school and would be leaving the orchestra in July to be replaced by others moving in at the start of the new school year. As Hugh explained, this meant that there was no point rehearsing anything until September. To do something earlier would be unfair on those who were leaving as they would not be doing the show, and unfair on those joining as they would not be as familiar with the material. The concert had been booked for 30th November which would give them just six rehearsals before the performance.

There was one other thing that should have rung alarm bells in our star's brain. During the conversation, John had brought up the subject of the orchestral arrangements and had asked if Hugh fancied doing them. "It wasn't just the polite emphatic 'no'," says Otway. "It was the look that came with it that should have warned me that I had no idea what I was getting into." But whatever it was that Otway was getting into, with a handshake at the end of the lunch he had rushed in where other rock stars might have been just a tad more cautious.

Meanwhile, something needed to be done about the declining numbers at the big Otway London shows, and John had a plan. There was an anniversary coming up: 1997 would be the twentieth anniversary of The Hit and this would be one year before the planned Royal Albert Hall show.

Long before that hit, when the local paper 'The Bucks Herald' still referred to John as 'Aylesbury's Singing Dustman', he found a way to pack out the larger venues in the town by putting on the annual John Otway Free Concert. Each July he ran up a large debt hiring the halls, the PA and the most popular bands in the town as support acts and let everyone in for nothing. He felt it was worth it as he got to headline successful events, even though what he was doing could be accurately described as 'vanity promoting'.

The idea of another packed Astoria from which to launch The Albert Hall a year before the big gig was, as John told Paul

Clerehugh, a pretty good idea. Would Paul promote the *Really Free* show?

"It is a good idea," agreed Paul. "But as it's your idea, you should promote that one. Leave me to concentrate on The Albert Hall."

Ever since Amy was born, John had resisted using the special accounting techniques he had previously been addicted to. But the urge was too strong, and he used one to figure out how the *Really Free* show could make a profit. His accounting technique took the two conventional 'Out' and 'In' columns and replaced them with ones called 'Predictable' and 'Unpredictable'. And whenever things looked a bit negative, he would simply apply a little more optimism to the 'Unpredictable' column.

The outgoings for the show were predictable, as he had already done three Astoria gigs and had a reasonably good idea how expensive it would be. The 'In', which was the 'Unpredictable' column, consisted of T-shirt sales, a special Otway jumble sale, and the video of the concert.

The fans were more than happy to turn out in large numbers to watch Otway and the Band celebrate the anniversary of The Hit, and the *Really Free* tickets were given away much faster than John would have been able to sell them. It was quite obvious from the time the concert was announced that once again the Astoria would be absolutely packed out.

This show was also the launch for The Royal Albert Hall, so Paul Clerehugh finalised the deal with them a week or so before, paid the deposit and arrived at the *Really Free* gig with a large pile of really expensive tickets: the boxes and the first rows of the stalls. These were the best seats of The Albert Hall – the ones that the most avid Otway fans would want to sit on most – and of course were the most expensive.

Both John and Paul were keen to do business, and so had booked a room in the pub a few yards from The Astoria to set up their shops and sell their respective wares a couple of hours before the show.

John had been there since the morning with Karen getting the jumble sale together, and Karen had offered to get her friends to help with it for the night. They would be selling a variety of Otway memorabilia: posters advertising gigs long gone, various T-shirts and badges that he had got printed over his years of stardom, and lots and lots of records that John was hoping would do better in the jumble sale than they had done in the shops.

There was stage clothing, too. During each show Otway would rip his shirt open and his mother would normally sew all the buttons back on again, but some were too badly ripped to be worth repairing and would only be useful as rags or jumble sale items. "Each one has done a gig" said a sign over the clothes rail. "We only need to sell 30 of these at a fiver and we've made £150," John had worked out.

At the height of his success, twenty years before the jumble sale, Lloyd's bank had allowed John to have specially-designed cheques with his photograph on them. The idea had been that if he paid small bills with them, people would keep the famous rock star's cheque rather than cash them. For very good unauthorised overdraft reasons, the bank account had long since been closed, however, John still had a couple of the cheque books left. On the night of the *Really Free* show, for a fiver John would write a cheque for however much you wanted. £1000, £10,000, even a million pounds. Aware, of course, that these items would instantly display their latex qualities should they find themselves in the proximity of a financial institution.

The once-free Gig 2000 and *Premature Adulation* newspapers were up for sale at 50p each, and there was of course the *Really Free* anniversary T-shirt for that night's show which, because of some ridiculous oversight, had the wrong date on it.

Karen brought in a friend who worked in the art department for feature films and would work on the sets for *Casino Royale* and *The Golden Compass*. He had a natural flair for design and within minutes what once had been one end of the bar was transformed into what looked exactly like a real proper jumble sale.

At the other end of the room, Paul Clerehugh's stall was a much simpler affair, with very little thought or effort put into it. He arrived shortly before the pub opened with a couple of waitresses from The Crooked Billet, carrying a small sign saying 'Albert Hall Tickets', a briefcase, and a cashbox. "Can I just borrow a couple of chairs and a table?" he asked the landlord, and in about three minutes he was ready.

After the show, Otway and the Band headed for the pub to see how Karen and Paul had done, and they had done very well. Most of the torn shirts had been sold and John signed-off twenty-two cheques for a total of six million, five hundred and seventy four thousand pounds, and made a whopping one hundred and ten pounds from them. The show was still in the red but "the video sales will take care of that," and they did. It would take the invention of the DVD and a deal with Cherry Red records, but six years after the *Really Free* show, John's accounting came good and the show was in the black.

Things happened a little faster for Paul Clerehugh. All his tickets had gone and the takings from his small table opposite the jumble sale was over ten times as big as Karen's. In fact, only a few days after paying the deposit, Paul's Albert Hall gig was in the black and would never again be in the red.

CHAPTER 12

One of the reasons Paul Clerehugh's big production did not go in the red was because Paul did not rely quite so heavily on optimism when working out his accounts.

When studying the feasibility of the project, he had identified a gap between the total costs and revenue from ticket sales: there was, he felt, a limit to what an Otway fan, used to paying a fiver for a pub gig, would pay to see John in a more prestigious venue. The really avid fans would buy the boxes and first couple of rows, but there would still be another 3,500 to go.

"And these really did need to be sold for a price the fans would pay," says Paul, "so I started looking for some sponsorship."

He approached Viz to sponsor the gig, because back in 1987 John had recorded a single for the magazine when it was still a cult publication. "It was one of the funniest things I had ever read," says John, "I suggested recording a song for it, so got together with Andy Partridge from XTC and friend Neville Farmer to record *Bags Of Fun With Buster* by Johnny Japes and the Jesticles."

Chris Donald, the magazine's editor, liked the single so much that in the April 1988 edition of Viz, the single went straight into comic's chart at Numbers One, Two, Three, Four and Five, the first time that these chart positions had been reached by one record since the Beatles stormed America in 1965. Since the *Bags Of Fun With Buster* single, but probably not because of it, Viz had had meteoric success, going from cult status to the fourth most popular magazine in the UK with a circulation of 1.2 million at its peak.

Viz was famous for its toilet humour and black comedy with often violent or sexual story lines, so "Viz presents John Otway at the Royal Albert Hall" would be very funny. But was it a joke that those responsible for maintaining the status and reputation of Britain's most prestigious iconic concert venue would appreciate? It came down to Paul Clerehugh's marvellous ability to use the English language to colour things in a way that made them more palatable, an ability that he had honed in his restaurant menus.

"He was wonderful," says Richard Holgarth. "Fish and chips would be described as something like 'lightly stunned slab of haddock on a bed of pomme frittes' and mutton would be dressed up as 'mature full-flavoured vintage lamb a la Cartland.'" These days a mild form of this technique is used in political circles and is called 'spin'; Paul's more virulent technique would be better described as 'gyroscopic' (as in the device that keeps a rocket heading in to space without falling back to earth – it was how man got to the moon and how Viz got to the Albert Hall).

John Haxby, a graphic designer who had done a great deal of artwork for Otway, produced a wonderful image of Otway flying over the building playing his ambidextrous guitar. It looked fabulous and was used for all the publicity.

All the successful promoting ideas from Gig 2000 were to be refined for the Albert Hall: there would be a newspaper, but this time in colour; instead of a free cassette there would be a free CD with some specially-recorded tracks; and the tour leading up to the big event would eventually be forty-eight shows in fifty-four days.

Since he had never learned to drive, Otway was a bit cavalier with how he routed his tours. Whether you groaned or smiled when you saw the random way it zig-zagged around the British Isles, depended on whether you were doing the tour or just taking an interest in it. On this tour there were two consecutive dates that would significantly alter the usual geometric zig-zagging by adding one line that represented a distance of 600 miles. John had received a call regarding his availability for the Penzance Festival, this would be the day following a show in Perth. "Well it's close alphabetically," he quipped. Otway could see a publicity opportunity and the gig was added to the tour. 'The Perth to Penzance Challenge' was announced in the special newspaper. "Anyone who comes to both gigs will be given back stage passes and will be able to lig with me, the band and the special guests at the Royal Albert Hall."

Since meeting Hugh Malloy, John had been wondering how best to use the Aylesbury Youth Orchestra at the Royal Albert Hall gig. He had used an orchestra once before, when he had recorded *Geneve*. Before he had become a pop star, when he was working for the Aylesbury Vale District Council as a dustman, he had fallen for a girl named Lisa: when she turned him down, John's response to the subsequent heartache was to write songs. *Genève* (spelt like that because that was how she spelt it on her letters), is probably his best known ballad, a song in which he spells out his feelings for her and his faith in his belief that he will eventually be a great star. A few years later, when *Really Free* was in the charts, John had recorded a new version with a huge orchestra and Polydor had released it as a follow-up.

It was one of the biggest mistakes of his career. The wild Otway and Barrett had endeared themselves to a generation of punk fans with their hit, and most of these were unimpressed with the six and half minute solo Otway orchestral epic that came next. Shortly afterwards John and Willy split up, and the spiral of descent his career took was only halted by his description of it in his 'Rock and Roll's Greatest Failure' book.

But John loved the song, and to be fair, so did a sizable number of his fans. No one ever thought they would get to see him sing it live with the 'big flop single' arrangement, but they would if John had his way, and it would be from one of the more prestigious stages in the world.

His original plan had been to use the orchestra to back him on *Geneve* at the Royal Albert Hall, but when he saw them in concert, he realised they could do so much more. "The thing I noticed was that they were doing a classical repertoire," says John. "The Aylesbury Music Centre had a dance band for lighter, popular music, but the Youth Orchestra was for those young people who had both the ability and appreciation for more challenging material. I knew that I couldn't bring the whole orchestra to the Albert Hall to play one romantic pop ballad, so I started thinking a great deal about what else I could do with them."

"John putting a great deal of thought into any idea was not always the best use of his brain," says Paul Clerehugh. "I often used to say 'Don't worry about that, I'll deal with it', because I could see the profits leaking away as he mulled something over – a simple concept could become a grand magnificent spectacle after a relatively short time in his head."

So what had his musings over the orchestra produced?

"I knew that getting the orchestra to do a bit of Brahms, Beethoven or Tchaikovsky wouldn't be very popular with the fans," says Otway. "Years before, after we had recorded the song *Birthday Boy*, I recall Willy saying that it would be really fun to do with an orchestra, and I could see what he meant: the intro had this simple passage that would just sound sumptuous being blasted out by the string and brass sections and there was a solo that was completely mad and modern that Shostakovich himself would have been proud of. The other thing that came to mind was *The Highwayman*."

The Highwayman was a long poem by Alfred Noyes that John had learned at school. It was very popular, and eighteen months earlier had been voted in at number fifteen in a poll seeking Britain's favourite poem for the BBC's *Bookworm* programme. It featured in many anthologies and many school syllabuses, which of course was how John had discovered it. When he was learning it, he had started strumming his guitar along with the words and found a musical riff that worked very well with the rhythm of the lines. He turned it into a dramatic performance piece for his very first gig, and his wild rendition of Alfred's poem remained one of the high points of his show for many years. There was even a version of it on his first solo album.

This was John's brilliant idea: a specially-commissioned orchestral arrangement of *The Highwayman*. It could be something akin to Prokofiev's *Peter and The Wolf* or instead of Benjamin Britten's *Young Person's Guide to the Orchestra* you could have an *Otway Fan's Guide To The Orchestra*. It would add real culture to the Royal Albert Hall Show, he thought, and the fans already familiar with the Otway treatment of the poem would be thoroughly impressed with a full orchestral arrangement. Now, not only was he going back to his old orchestra and getting them the Royal Albert Hall stage to play on, John was also getting a new classical work specially written for them: *The Highwayman* for John Otway and Orchestra.

"When I thought this through, I got really excited," says John. "It just seemed the perfect way of using the orchestra. And the fans, a lot of whom might never go to a highbrow classical concert, would get to hear something a bit special."

Unfortunately, John had no idea how to progress with the orchestral arrangements. He had used strings and brass a few times on his recordings, but from a few brief enquiries he had discovered that arranging for a full symphony orchestra was in a different league altogether. But then Karen mentioned Frenchman Jean Paul Metzgar, who had started going out with her friend Julia Donnely.

"He's a composer," Karen said to John. "Do you know what he does? He gets orchestral scores and reads them like books. He often prefers doing that to listening to the music, isn't that interesting?" John agreed that it was very, very interesting and suggested that Julia and her new boyfriend should be invited around for a meal. A few days later John could be seen in the kitchen cooking coq au vin "to make Jean Paul feel at home", and over dinner John shared his excitement with Karen, Julia and Jean Paul.

Fortunately or not, Jean Paul found himself "au bon endroit au bon moment" (in the right place at the right time) and was impressed by John's cooking, the wine he had carefully sourced and the enthusiasm he had for his new project.

There are two important facts about Jean Paul that should be borne in mind: firstly he had never done the score for a complete symphony orchestra before and secondly he had never witnessed a John Otway performance. Because firstly, if he had, he might not have taken the £500 commission Paul Clerehugh had earmarked for the six month's work and secondly as he says himself, "Had I seen one of John's performances, I would have done the arrangements a little differently."

For the composer though, there was something seductive about what John was suggesting. He had written several pieces for various ensembles for both performance and recording, but his ultimate goal was to compose for a symphony orchestra. As Otway pointed out over dinner, "Doing it like this you've got the added benefit of The Albert Hall."

A week later Otway arrived with a guitar at Jean Paul's flat in North London to go through the ideas in more detail. *Geneve* would be relatively simple, because John wanted it to sound as it did on the record, so for Jean Paul it was just a matter of copying the original. *Birthday Boy* too didn't pose too many problems and it was fun. Jean Paul could easily see what Willy envisaged when he said that an orchestra would sound great doing what he was playing on the guitar.

The fifteen-verse *Highwayman* was what would take the work and the creativity. John had given Jean Paul a copy of the recorded versions of *Geneve* and *Birthday Boy*, but wanted to give Jean Paul as much artistic freedom as possible with *The Highwayman*. "So I just took a copy of the poem and played him the riff on the guitar," says John. "I didn't want to give him too many preconceived ideas as to how it should work out."

Together they went through the poem verse by verse. John had traditionally left out several verses in his live version in order to make the song a suitable length, but when he talked it through with Jean Paul....

... Tim the ostler listened, his face was white and peaked
His eyes were hollows of madness, his hair like mouldy hay
And he loved the landlord's daughter ...

"You have to keep that verse in," said the composer to the star, "I can do wonderful things with that."

... When they shot him down on the highway
Down like a dog on the highway,
and he lay in his blood on the highway
With a bunch of lace at his throat ...

Karen, John and Amy.
(Kim Furrokh)

On the set of *Forever Green*
with Pauline Collins & Brian Coburn.
(Courtesy of Picture Partnership Productions Ltd)

Karen at the
Edinburgh Festival 1988.
(Otway Archives)

The Otway & Barrett Re-Union tour. *(Otway Archives)*

Headbutts & Halibutts
with
Attila the Stockbroker.
(Otway Archives)

With Richard Holgarth.
(Rebecca Marr)

*The Otway Big Band –
(l to r)* Seymour, Murray,
Richard & Adam –
a youthful line-up.
(Otway Archives)

The Sinclair C5 at Gig 2000. *(Kev Dutton)*

The Dunkerque Dip. *(Otway Archives)*

The 20th Anniversary of the Hit at the Astoria. *(Otway Archives)*

The 20th Anniversary of the
Hit at the Astoria.
(Otway Archives)

Paul Clerehugh –
successful promoter
and restaurateur.
(C J Photography)

Jean-Paul Metzger, Otway and Hugh Malloy
study the orchestral score.
(Julian Hill)

Otway, Hugh and the Aylesbury Youth Orchestra. *(Brian Thomas)*

Amy & Paul Bradley present the Star with his bouquet. *(Brian Thomas)*

The Royal Albert Hall. *(Brian Thomas)*

The Royal Albert Hall – *You Ain't Seen Nothing Yet!* (Brian Thomas)

Seymour at The Royal Albert Hall. (Brian Thomas)

The Royal Albert Hall. (Brian Thomas)

The Big Band at Ingmire Hall.

above left:
Roadie Brian Blunnie (324 gigs) with
'instruments' on stage at the RAH.
(Julain Hill)

above right:
Roadie Bill Masterson (228 gigs).
(Otway Archives)

right:
Roadie John Padget (743 gigs).
(John Haxby - Art Surgery)

And other verses too, that John would not normally have included, were re-inserted into the new version as the pair of them got carried away with the concept of creating mood, excitement and drama with a full complement of strings, brass, woodwind, percussion, Otway and horse.

"Paul, you know that Lloyds Bank advert on telly?" John asked Paul Clerehugh on the phone the next day. "The one where a great black stallion goes upright on two hind legs and does this whinny thing. Well, I was thinking, do you think we could do something like that at the Albert Hall? Coming up to the end of *The Highwayman*, as the orchestra bring the thing to a climax, we could get a stunt rider to gallop centre stage do the big whinny and gallop off the other side. It'd be brilliant, no-one would expect it and it would be an astonishing climax to the piece."

Paul promised John that he would get straight on to the Albert Hall and ask them if it would be possible to put this very expensive idea on the Albert Hall stage. And he was very efficient and called back minutes later to tell John that they had said "No".

"Well did you ask if it was OK if we just had the gallop and didn't do the whinny?"

"They wouldn't even discuss it," he told John. "They just said 'No horses'."

CHAPTER
13

A few weeks before the big tour kicked off, Paul organised a production meeting at the Albert Hall for everyone involved in the show. Hugh, the conductor, was coming to sort out the logistics that affected the orchestra, so John arranged to meet him and Jean Paul at a Kensington pub beforehand. As it had been several months since John and Jean Paul had talked through the ideas there was a lot of interest in how the compositions were progressing.

"Jean Paul had these huge pieces of manuscript paper containing bits of the score that he and Hugh poured over with great enthusiasm," recalls John. "I hadn't read music since my days at the Aylesbury Youth Orchestra when I was eighteen so there was not much I could glean from what was on show. But they looked wonderful, handwritten musical sketches that would not have looked out of place in the British Museum along with other great classical originals.

"Jean Paul would point to a crotchet here and a semiquaver there and hum a little bit of melody. The only time I felt I understood anything was when he pointed out a very neat bit of handwriting which read *The wind was a torrent of darkness* and said 'That's where you come in'."

Hugh Molloy seemed very impressed with Jean Paul's months of composing as more of the great sheets of manuscript were laid on the pub table for further scrutiny. Just looking at the huge amount of work involved, John for the first time truly appreciated why Hugh had looked at him the way he did when asked if he fancied having a go at the arrangements.

It was a great precursor to the Albert Hall meeting. If Hugh had reservations about what John was going to give his orchestra to play they were now gone, and Otway basked in the reflected admiration. Even if he had not written and composed the work, even if he couldn't understand it, he knew from the reaction that it was good and, most importantly, it had been his idea. This was one of those wonderful days that Otway loved, when he both felt like a rock star and was treated like a rock star. And what rock star wouldn't be delighted with a day that started with "Here are the orchestral arrangements for your orchestra" and went on to questions like "And where on the Royal Albert Hall stage should we put your orchestra?"

Richard Holgarth was enjoying it too as he and his favourite sound engineer explored the venue and discussed how they would reinforce the sound the Otway Band would create to entertain the thousands of fans who would turn up to see the star on the big day.

They took a lengthy tour of the building during which Otway and to a lesser extent Holgarth spent a considerable time on the stage doing what looked like (but we are reliably informed by both, was not) air guitar. There was then a meeting for all in an ornate room just off the side of the auditorium to sort out production issues. Once the most pressing item had been dealt with – "What time would the back stage bar open?" – it was time to sort out all the other issues such as: Who would sound-check when? What parking was available for the two coaches that were coming from the Aylesbury Music Centre? How was the stage going to be lit? Who was organising the catering? What was the running order for the evening? And so on. By the end of the meeting there was a general confidence that all the major issues had been covered: Hugh was fine with what had been sorted out for the orchestra; the PA guy knew what he was doing with the sound system; Holgarth knew what he was doing with the band; Otway thought he knew what he was doing and the backstage bar would open at 4:00pm.

September and October of 1998 were to be two of the busiest months in John's life. He had decided to do a solid tour leading up to the big gig as he thought it was important. Not only would it encourage sales, but posters going up in all the fifty-odd venues would be telling people that John Otway was headlining the Royal Albert Hall, making people aware of the fact that he had reached a point in his career where he was big enough to do that. "I mean that was part of the point of doing it," he says.

There was one thing that made this particular tour even harder than most: arranging rehearsals with the Aylesbury Youth Orchestra. The best days of the week to do a gig, both financially and for the size of audience are Friday and Saturday, but the Aylesbury Youth Orchestra rehearse once a week on

Saturday mornings. This meant that each weekend John would have to travel from wherever he was playing on the Friday night to Aylesbury and then from Aylesbury to wherever the gig was on Saturday. It would have been impossible to book all the weekend gigs near Aylesbury, so there were a lot of miles that John would have to cover on those days each week.

He had brought the subject up with Hugh at their meeting. The first rehearsal was particularly difficult because the Friday and Saturday dates were in Sheffield and Alston in Cumbria – a trip to Aylesbury between the two to fit in a rehearsal was not something to be relished. Fortunately Hugh felt that as this was the first time the new orchestra would be together, John might be a distraction. "I think it would be useful for me to have a talk with them and to look at the music. Then you can turn up the following week, once they've got the idea of what they are getting themselves into."

"I was relieved when Hugh suggested that," says John. "It made that bit of the tour so much easier."

John and Hugh agreed that it might be a good idea to have a dress rehearsal, so they agreed to have one on the last weekend before the Albert Hall. Pendley Court Theatre near Aylesbury was suggested as a suitable venue. John had not booked it before but Willy had, "I'll give him a call and ask him to put the date in for us," he told Hugh. This would give them a chance to run through the material in front of parents and loyal fans, and would give the band a chance to play *Geneve* with the orchestra.

John now had five Saturday mornings and one dress rehearsal with the orchestra to get the pieces Jean Paul was writing for them up to scratch. Not a lot of time, but the consensus was that there was enough.

The tour started in Newcastle, home of the Viz offices, followed by a gig in the editor's local pub, The Plough Inn at Powburn near Alnwick. Chris Donald was after all the perks he could get from the sponsorship, and getting Otway and Holgarth to play his local boozer a mere twenty yards from the driveway to his mansion could really help to increase his status amongst the locals. After a few more duo gigs the rest of the band joined them for the Sheffield, Alston and Bradford dates.

Meanwhile Jean Paul was discovering the logistics of writing for a full orchestra. He was using a computer program called Finale, which enabled him to write in the whole score and then the program would separate out each part. He still had to check and neaten up the music that would be given to each different instrument, but it was a great deal quicker than writing each part out by hand.

The process was taking more time than envisaged but Hugh had the score and parts for the easiest piece, *Birthday Boy*, to present to the orchestra. John had no idea how the pieces were going to sound as he could not read the music, so he had to wait until he phoned Hugh to find out. "*Birthday Boy* is absolutely mad," laughed Hugh, and from the tone of his voice John could tell that it had worked a treat.

Jean Paul was quickly trying to finish off *The Highwayman* score for the next Saturday morning. It took most of the next week to put it all into Finale and check all string, brass, woodwind and percussion parts, so he was relieved when the huge job was complete with enough time left to output the 600 pages of music and to courier them to Hugh in Aylesbury. Then his printer broke down.

"There's not much point in you coming down this weekend as we haven't got the music yet," said Hugh. "Let's start next week, that still gives us five rehearsals." It was a little disconcerting for John as the concert was now getting close and he had absolutely no idea what the pieces were like.

There was no danger of the music not happening. Jean Paul had worked on little else since April and, as he himself said, "If I can do this, and write for a full symphony orchestra, I know there is no challenge in music that will ever be too great for me to accomplish." Otway was well aware of how much it meant to him. But it still meant that Otway would have to play Bradford, York, Chester, Manchester, St. Albans and Scunthorpe before getting his opportunity to sing with the orchestra.

Bill Masterson, who John had met in his local pub, had offered to do some driving and was doing a lot of the duo dates on this tour. He wouldn't be what Otway would call a proper roadie, as he had too much nous to go anywhere near the stage when John was performing on it. Bill had a Honda Civic which is a tiny car and not a vehicle normally associated with a rock band on the road, but because you could fold down two thirds of the back seat you could just get all of Otway and Holgarth's gear in the back with the star in the front and the guitarist on the bit of the seat which could remain upright. "We travelled thousands and thousands of miles like that," says Richard Holgarth who remembers the cramped conditions better than John.

And that was how John, Richard and Bill travelled from The Cross Keys Hednesford in the Midlands to a hotel in Aylesbury for a few hours sleep, and then on to Aylesbury High School where the rehearsal was due to take place in. In subsequent weeks, to save John money they would stay at John's mum's house and on arrival Richard would transfer himself from the back of Bill's car to Mrs. Otway's living room floor.

John did not look his best when he arrived at this first rehearsal: he had overslept, was running a little late and looked a mess. So, instead of his hoped-for grand entrance, it was just John shuffling in with Richard Holgarth and Bill in the awkward manner he did everything, but with the added look of a man who had just done a pub rock gig the night before. And because he knew this was a special moment he had got Julian Hill, who had filmed the *Really Free Show*, to capture it.

Hugh introduced the star to the orchestra. Since John had been the leader of the Youth Orchestra, Hugh said to the current leader "You never know, one day this could be you". They were words that beforehand John would have thought great for some future documentary on him. But as this bright, smart young lady looked at the forty-five year old unshaven balding character who had just crawled out of a Honda Civic, the words took on a different meaning entirely.

Mercifully the focus did not remain on the star too long and the attention shifted to the composer. Jean Paul was tall, dark and handsome and his strong French accent for some reason gave his work much more authority. There was a real sense of excitement when the parts were handed around, and John within a short time could hear variations on the musical riff that he had played to Jean Paul all those months before.

John had thought he would have no difficulty adding the vocals to the music. He believed it would just be like working with a very big rock band. But it wasn't, he was finding it difficult to fathom where to come in with each verse. As he listened for the first time to the lovely and complex textures, he became aware that this was going to be a great deal harder than he had envisaged. He sat next to Jean Paul for the second run through and the composer carefully pointed out where everything fitted. To him it was obvious, to John it was anything but.

Jean Paul thought John was just having a little difficulty, but Holgarth knew why John was looking confused and worried – he had been working with John and recording with him for several years and knew his capabilities well.

Though few in the orchestra knew who John Otway was, a couple of them had heard stories from their parents, and another had discovered his autobiography in the local history section of the town's library. Word had got around that he was a bit eccentric so no alarm bells rang when Otway did not do his part with the same enthusiasm as the others. And no-one thought it odd when he said, "where's that?" when Hugh said "OK let's take it from bar fifty-four".

It is fair to say that Otway's input that day was minimal. He didn't know what he was doing at all. It didn't help when Hugh kept stopping the orchestra and going back to bits that he or Jean Paul thought they could do better, because John simply had no idea where they were going back to. Richard Holgarth knew, and kept prompting him, but this either added further confusion or made John avoid looking at him because he didn't want anyone to notice he was in difficulties and needed help.

As John's worries grew Jean Paul's receded fast. The orchestra was well up to playing the pieces he had written for them and he remained unaware of Otway's problems as he discussed with Hugh small subtleties that they felt the orchestra could work on.

"What I would find useful," John said to Hugh towards the end of the first rehearsal, "is if the orchestra played the whole piece all the way through without me joining in." He had brought a cassette recorder with him and thought if he could have a recording of the piece he could play it on his Walkman to his heart's content until he got it right and knew what he was doing.

On the way to that night's gig in Birmingham, John decided that he would use the two hours journey to "nail *The Highwayman*". He was going to sit in the car with a copy of the poem and the cassette in his Walkman and get it so he could perform it for the next Saturday morning. He failed miserably. Over those two hours he discovered that the piece was considerably more intricate and complicated than he had envisaged and the process of just going over it again and again was not helping him get it right. In fact, it was no better half way through the journey than it was when he started. And there was this awful thought which was like hitting a brick wall. "What if I just can't do it?"

It was then that he realised that he had gone too far down the path and there was no turning back: he couldn't simply go to Jean Paul and say "Sorry I can't do it," or go to Hugh and ask him to tell the orchestra that "The Albert Hall's off – Otway can't do his part." One way or another he just had to go through with it, and he knew what the consequences of going through with it and getting it wrong were. Before joining the Aylesbury Youth Orchestra, John had been in the beginners' orchestra, and could still remember a concert to proud parents that went completely wrong. By frantic gesturing the conductor had eventually brought all the musicians to a standstill. He then apologised to all present and with a forced smile said, "Let's try that again from the beginning." It had been very embarrassing, even for an eleven year old in a beginners' orchestra. Half way between Aylesbury and Birmingham John Otway was staring at a scenario that was much much worse. It was a nightmare and a nightmare of his own making. He tried with renewed determination to get the words to fit, but an hour later as they pulled up to The Hare and Hounds in Kings Heath, Birmingham, things were no better. Listening to the tape on the way to Cambridge, Milton Keynes and Oxford that week didn't help much either.

The Friday before the next rehearsal was John's birthday, which was his traditional Birthday Gig in Coventry. And so the sight that greeted the leader of the orchestra for the second rehearsal was a forty-six year old unshaven, balding character who had just crawled out of a Honda Civic, with a hangover.

From his hours of work with the Walkman, John knew it was not going to be the easiest of rehearsals and did not surprise himself a great deal when he started the second verse several bars early. But he had made a decision that one way or another he would get it right, so there was no point in freaking the composer or orchestra with the knowledge that the front man had no idea what he was doing.

The problem was that Jean Paul had treated John's voice as an instrument, the same way he used the violin or the timpani. John had never treated his voice as an instrument, and he didn't know how to.

The only person who really appreciated the problem was Richard Holgarth.

"Otway was used to people following him," he explains. "He would start singing a verse at a different place each night – sometimes four bars after the solo, sometimes eight and occasionally even three or five, and he didn't even realise he was doing it. He was up in front posing away and the band got used to following him. He really could be all over the place and miss the odd verse out, but it was Otway and that's what you expected. The thing is you can't do that with an orchestra. If you don't come in when you are supposed to, they don't wait for you they keep going, and watching them keep going after Otway hadn't come in and seeing him trying to catch up would have been hilarious if it wasn't for the fact that he looked terrified.

"I could have done his part with my eyes closed" he says. And he could, and in fact had many times as he tried to doze off in his cramped quarters in the back of the Honda as he heard the orchestral hissing from John's Walkman earphones.

That Saturday John relied on him to get him through the morning. A vigorous shake of the head meant he had got it wrong and the mouthed count of "one, two, three, four," meant start singing at the point one imagined the word five would come. It says a lot for Richard Holgarth that he never said "told you so," about the orchestra and that he turned up unpaid to every single rehearsal to try and help Otway get it right.

Jean Paul, Hugh and the orchestra did not notice any of this – the composer had picked up on a few little improvements he could make to the score and they were all too absorbed in interpreting the new work with as much flair as possible to spot anything amiss. Quite simply it would not have crossed their minds that the professional pop star who was headlining his Albert Hall show would have a problem doing the numbers that he had picked himself.

Jean Paul shocked the orchestra the following Saturday morning when he presented his improvements to the score. "I couldn't believe it," said one of the orchestra later. "They just took away all our parts and gave us new ones." Being an orchestra used to a classical repertoire it was like someone coming up and saying, "We've just made a few changes to Beethoven's 5th, please throw your old version away." Though surprised the orchestra enjoyed the challenge of working with someone who was creating original music especially for them. It didn't help John though, who still hadn't got a handle on the first version. And this would be the last rehearsal of *The Highwayman*, the following week's rehearsal had been set aside for *Geneve*.

As a performer, John was familiar with the phrase "It'll be alright on the night" – when faced with an audience, with adrenalin rushing around the system things more often than not fall into place. Also there was the dress rehearsal at Pendley Theatre where there would be an audience. Five days before the Albert Hall he would know. He would give it his best shot and work out what to do from there. At Pendley, if he messed it up and the orchestra had to be brought to a halt, he could make a joke out of it and announce to the few parents and fans, "Whoops, I better not do that on Saturday." He knew he could get away with that.

John called Paul Clerehugh to ask him if he could speak to Willy and sort out the Pendley Theatre show, as "there appears to be a bit of confusion about the tickets and the logistics that need tidying up."

"It was the old Otway/Barrett thing," says Paul. "John and Willy were diabolical at communicating with each other, and there was nothing properly organised for the Pendley show. I did my best to sort it out but it had been left too close to the date and I had to pull it."

There was good news and bad news for Otway when they spoke later that day. One would have thought that the very exciting fact that nearly 4,000 tickets had now been bought for the big show – meaning John would be headlining a packed Royal Albert Hall – would have dwarfed the news that unfortunately the 150-seater Pendley Theatre show the week before had to be cancelled. But it didn't. It now meant John would not find out until October 30th 1998 whether or not he could do *The Highwayman* with the Aylesbury Youth Orchestra all the way through... without stopping.

Because of the cancellation of the Pendley Theatre show, Hugh arranged a couple of hours at the High School a few days before the Royal Albert Hall so the orchestra would have a chance to work with the band. The *Geneve* rehearsal with the band was the one occasion where John got the chance to really enjoy the orchestra. He was completely in his comfort zone, singing one of his own songs scored as it was on the record. Since John is one of the few artistes who listens to his own records a lot, he was able to enjoy this moment to the full.

Understandably Richard Holgarth did not want to do the Perth to Penzance challenge screwed up in the back of the Honda Civic and Bill didn't want to do the drive either. So for the final leg of the Royal Albert Hall Tour, John hired a comfortable people carrier, and Sandra (who had been helping on the tour selling merchandise) and her friend Jacky offered to drive. "And all the way round Scotland, you could hear Otway swearing at his Walkman and Holgarth telling him that he had to get it right as he had got less than two weeks to go," recalls Sandra.

After touring solidly for a couple of months, John had not been looking forward to the Perth to Penzance journey that he had so cheerfully popped into the itinerary early in the year. "In the end though it was OK for me," he says. "I had a couple of extra whiskeys at the Glen Farg Hotel in Perth before climbing into a comparatively luxurious vehicle and dropping off to sleep. When I woke up I saw a sign whizz past saying 'Welcome To Exeter'. It was around nine in the morning and we had done nearly the whole journey."

For that evening's gig there were eighteen fans who had taken up the Perth to Penzance challenge: they had been at the Glen Farg Hotel the night before and would get back stage passes to the Royal Albert Hall. A special mention must go to Steve Lloyd, who had hitchhiked to every single show on the tour.

CHAPTER 14

The producers of television's *London Tonight* programme liked the story of *Rock and Roll's Greatest Failure* taking over the Royal Albert Hall for a night: in the week leading up to the show they found a person called Albert and filmed John playing in his hall; on the day of the big event they interviewed Otway live, standing outside the venue with Paul Bradley. Bradley played a major character in the TV soap opera *Eastenders*, and years earlier had co-written and co-starred in a play with Otway.

"Thank heavens Paul Bradley was there," says John. "Paul Clerehugh had promised the TV crew that there would be loads of celebrities and he was the only one I knew. He had offered to come and compère for the night and he really helped me out of a hole."

As John was broadcast live to the citizens of London, the band, guests, Perth-Penzance veterans and crew were watching backstage. Halfway through the interview Karen and Amy arrived. "Oh there's Dad on telly again," announced Amy unimpressed – at the age of nine she had already seen hours of John's video footage at home.

It was a good interview. Paul Bradley called John a 'National Treasure' and Otway was able to say, quite honestly, that the show was almost a sell out and there were just some seats left in the gods if anyone fancied heading across town to his show.

Shortly after the interview Hugh had sorted out the orchestra and was ready to do a sound-check. "Do you think we could run *The Highwayman*?" John asked. He was in luck, he would get the chance to see if the work he had put in over the last two weeks had been enough. "Whoops better not do that tonight," he said halfway through after coming in with the wrong verse.

John had laid out a large number of crib sheets on stage and after the run-through made one more to remind him where he had gone wrong.

The evening was going to have two sets, with the orchestral numbers ending the first half, but as getting the orchestra on the stage would take a while they were in position from the beginning. As they took their positions, all in uniform 'Viz Presents John Otway at The Royal Albert Hall' T-shirts, the huge auditorium was already packed.

Backstage John and Paul Bradley were very excited – both were Bob Dylan fans and Paul had spotted that they were standing in the same spot in the dressing room as Bob had in the film *Don't Look Back*.

Then it was show time.

The applause after Paul's introduction was every bit as loud as Otway had dreamt it might be, as he came on with Richard Holgarth and started *House Of The Rising Sun*. "I just fancied the idea of starting the evening by singing the words 'There is' and having the whole Albert Hall yelling back 'What?'" says John.

After that number, and the audience's opportunity to ask "Who's a prat?" Willy joined them for *Louisa On A Horse*. The next guest was Attila to do *The Glue Medley* and then Wilko and Otway did a version of *21 Days*. The orchestra on stage waiting had only seen John in rehearsal and had no idea what his live show was like, so they were probably a bit taken aback by *Body Talk*, which involves Otway hitting himself quite violently in order to activate electronic switches placed around his body and so trigger-off drum sounds. It made him look ridiculous, but Otway hitting himself was very funny and always went down very well. After Gloria Gaynor's *I Will Survive* (which John sang in a Bob Dylan voice so someone in the audience could yell "Judas") and two songs with Richard Holgarth from the *Premature Adulation* album, it was time.

"I'd like to introduce my first ever band, The Aylesbury Youth Orchestra."

Hugh raised the baton, there was a roll on the timpani and they were off. So far the show had simply been John with at most a couple of guitars and Willy's fiddle. Now suddenly sixty members of a symphony orchestra created this big, big sound, with Otway dancing around in front of them.

The day has come you're still alive, you're going to carry on
You're having a big party with all your friends along
They're all going to shout and cheer the moment you walk in
Who's a lucky birthday boy everybody's going to sing

He knew what he was doing in this song which was short, snappy and mad, and three minutes later the audience were out of their seats and cheering.

John's mother had sat through many an Aylesbury Youth Orchestra performance supporting her son and she could now watch the Aylesbury Youth Orchestra supporting him – at the Royal Albert Hall.

But how long could they support him? John announced that he was about to do an epic and that he hadn't managed to get it right in rehearsal but it just came across as a bit of humour. Most of the people there did not know there was a potential disaster looming – certainly not John's mum or the 4,600 audience, or the sixty orchestra members, or the box full of sponsoring Viz people along with their friend Screaming Lord Sutch, one composer and one soap star. But Sandra and Bill realised – they'd driven John around while he practiced. And so did Richard Holgarth.

"I just kept asking myself, is there a point when it would be right to go on stage and help him out if it was going terribly pear shaped," he says.

"OK let's go for it," John said to Hugh off mic. The baton was raised and Otway braced himself for the climax of Jean Paul's six months' work and the orchestra's two months' rehearsals.

The orchestra powered into the first riff – there were two of them, then a couple of bars where the brass stopped and the strings played four notes, then there was one low note. John knew that he had to count "one, two," then start singing. It never felt like the right place, but after he had done the first line, if the violins went "diddly dee" he had got it right.

The wind was a torrent of darkness among the gusty trees, and there on cue came the violins. The next line and another *diddly dee* and he knew he could manage the rest of the first verse. Then, just one riff and straight in, don't wait, just a quick check of the sheet on the front of the stage for the first line of the next verse.

So far so good. In big letters on the crib sheet is the reminder that coming up there's one of the extra verses Jean Paul added *Eyes were hollows of madness*, had the correct orchestral backing, as did *hair like mouldy hay*.

Next came the fourth verse, which John often sang third, one big hurdle that had already been safely cleared. Fifth verse, one that had often been missed in the hurry to get to the more familiar sixth. However the more familiar sixth had four bars of instrumental after the first line, which Jean Paul had put in to add some musical colour, and this little unfamiliarity often bred incompetence. But both pitfalls were marked in big letters and when John sang *Tugged at his reins in the moonlight, and galloped away to the west,* orchestra and star were still in sync.

Traditionally, John had got the next few verses right but, having got further than he had ever got without screwing up, he carefully read the first line of each verse. Then came the acapella section where John recited some verses on his own, running around the stage in dramatic fashion as the landlord's daughter tops herself. And the highwayman? *They shot him down on the highway, down like a dog on the highway.* Just two more lines then the reprise of the first verse – the riff twice, four notes, the low note, count "one, two," the first line and the *diddly dee* is in the right spot. Both John and Richard Holgarth, who was holding his breath backstage, knew that if the *diddly dee* came in right after the second line, they were home and dry.

When the moon is a ghostly galleon tossed upon cloudy seas and there it was *diddly dee.* Just four more easy lines that could be sung with confidence and then Otway could shut up and leave the orchestra to play the piece to the end. A triumph.

As the applause echoed around the Hall, the band, (Holgarth, Seymour, Adam and Murray) came on to do *Geneve* to close the first half. And John at last was able to enjoy the event. "This is *Geneve* as you've heard it on the record," he proudly announced.

Yet even though the version of *Geneve* they produced was lovely and Richard Holgarth's solo probably surpassed the original, it did not get the biggest standing ovation of the night, it did not happen when Paul Bradley presented the leader of the orchestra with a huge bouquet nor when Amy presented her father with a smaller one. This ovation was not obtained by the band, or by Brian the Roadie who had returned for the night to bang his bits of wood and headbutt the breezeblock. It wasn't the skateboarding, Sinclair C5-driving star either or the four encores Adam, Murray, Seymour, Holgarth and Otway were awarded at the end of an incredibly successful night.

"It was one of the brass players, it could have been Duncan Hamilton," remembers one of the Youth Orchestra members.

"Well, it had to be him," says another.

"It would probably be a brass player," says Hugh. "And I would say with some certainty it would have been the trombonist, Dunc."

The biggest ovation happened during the interval whilst John was in the backstage bar. Because the Royal Albert Hall does not have the best sites for setting up merchandising stalls ("and they charge commission on sales," adds Paul Clerehugh) the promoter had found a rather good method of selling John's CDs, videos and T-shirts: for a small cost the venue would put a flyer on each seat, allowing everyone watching the show to mail-order a souvenir item for the event. After they had done the three numbers, the orchestra members were given free seats right up in the Gods so they could, if they wanted, watch the rest of the show. The first paper aeroplane did not travel very far at all, but the fluttering piece of paper flying down from the top of the building caught most people's eye. Several other planes took off, and soon the ones that flew as opposed to just plummeted attracted a round of applause.

Then, what must have been a piece of near-perfect aerodynamically folded sheet of A4 was launched. It could have been just luck and that this plane just caught a thermal caused by the excited crowd below, but this particular mail-order form glided straight to the middle of the hall, until there it was, way above the stalls, right under the centre of the great dome – then it just kept going. A hush fell over the crowd as it gained momentum and landed back in the Gods directly opposite the point it had taken off from. The place just went nuts.

So the big prize of the night was achieved by a brass player for a piece of spontaneous origami.

"Did you see the aeroplane?" was the first thing John's mum said to her son when she greeted him after his big show.

"It was pretty spectacular," agreed his Auntie Margaret who had come with her.

And, to this day it is still common for people to say, "Ah yes, the paper aeroplane," when asked if they made it to the Viz presents John Otway at the Royal Albert Hall show.

CHAPTER 15

"The audience could have been yelling, 'who's a prat' in *The Highwayman* instead of in *House of The Rising Sun*," thought John as he sat in his living room and contemplated the wisdom of what he had just done. Karen and Amy had gone to bed and he was winding down with a couple of cold sausages from the fridge and a bottle of Glenfiddich whiskey a fan had given him at the Albert Hall.

He concluded that "It'll be alright on the night" summed up the performance: he'd got stuck in and held his nerve, and things had turned out OK.

The following day the fax machine in the corner of the same room printed out a congratulation message from Hugh and the orchestra thanking John for a fabulous night. The following week the Aylesbury Youth Orchestra were back at the Royal Albert Hall, as they had just won a nationwide competition to find the best Youth Orchestra in the land and would be playing a piece at the School Proms. "They were that good," says John.

The majority of the inhabitants of Flat One, 9 Melrose Road had not found the experience of a nervous Rock Star planning the campaign as rewarding as one might expect. In fact after the event the family opted to engage in what is often described as the third most stressful event in life after bankruptcy and divorce – they moved house. Their new home had a loft conversion which John could have as an office: it was two floors up from the living room and kitchen and if all doors were closed you would never know he was there.

"Heaven," agreed the two girls in his life.

Over the last few years the internet had become more and more important. Otway had found it a valuable tool and with some very talented computer techie fans had started to unleash its power. Steve Pond had introduced John to the internet forums as early as 1994, inviting John round to his house to do a Rocknet real time conference using an old modem attached to the telephone handset. By 1995 Steve had an Otway web page running and shortly afterwards Xav, a student at Manchester University, got a fan web site working. By the time of the Royal Albert Hall, John had found the ability to communicate directly to his fans incredibly useful and replied personally to each e-mail he received.

In January 1999 Steve Pond set up a newsgroup for Otway fans which soon became an important influence on John's career: suddenly the fans had the ability to affect the decisions of John and those around him. The company that ran these groups was called Onelist and even though the group would be taken over by Yahoo! the original name stuck.

"Suddenly we had to take into account what the Onelisters wanted," recalls Richard Holgarth. "John would arrive at a gig and say 'The Onelist wants us to do this' and if I suggested doing something Otway would say, 'I'd better run that past the Onelist see if they think it's a good idea."

Within six months the group started to have a significant effect on John's career. It began with Q Magazine's poll of the hundred greatest acts of the past hundred years. A lot of the members of the Onelist genuinely believed that Otway was, if not the greatest act of the past hundred years, certainly one of the greats. They got quite excited, and many posts on the Onelist site were about how to make one's Q vote most effective. For this particular poll one had to nominate four great acts, and much of the discussion on the forum concerned which other acts deserved to be on the same ballot as Otway... bearing in mind, of course, that if everyone agreed to pick any one particular act then this act would be in competition with John when the votes were counted.

Q Magazine held a different view to the members of the Otway Onelist. They did not think that John was one of the hundred greatest acts of the 20th Century and he did not make the chart. "John Otway – despite what was a bravely contrived election campaign by someone quite close to him (possibly himself) – didn't quite make it," the editorial of the magazine said.

This was like a red top to an Otway fan. "I know a lot of us voted for him sincerely," Patsy Andrews put on the list and she fired off an angry e-mail to Q which they subsequently printed.

"What is the point in asking us to vote for an act if you are going to disqualify them if they are not the people you want in your chart," was the gist of her message.

A couple of weeks later there was another poll – The Observer newspaper was trying to find the greatest moments in the history of television. To those who subscribed to the John Otway Onelist Newsgroup this was a no-brainer – the greatest moment on TV ever was during an episode of *The Old Grey Whistle Test* in 1977 when a leaping Otway had missed his footing and landed on his testicles astride Wild Willy's amplifier. And in went the votes. Once again Otway didn't quite make this chart but Ali McClean's letter about this Otway clip was mentioned in the editorial. No huge achievements but they were starting to make an impact. Otway's name was appearing in the pages of Britain's most respected magazines and newspapers as were the names of some of the Onelist members. (As a postscript to this particular story, much later, when a poll appeared for the worst moments on television, a more organised and efficient Onelist group achieved the 89 spot for Otway's Whistle Test moment.)

In July Karen Wintle posted the following message on the Onelist:

> *Whilst missing the Otway Bristol gig at the weekend (hubby dragged me off for a few days away from the kids) we ended up watching the Old Rope String Band. They were great, if you get the chance go and see them. They are to folk music what Otway is to rock.*
>
> *Anyway, as part of their act one of them played a Theramone (or something like that). It is played by waving your hands (or anything else!!!) near two metal rods, one controls the pitch, the other the volume. The possibilities in Otway's hands would be limitless. Apparently it was invented in the 1920s by a German or something (I'd had a lot of beer) and they cost about 250 quid. Maybe we should have a whip round and get one for Otway. I'm sure we'd get our money's worth.*

Some of what Karen wrote was wrong as subsequent messages on this topic were quick to point out. The instrument Ms Wintle had seen was in fact a *theremin* – named after its Russian inventor Leo Theremin. However, other parts of her note were spot on: you did play it by waving your hands near it, and they would get their money's worth if they got John one.

'Get That Man A Theremin' was the heading for the next string of postings to the group, and on John's birthday a large number of Onelisters from around the country headed for his traditional birthday Coventry show to give John the present they had imported for him from the USA, and hear him play it.

Some of the members of this group were Dunkerque veterans, from the annual Otway trip, who had already met each other, but for the majority it was a chance to put faces to the names they were so familiar with on-line.

Ali McClean was there, he was canvassing support for another poll he had discovered. In the run up to the millennium, the BBC had chosen to have a ballot on what the nation felt were the greatest song lyrics written in the past two thousand years.

The Onelist had previously worked out that people like Burt Bacharach, Paul Simon and Bob Dylan had written many good lyrics and votes from their fans would be spread over their catalogue of fine material. If the Otway fans could agree on the same song this could put their star at an advantage over Burt, Paul and Bob.

Otway watching these events unfold daily on his computer monitor marvelled at the democratic process at work. "They just got the nominations together and then chose which song to go for."

Beware of the Flowers (Cos I'm Sure They're Going to Get You Yeah) was the B-side to *Cor Baby, That's Really Free*, John's Hit. Many times it had been suggested that if it had been saved for a follow up, John would have had more than the one significant chart position he had. It was still one of the most popular songs in the show and was the lyric the fans opted to go for.

Whilst Ali scoured the venue for those who had not yet voted for *Beware Of The Flowers*, Otway was with Holgarth working out what to do with his new instrument. It was exactly as described, you just waved your arms around the aerials sticking out of it and it made a noise.

Richard Holgarth, although having a natural aversion to such an instrument, saw an opportunity to get out of the chicken and portuguese man of war noises and avoid the lemming leap from the ladder. "*Crazy Horses* would sound great played on that," he said. He was right, it did, a big extravagant wave of the arm towards the bit of metal sticking up in the air produced a pretty good "whoop". Otway waving his limbs around always looked a little comical, and when these same actions produced "whooping" noises the effect was greatly intensified.

"Best present I've ever had," he told the fans who bought it for him.

The following morning he set up the instrument in the front room of the new family home and showed it off to Karen and Amy.

"Lovely," they said.

CHAPTER
16

"Just got back from the filming of the BBC's *Poetry Week*," said the e-mail, "you were number seven in the lyric chart."

John could not believe it, "Are you sure?" he e-mailed back.

"Yes, they announced the results, and there you were," came the reply.

Sure enough, when the programme was broadcast, there he was at number seven. And the Onelist were ecstatic.

All the major national papers covered the story too. The Independent even headlined their article about the *Poetry Week* poll "John Otway 'a better lyricist than Dylan'". The Daily Telegraph and Daily Express called the result 'surprising'. However Q Magazine who had already encountered the Onelist, ran the following:

> *Fix! Fix! Fix! Fans of '70s pub poet John Otway conspire to make a mockery of BBC pop lyric poll. John Otway fans are celebrating their manipulation of the BBC's poll for the country's favourite pop lyric which put Otway's* Beware Of The Flowers *at Number Seven.*
>
> *The chart was compiled from e-mails and phone calls received between September 22 and October 6, a period when Otway's fanbase was extremely active. On the day of the result they e-mailed each other saying 'well done everybody' and one fan confessed his disappointment: 'a little too low on the list for my liking, but there you go'.*
>
> *Otway himself reacted 'Yes Yes Yes Yes... I'm a happy microstar.'*
>
> *Meanwhile a BBC spokesperson insisted there was 'no duplication, and if Otway fans organised themselves that's hardly a ghastly affront to democracy, is it? If we'd changed the result we'd rightly be accused of tampering with the votes.'*

John's book was now in its third edition: when Omnibus had sold out its print run, John reprinted it himself, and when this edition ran out publisher Cherry Red took it over. Towards the end of 1999 a film company approached Otway with an offer to make a movie based on his autobiography. John asked his acting agents Peters Frazer and Dunlop, to negotiate for him.

"It's period," said the agent, "so the budget is going to be quite substantial."

"It's what?" replied John.

"Period, a great deal of the book is in the 60s and 70s," he explained, and went on to secure substantial option rights for him.

"They are going to make a movie of my book," John excitedly told his sister, Margaret. "According to my agent, they have to consult me on casting, who would you like to play you?," This news though would eventually make her feel her age, when her daughters told their friends that someone was going to play their mum in a period costume drama.

John met the producer and director for a drink. "What did you think the day someone rang up wanting to make a movie about you?" they asked. "Normal," replied Otway. "It's every other day of my life that's felt a bit strange".

In the January 1st 2000 edition of The Times, the paper included some facts about the previous millennium and printed some charts and statistics. Among them was a reprint of the greatest lyric chart. "I felt it was a great way to start the 21st Century," says John. "The Times had me contributing something to the 20th Century and as I'd just sold my life story to a film company I had something pretty good to look forward to in this one." Even though the option ran out without the film being made, the fact that he had secured a substantial sum for the tale of *Rock and Roll's Greatest Failure* made him feel he was definitely on the right track and heading back to stardom.

Before he got too carried away with how things were going, one thing brought him down to earth and kept his feet on the ground: his appearance on the 'Where are they now?' section of the TV show *Never Mind The Buzzcocks*. An old clip – in this case his 1977 *Top Of The Pops* one – was played, then John was lined up with three other forty-somethings and the panel had the task of working out which was the real Otway. The fact that John was offered the job meant that the producers obviously felt he was a has-been and the headlining of the Albert Hall and being the nation's seventh favourite lyricist hadn't appeared on their radar.

But the Otway size elevens would not be kept on the ground indefinitely.

Sean Hughes was on the panel and John had worked with him in Edinburgh. "I know Otway, he's one of my mates. Hi Number Two," he said. And when it came to the bit where the host announces what the has-been has become, Mark Lamarr said simply "Otway, still a genius".

Ego saved. Feet back in the usual position.

CHAPTER 17

There is no way that one could have called the solo show John played at the HQ Club Camden Lock in February 2001 a success in the conventional sense. The promoters of the venue had assured our star that it was a 'happening' club, and that with someone of John's stature playing there the place would be heaving.

When one is paid a percentage of the door take, there is often confusion about the exact total due to the artiste. This confusion is not significant when the size of the audience appears to be less than twelve – and even easier to deal with when two of them are on the guest list.

John's guests that night were Maurice Bacon, his old manager and music publisher and Steve Barker. Steve had a long career in television and was currently working for Associated Press. He had been on a New York trip with John had taken over a small crew to get some footage of Otway playing the Big Apple. They enjoyed each other's company and were not averse to cooking up some very ambitious plans over a few pints of beer.

Otway was a little embarrassed as he sat in the club with Maurice, Steve and half a dozen or so others who had braved it out to see someone of John's stature on a cold night. But the gig was quite enjoyable: some people find it difficult to play to very few people in a very big room, but one of John's talents is his ability to engage particularly small crowds. "That's because he's had a lot of practice," someone, who was not a fan, once unkindly observed. And this small gig was the birthplace of the most successful campaign of his career, something that would, for a short period, have the effect of losing him the *Rock and Roll's Greatest Failure* tag.

Despite the progress he had made with his career he was not finding it that easy to let the tag go. His merchandising stall would still feature T-shirts with slogans like 'John Otway One Hit WONDER!', 'It's Nearly Rock and Roll But I Like It' and 'John Otway, I Can't Believe It's Not Better'. And on the BBC's Glastonbury coverage John Peel introduced him as *Rock and Roll's Greatest Failure*, after Otway had given him one of his books.

"Do you know what you should do?" Maurice said. "You should ask your fans to get you a hit for your fiftieth birthday. Single sales are so low now that if you all worked on it, you should be able to get a single into the top thirty. You're never going to get a Top Ten hit or anything like that, but you might beat twenty-seven." Being a pop star, ideas that included the word Hit had a very special appeal, and the one Maurice was suggesting was particularly exciting.

As everyone who had seen Otway over the last twenty years knew, John had one hit. *Cor Baby, That's Really Free* had reached twenty-seven in the charts almost a quarter of a century before, and his live show almost revolved around it. "I'm going to start with a medley of my Hit," he would announce, and after performing it would say, "I'm now going to play the B-side of my Hit. It came out the same year and sold just as many copies". After that, he told the audience that as he had now run out of hits, he would have to move on to his flops.

The second half of Otway's book had chronicled John's desperate attempts to try and get a follow up by fair means or hyping the charts. He had some small successes. He had done a whole tour whereby you could get in to the shows if you had a copy of the *DK50/80* single and not at all if you hadn't. A frantic tear around the country, playing only towns which had chart return shops (retailers from whom the chart compilers sampled) scored John Otway and Wild Willy Barrett a number 45. "It could have been higher," says John. "We got booked to do *Top Of The Pops*, then the Musicians Union went on strike and the BBC cancelled the show."

Give It Headbutts almost made it too. This song, which involved Willy hammering John's head against the microphone, was very popular with the fans, but the song's particular appeal, mindless violence, meant that the BBC did not give it a great deal of radio play. It was a cult hit and stayed at number 76 for a few weeks. Had it just made one place higher it would have been stocked by most of the major shops and almost certainly got a lot higher, but Maurice Bacon's small label that released it did not have the clout that the major record companies had and could not get it through that barrier.

Far less successful was the vocal-less single competition. Amongst the many copies of *Frightened and Scared* distributed to the shops, three of them had music but no singing on. The idea here was that fans would keep buying copies hoping to get an Otway-less one, because if you had one of these the man himself would come to your house, stand between your stereo speakers and add them live. But unfortunately people who had seen the live show would not want to stage it in their own home and so this particular record got nowhere.

By now, John had given up trying to have another hit. He had worked his show around making the most of the one he had, and because of his continuous live work, the internet and his comprehensive mailing list, he could sell directly to his fans. The last album *The Set Remains The Same* was a studio recording of all the material the band played live. It was not sold through the shops at all and made a reasonable profit, the first of his albums to do so for many years.

"Until Maurice came up with that idea, I hadn't thought about the chart in years. I had resigned myself to the one hit for the moment and concentrated on other routes to stardom, like a movie, a TV series or my book. And then hits would come naturally as a by-product," John says. "But as soon as Maurice mentioned this idea I knew instinctively that it would work. Maurice's concept of combining my special fiftieth birthday present with another chart to have a go at was magic, the fans would love it."

Another reason Maurice felt it could work was that John was still only 48. Most single campaigns lasted about six months: John would have over a year extra campaigning than anyone else. No other acts in the UK knew in February 2001 that they would have a single released on September 30th 2002 but by the end of that gig in Camden Lock Maurice, Steve and John did. Otway's days as a one hit wonder were numbered – 519 to be precise.

There were obstacles because of the way the charts and shops worked. It was almost impossible to get the major chains to stock a record if you were a minor record company, and if you managed to get past that hurdle the shops would only take them on a sale-or-return basis. If you wanted a big hit with say 30,000 sales in one week, you would need around 100,000 stocked in shops around the country. Pressing them would cost around £70,000 and you would also be liable for the cost of returning unsold records, so the total exposure to a record company would be £110,000 to £120,000 – a lot of money.

"And you won't get anyone to do that," said Maurice. "However, there are enough independent shops that if you and your fans are organised you should be able to shift the three or four thousand needed to make the top thirty."

None of this was news to Otway. Whenever he had battled to have a hit record the first problem he encountered was the complaint "Yes we'd buy it, but you can't get your record in the shops," from the fans. It was actually easier to get people to buy singles than it was getting the record shops to stock them.

Back in 1977 *Really Free* sold 125,000 copies and reached 27 in the charts. In 2001, as few as 4,500 would get you the same position. If just everyone who bought an Albert Hall ticket bought a copy of John's single in one week, he could justifiably announce that he now had two hits. Maurice was right, it was quite achievable. But John was already thinking bigger. Much bigger.

"There were a couple of things that I thought were relevant," says John. "Firstly, I remember doing a gig with Willy just after *Really Free*, and we got blown off stage by a college support band. Turns out they'd been working on this one gig for over a year – costumes, lights and props and every friend, relative and fellow student had been involved in some way over that time preparing for their thirty minute slot. It was the only show they would ever do – all that huge effort compressed into one small event. There was no way we could compete when we were doing an hour show every night on a thirty date tour. With this campaign I could use the same technique, I would have a year and a half to get one week's singles' sales right.

"The other thing worth recalling was something Chris France had said a few years before. He had told me that Woolies, HMV, Virgin and all the major chains had the most amazing demographics for ordering that worked spectacularly almost all the time, but they could be thrown completely by as few as 2,000 avid fans causing havoc in the market place."

Over the next week or so John started fleshing out Maurice's amazing idea. His first dilemma was deciding who would choose what The Hit was going to be. John did not have a very good track record of picking hits, but didn't want anyone else to pick one for him either. He had disliked *Really Free* when it was released and had let the obvious second hit, *Beware of the Flowers*, be used as its B-side. The follow-ups were *Geneve* and seventeen other flops. He had been in meetings to choose releases that went on for hours, where arguments had only ended when a song nobody minded too much had been picked as a compromise as opposed to a song somebody loved. There were many people who would say "I know a hit when I hear one," but John believed they only actually knew it if the presenter on *Top Of The Pops* had just told them it was. It would come from all angles: the band would have their view, whatever record company put it out would have theirs and John would not be safe at home either, because Karen knew what songs she liked and Amy was now old enough to tell her dad what she thought of his singing.

"My first thought was of course 'ask the Onelist', and then I thought, 'let them vote for it, they like a good ballot'," says John. And that's what he decided to do. He would get a CD together with as many suitable songs as he could, and the fans could then choose which one of them should be The Hit.

This plan would meet with a certain amount of opposition, especially from those within the music business: the concept of the fans choosing what should be released was basically taking away their jobs. Plus there was the issue of sales: if the fans already had the single, what was going to encourage them to buy another copy when it comes out?

But John was now seriously contemplating a Hit and that automatically triggered other ideas. "What do you reckon? The chart gets announced on the radio around 6.00pm, so why don't we play our own *Sunday Night at the London Palladium* an hour later?" said John excitedly as he explained the Hit idea to Paul Clerehugh. "My first gig as a two-hit wonder. Everyone will know we're very serious if we've booked the London Palladium over a year in advance to celebrate." And Paul Clerehugh went along with it. He was a fan and he wanted Otway to have another hit, there can be no other explanation.

It was time to tell the Onelist.

CHAPTER
18

Wed Mar 21, 2001 1:03pm

Hi all

All the recent mail about Popstars has prompted me to let you know what I would like for my 50th birthday.

Another Hit

I'm sure you can do it – and in anticipation I've already penned out the first and last paragraphs of my new biog:

...... On the 8th October 2002 John Otway will have just reached the age of 50 and for his birthday present his loyal following have promised him another hit record. The London Palladium has been booked for the night the chart comes out so Otway and his fans can celebrate being in the charts again 25 years after his original hit.

"I know what I'm getting for my Birthday," says Otway. "I've felt the parcel, but it doesn't spoil the excitement because I just don't know how big it's going to be."

This is a good time to catch Otway live, you have from now until October 2002 – while he is still a one hit WONDER and before another hit goes to his head in the same way the last one did... Single sales are at an all time low – I've looked at the figures and it is feasible.

Let me know what you think of the idea – and if you lot fancy manufacturing me into a popstar again.

I'll be on the live chatroom tonight at 8:00 if anyone fancies discussing it

Love

Otway

The Onelist response was both immediate and enthusiastic. This was the ultimate poll – the chart that everyone wanted to "fix, fix, fix" the one that actually defined whether one was or was not a pop star. Within weeks the Onelist had organised themselves, were headed by their own war cabinet and there was a gig coming up that would present a good opportunity to plan and discuss the next hit.

There is a tradition going back over 500 years in Oxford that at 6 o'clock on May Day morning a crowd of students gathers to hear the Magdalen College Choir sing the hymn *Hymnus Eucharisticus* from the top of Magdalen Tower. And, because the council grant the local hostelries a license to open and sell beer at this time there is another tradition going back over twenty years: in Oxford at 6am on May Day morning a crowd of fans gathers to hear John Otway sing The Hit *Cor Baby, That's Really Free* in a pub just down the road from Magdalen Tower.

Quite a number of Onelisters made it to this event including Xav, who turned up with a laptop containing the template for Otnews.net the new fans' website. At eight-thirty in the morning – after the gig and a few beers – John, Xav and a couple of others from the war cabinet left the Gloucester Arms and headed to a cafe for breakfast where they could discuss launching the new website and talk Hit.

"It was great. By this time they had already checked out the chart rules, scoured the web for other acts that had tried similar campaigns and discussed on-line a lot of the main problems we were going to face," says John.

With the fans now on board John started looking at what The Hit might be. He had a new introduction to his show, which instead of the simple "We're going to start with my Hit," went thus:

"Next year I'm going to be fifty and I've been promised another Hit for my birthday, but we don't know what it's going to be yet. So in order to get an idea of what might work the best, I'm going to start with The Hit I've already got – so you know what a hit sounds like – and if I play anything else in my show that sounds like one, just yell 'hit, hit, hit' so I know."

At Shene Secondary School Miss Mbanifo had given class 8S1 some chemistry homework, and John heard about his daughter's assignment as Karen was driving them through Battersea. "We've got to do something on a Bunsen Burner," Amy told her parents. "Do a song," suggested her father who started singing "Let me be your bunsen burner" to the tune of Elvis Presley's *Let Me Be Your Teddy Bear*.

John's Elvis impersonation was not particularly good. "Awful," remembers Karen – one of the two-girl audience to hear this first embryonic performance from the driving seat of the Austin Metro.

"I was quite surprised to find that they were still using bunsen burners in Chemistry lessons," says John. "I asked around and everyone I spoke to seemed to have a bunsen burner story about what they or someone else in their class had burned, set fire to or exploded. It occurred to me that anyone who had been through some form of secondary education, including the present generation, would understand any references I put in, so I put some more work into it."

During a short solo North England tour, he wrote a few verses and a chorus. The *Teddy Bear* tune wasn't working so he got up on stage in York and gave it a go without one. "I just announced that I had made a start on my birthday present and read out the lyrics. As soon as I had finished, there was this chant of 'hit, hit, hit' so I thought, 'great, that's one for them to vote at'."

Soon the whole postal mailing list was to learn what Otway wanted for his 50th birthday. John Haxby, who had designed all his recent CD covers, had produced a flyer which explained what present he was hoping for and also what he was doing for his 49th.

For the Coventry birthday gig that year "I'm going to have a 'Hit minus One' party to celebrate the anniversary of next year's Hit and my last year as a one-hit wonder."

All this publicity was starting to work, and by the time that John had contacted William Hill, the bookmaker, to place a bet on a big Otway Hit in October 02, he discovered that quite a number of others had had the same idea and the bookies were aware that some serious chart rigging was underway, and bets were off.

John, as always believing in the great importance of what he was doing, managed to persuade producer Mark Pegg to film The Hit campaign for a possible lucrative documentary. He was there to capture the 'Hit Minus One' party as well as that year's Dunkerque trip, which had the title 'The Trip Before The Hit Hits the Fans'.

John had found a new roadie too. John Padget had been driving John to a lot of gigs and was taking more and more time off his work as a jeweller to fit in the shows. "One night after a show, when he was staying at my place, I sat and drank brandy with him until the early hours," Otway recalls. "I just kept going on about what an amazing year it was going to be and how he would never forgive himself if he missed out on all the fun that we were about to have. It must have worked as he gave his notice in the next day and managed to last in the job for four years, twice as long as any other roadie has ever managed."

Another character is about to enter the story, one who would be as divisive as it is possible to be in the world of rock and roll. Once Otway had opened the following e-mail things would change, and musically things would never be the same again: for Cotton it was Otway saving his soul, for Holgarth it was Otway selling it.

Hi John,
   Great news about your forthcoming hit! Great idea and I will try to be on it if my schedule permits (I am a pop tart after all). I know Abbey Road well having recorded there a few times (including one football hit).
   My hits 5-6-7-8, Last Thing On My Mind, and One For Sorrow are currently at number 1 in the album charts on STEPS GOLD (Greatest Hits). WE KNOCKED KYLIE OFF. How many times in your life is that gonna happen. So if you need any cheesy advice on the production for your A side, let me know.
   See you soon
   Barry

Barry Upton had a fascinating history. John had first met him at a solo gig, where Barry had really enjoyed the show and introduced himself. At that point in Barry's career he had already left the pop group Brotherhood of Man and was producing the group Steps to perform 5-6-7-8 for the group Steps – a line dancing song he had co-written.

They kept in touch over the years as Barry's group became a huge pop sensation, but no one would imagine that John and Barry would have enough in common to work together. Otway could never fit into a band like Steps or Brotherhood of Man: he did not have the co-ordination, the voice, or the looks – plus he was balding and in his late forties.

"And anyway, I thought the fans would hate it if I put out a cheesy pop record," says John, "so it never occurred to me until I got that e-mail."

John wanted a diverse selection of tracks for the fans to vote from, a few favourite original tracks, some re-workings of popular old Otway songs and a number of completely new and original tracks specially recorded as potential chart busters. Reading Barry's e-mail it occurred to John that it would be fun to have tracks that ranged from absolute pure pop to complete outrageous punk. It hadn't escaped his notice that dropping lines like "We even had Steps' producer in to help get us a hit" would work very well in the hundreds of interviews he suspected he would do nearer the release date.

John wouldn't normally be able to take a successful producer, try them out and then fire them and refuse to put out their work saying "It doesn't sound like a hit to me."

Richard Holgarth and the band had spent so many years making John both look and sound credible that to go and tell them that they were going to have to change their image and they would not be the next Clash or Oasis but would be the next Bucks Fizz or Dollar and do something like the *Birdie Song* – would not have been appropriate. However, with the fans themselves choosing The Hit, these issues would be irrelevant. If something didn't "sound like a hit to us" or resembled the *Birdie Song*, it would suffer the fate of a recent Norwegian entry for the Eurovision Song Contest and get Nul Points. John with confidence could say to Barry, "Make whatever you think is a hit."

"I admired Barry," says John. "He knew that the fans were going to choose what track they were going to have. Not only could he be wasting his time, he could also be exposing himself to a dose of pride wounding. But when he came round he seemed very confident about doing it, and must have felt he was going to get some votes."

Two strong ideas came out of the meeting between John and Barry at Otway's house in the first weeks of 2002. Barry's idea was that the iconic Otway song *Beware of the Flowers*, the number seven favourite lyric and punk number second only to *Really Free* in the fans' affection, should be re-worked into a disco dance track. And John's idea was *Bunsen Burner*.

Over the past few months John had tried to get Richard Holgarth to do something with *Bunsen Burner*. He had been reciting the lyrics at all his solo dates and so far it was the only new idea. Because he told the audience that it was a contender they regularly yelled, "Hit, Hit, Hit!" so he felt that some sort of version should be on the voting CD, even if it wasn't very good. At a band date at The Half Moon in Putney, John had opened the second half with it, to demonstrate how well it was going down. "It's a poem," said Richard Holgarth. "That's only 'cos it hasn't got a tune yet," replied John, who went off to find someone who could help create one.

Paul Clerehugh could play a bit of guitar, so John asked him if he fancied spending the afternoon in a studio to try and help get a melodic version together. A few days after the session Otway played the new 'song' version of *Bunsen Burner* to Holgarth on the way to a gig. But again Holgarth was singularly unimpressed. "It's just *Really Free* without the chorus or the hook," he pointed out. And he was dead right. If you ignored the new lyrics and did the verses of John's first chart record they fitted perfectly. And, as Holgarth said, "All that's missing is what made *Really Free* a hit."

After John had given Barry the OK to do the dance version of *Beware of the Flowers*, he read him the lyrics of *Bunsen Burner* and played him the Clerehugh version. Although Barry did not do what the audience did and yell "Hit, Hit, Hit", he showed a great deal more enthusiasm for the idea than Richard Holgarth and, with hindsight, it is not to difficult to see why. Barry's greatest international smash success and the seeds to his empire began with the following five lines:

My boot scootin' baby is drivin' me crazy
My obsession from a western – my dance floor date
My rodeo romeo, a cowboy god from head to toe
Wanna make you mine better get in line 5-6-7-8

And Barry had known what to do with them. So when presented with lines like:

You are the kind of carbon I can date
You're the element that makes me passionate
and
You're my little pipette
My favourite piece of apparatus in my chemistry set

He felt they were perfectly adequate for the verse of a pop song, and

Science tells us love is just a chemical reaction in the brain
Let me be your bunsen burner, let me be your naked flame.

could be made into a pop chorus. If the song had no hook, no problem, just find one that someone had made earlier.

"Do you know the song *Disco Inferno*?' he asked Otway. "It doesn't matter if you don't, a lot of your fans will. It's got this bit in the chorus that goes 'burn, baby burn', I'm sure I can make it fit with this." Which he did, and eventually it was discovered that The Trammps' *Disco Inferno* worked a lot better with the *Bunsen Burner* words than Elvis' *Teddy Bear* or Otway's *Really Free*.

CHAPTER
19

A gig at the Boardwalk in Sheffield saw the launch of a brand new ale brewed by Essex firm Crouch Vale. They were fans and had offered to brew a commemorative beer for The Hit Campaign. If you visited the bar that night, as well as ordering a whisky, gin and tonic and a lager, you could also order a pint of OTWAY'S NEXT HIT, a fine pint of bitter with an ABV of 4%.

"I don't want to hear of anyone ordering half a Hit," John told the audience. "'Can I have two hits please?' is quite acceptable, but what I'd most like to hear you requesting is a Hit Top."

The Hit Squad, The Beer and the Otnews web page were all having an effect and increasing the awareness of John's birthday present. John had been thinking of other ways to involve the fans in The Hit; one of them was to actually have them on the CD. "I thought why not do *House of the Rising Sun* at a gig and record it with all the heckles for the B-side. We could then take all the names of every member of the audience and credit each one of them as backing vocalists. So I called Paul Clerehugh and asked him if he could book somewhere big so we could record the B-side. He came back to me a couple of days later saying he had it sussed – 'don't record it at a gig, book Abbey Road Studios.' I wasn't sure, but Paul was, he just kept saying 'trust me, it will work the fans will love the opportunity to record with their star at the most famous studio in the world'."

Having still not quite recouped the outgoings from the Really Free Show five years before, John was determined that The Hit should not lead to outrageous personal debt. As Maurice had mentioned and Otway was all too aware, big hit campaigns can cost as much as a two bedroomed house – Monopoly money literally. He couldn't afford to book Abbey Road and pay the expenses so those that were coming paid twenty pounds, for which they received a limited edition CD and a ticket for the celebratory concert in the evening after the session. That meant if the three hundred he was hoping for turned up, John should break even.

But far more people than that wanted to be on the B-side. The total was a thousand. John had figured that as well as putting their names as backing vocalists on The Hit single, he could also get them printed legibly on a T-shirt and from the orders coming in it became apparent that pretty much everyone who was coming to the studio wanted both one of these and an enamel Abbey Road badge.

John had got Paul Clerehugh to negotiate the deal with Abbey Road, and Paul had suggested that anything left over after the studio costs should go into the campaign funds. It soon became apparent that the profit from that event would pay for something that would make a big difference to the success of what John was aiming for – Richard Cotton. Cotton was now living back in the UK and he had discussed The Hit many times with Otway. Richard had been the only knowledgeable person who had voiced something that John had always secretly believed – that the Top Ten was possible.

So John really wanted him on board. The problem was that the more successful a single was, the more money it cost. Long gone were the days when a big hit made a small fortune. That happened in the big singles sales days of *Really Free* twenty-five years previously. Now, as John was approaching fifty, they were loss leaders – a device for raising the profile and selling the new album… and there was not going to be a new Otway album. If Cotton was going to work on the project some other way of paying for him would have to be found – and Abbey Road would do that.

It wouldn't be a big earner for him but John asked him at an ideal moment. He had just been elbowed out of a company that he had helped make successful, and to rub salt into the wound had seen one of the acts he had found for them reach number 17 in the charts. *The Wheels On The Bus* by Mad Donna would have been his first hit record. He wasn't happy about it and he had a point to prove.

Paul Clerehugh needed a generous amount of gyroscopic explanation in order to make the booking at Abbey Road, as they guarded their reputation very carefully and sightseers were expressly forbidden. It was regarded as one of the best studios in the world with the latest and most advanced sound recording equipment. The acoustics were admired by the world's greatest artists in both the popular and classical fields, and the large room needed for the recording of John's version of *House Of The Rising Sun* was almost fully booked and most commonly used to record large symphony orchestras putting the soundtrack onto the latest James Bond movie or similar blockbuster.

The request to use the studio for the purposes of capturing the sound of Otway fans heckling "Who's a prat?" was possibly not going to be received very well and would need to be carefully worded. "We need to record a large choir," was all they had been told when John and Paul went for the production meeting.

"We went into that meeting knowing that what we wanted to do might be a bit sensitive and I was a bit nervous having sold so many tickets," says John. "I remember the administrator saying the large studio could take up to three hundred people, and me and Paul looking at each other thinking 'which of us is going to tell them we've got a hell of a lot more than that coming?"

"I think we're going to have to do it in three takes," Paul eventually told them. "We want to capture the sound of a thousand people."

"Goodness, what is it for?" the administrator asked with genuine interest, and on being told that it was for the B-side of John's hit, enquired with even more interest what they had planned for the A-side.

"The funniest thing I remember from that meeting," remembers Paul, "was when the chap had finished showing us around and asked us if we had any questions. Otway piped up with 'I was reading about you recently in the paper and the article was about all the things that had been recorded here. Can you tell me which studio was it where ...' and you could see the poor man's eyes glazing over as he prepared himself to answer a question he had been asked countless times before. Then Otway continued with '... Benny Hill recorded *Ernie*' and the guy just looked at him dumbstruck."

There would obviously come a point when those responsible for the smooth running of the studio became aware of the true nature of the Otway choir. If John and Paul hoped it would not be until the sound engineer was modifying and mixing the massed yells of "Where?" and "What's it called?", they were to be disappointed. It happened after John had done a local newspaper interview and had gleefully told the reporter of his plans. The article reported that "Outrageous punk lunatic and rock's great failure has invited all his fans to the famous Abbey Road Studios," and delighted its readers with a pretty graphic description of the singer's wild live show and innate ability to create mayhem. The piece had also implied that there was an open invitation to all who revelled in this behaviour to pile down to the studio and join in.

Abbey Road Studios rang up with the intention of cancelling the session. "That was pretty scary," says John. "Not only was Abbey Road the big plan for the B-side, but one thousand fans had made travel arrangements, we had already ordered the T-shirts and badges and I had just taken Richard Cotton on."

As organiser of seven Dunkerque trips and a man used to dealing with Otway fans in large numbers, Cotton was sent to the studio to calm fears and assure the nervous guardians of Britain's greatest musical heritage site that there was not an invasion planned – just a session in which a number of enthusiastic people intended to record a song. Eventually Cotton was able to persuade them that he had the names and addresses of everyone attending the session and there were plans to get them all in and out of the studio in an orderly and professional manner. With a little nervousness, the studio allowed the recording to go ahead.

It was the first of rather a lot of very uncomfortable close calls that this project would have.

For a large number of the fans, Abbey Road was the start of a very exciting journey with their star. Up until this point it had just been flyers, beer and a poem read from the stage, but being able to tell their friends and family that they were booked for a recording session at Abbey Road Studios was different. Paul Clerehugh had understood what an important event this would be for the fans: he was a fan, he wanted to go and record with Otway at Abbey Road, and he knew he wasn't alone.

"Even the band, who seemed to take everything in their stride, were impressed by recording there," says Otway. "Adam and Murray, who were the cool members of the band – by that I mean they were easy to amuse and almost impossible to excite – got really quite carried away by the idea."

For all involved it was like entering a secret temple – one that you could only gain admittance to by having the correct musical qualifications. And for just one day being an Otway fan would do.

"There was no question of any inappropriate behaviour," says Cotton. "Everyone just seemed in awe of the place."

Richard Cotton has a recording contract with the signatures of all those who attended that day. "Well, they were all artists," he said. "And I didn't want anyone after me for a royalty, so I got Patsy Andrews from the Onelist to get them all to sign away their rights as they came in. She was incredibly efficient – she got Otway and the band to sign away their rights too."

To make the recording session a bit more challenging, the band had come up with an addition to the live show version. When they played *House Of The Rising Sun* at gigs, they missed out the last verse; for the full length B-side version, instead of the masses heckling Otway why not have Otway heckling them? Therefore upon arrival, each Otway fan was given a cue sheet with both what they were to yell at Otway and what Otway was going to sing back, plus what Otway was going to yell at them and what they were expected to sing back to him.

So as well as the "whats" and "wheres" there was also:
Otway: *Where's your foot?*
Fans: *One foot's on the platform*
Otway: *Where's your other foot?*
Fans: *The other's on the train*
Otway: *And where are you going?*
Fans: *We're going down to New Orleans*
Otway: *What are you going to wear?*
Fans: *To wear that ball and chain.*

Throughout the day there were three sessions. In the first the band put down the basic track with the first three hundred and fifty voices, then the second group overdubbed and added theirs to make a total of nearly seven hundred. The final overdub brought the total to one thousand for most of the song, though with one less at the end. "I'm not yelling the big 'who's a prat!' at the end," insisted Patsy, "because he's not."

"I was, and still am, amazed at how seriously everyone involved took the whole process," says Cotton. "John told them all that this was a very important place, Benny Hill had recorded *Ernie* there and that had been a huge number one, and that we were aiming just as high, and they all laughed and there was a great atmosphere. But as soon as the red light came on there was absolute silence, apart from Richard Holgarth counting, "Five, four" then doing three, two, one with his fingers, so it didn't interfere with the take. And then there was this huge wall of sound that would have shocked Phil Spector going '*WHAT?*' It really was impressive."

As well as the B-side the band also recorded five other songs for the commemorative *Live at Abbey Road* CD, and Murray even managed to add the famous first chord from *A Hard Day's Night* inappropriately at the end of one song. "I couldn't help myself," he says.

After the session, producer Phillipe Bertrande made a quick mix of the recording and the band, then the whole choir headed to the Mean Fiddler in Charing Cross Road to party and film the video.

CHAPTER 20

Since Maurice had first brought up the idea of The Hit, John had given a lot of thought to how to get around the problems of having a proper big hit record. In fact he had thought of little else.

For him the arithmetic worked like this: 4,500 fans came to the Albert Hall and for each person that had come there must be at least one more who would have liked to have come – that's over 9,000 people. You were allowed to release a single in up to three formats – CD, cassette, 12-inch single, 7-inch single or any combination of these, including 3 CDs with a different mix and different B-sides. And each and every variation counted as a sale. 9,000 people buying all three formats would total 27,000 sales which was so close to a Top Ten Hit that it was scary.

The big problem was the cost: all three formats would need to be in the shops on a sale or return basis and if you wanted to sell 30,000 CDs in one week. The general rule of thumb was that you would need around three times this many spread around all the retail outlets in the UK. As Maurice had pointed out, this was a considerable cost that John was not in a position to afford. Most independent small labels could not afford to gamble in this way either. The major record companies did not have this problem, because shops could only return an agreed percentage of unsold stock from a large catalogue of items including both albums and singles. In this way they were less exposed, but even then singles were still unlikely to make them money. Record companies released singles because a hit could establish a career and then the more lucrative album sales should follow. Also, a UK hit often triggered international success. As far as the major record companies were concerned, that is pretty much all they were interested in.

So John did not expect to have a major record company take his hit project on. His 50th Birthday present was unlikely to trigger international success and there was no follow-up album planned. But there were, he believed, enough people who would buy his single and if he could get them in the shops he would be able to have that second chart record he had been wanting for all those years.

Back in the middle of the previous year, Otway had played a club called Bar Cuba in Macclesfield. Promoter Andy Wood (not the Shure Microphone Andy Wood) and his friend Andy Payne chatted to John on the night: they were both fans and up to speed with his chart idea and they suggested they could put out his single on Andy Wood's small record label. This was not the fantastic news that it might sound. Although he was pleased and needed all the help and support he could get, Otway already had a small label 'John Otway Records', Richard Cotton had his 'Amazing Feet' imprint and Maurice Bacon had a small label too, and together their small labels had released a considerable number of flops.

"I tried to explain as best I could about what I thought was involved but it didn't put them off and eventually we met up in London to discuss it further. I didn't really expect anything to come out of the meeting, but I felt it was terribly important not to put anyone off if they were trying to help," says John.

Both the Andys had been very successful in the computer industry. Andy Payne had a thriving company which specialised in flight simulator games and was not fazed by the idea of manufacturing a large amount of stock to put into retail outlets – it was a calculated risk that his company took regularly.

"One thing I felt, the fans felt and I'm sure the Andys did too, was the sheer romance of the music charts. We'd all grown up with *Top Of The Pops*, and however successful anyone became in another industry, being involved with a big hit record had a magic that nothing else had," says John.

So with the promise of as many copies as necessary on sale or return in the shops, John felt he could now phone Maurice and Cotton and tell them the unbelievable good news that they were not looking at just a top thirty hit, they were looking at something quite a bit higher. He had just cleared the big hurdle they faced in the project.

Unfortunately it was just the first hurdle, there would be several more. Small record companies don't deal with record shops themselves, they use distributors who have the task of getting the buyers for key accounts (like Woolworths, HMV, Virgin, major supermarkets) and the independent shops to take stock for their stores. Andy Wood's U-Vibe label was distributed by Pinnacle.

"As soon as I found out who U-Vibe's label manager was at Pinnacle, I knew we had a problem," says Cotton. "You've got this really trendy chap with all these cool record companies to look after. When he has a meeting with the big buyers he's got a big pile of releases and he'll be lucky if they even agree to stock one or two of them, so what's he going to ask them to stock? Is it going to be a single from a young happening band with a great album that he'll be able to sell thousands of pounds worth if the single makes the charts? Or is he going to ask them to help out with John Otway's birthday present because he hasn't had a hit for twenty-five years and his fans would like him to have another, when it's a one-off event with no new album and no way of capitalising on any success?"

So John found out the hard way that just because one could press up one hundred thousand records and be prepared to pay the cost of the returns if they didn't sell, that didn't mean the major chains were going to take them and have them in stock. And if they didn't, the chances of getting anything better than top thirty was zero.

And yet on offer was a substantial fan sales base and, for a single release, a pretty large budget. So Cotton and the Andys had meetings with a couple of alternative distributors.

Nigel Reveler was Otway's choice and he would prove to be an exceptionally wise one. The two had first met in 1978 just after *Really Free*, when Nigel became head of singles marketing at Polydor and he remembered fondly Otway's desperate attempts at getting a follow-up. He had even helped put into action some of the schemes like the single without vocals, and was amused that twenty-five years on Otway was still desperate for that second hit. So with a combination of "let's do it for old times' sake" and "I might as well finish the job I started as it's obviously not going away" he agreed to take the task on.

There was another reason why John was so keen to get Nigel on board – he was the distributor that Chris France had gone to in 1994 when offered Prince's *The Most Beautiful Girl In The World*. And between them they had managed to get a number one. It was a magnificent achievement – the small label and the independent distributor giving Prince his biggest hit and reaching the top of the UK charts, something John had never forgotten. "That's the man we want," Otway told Cotton. "He's been there and done it, and it's always hardest the first time."

But even with Nigel on board, Chris France was not convinced.

"The problem is John, you're not Prince," Chris had told him. "The shops choose stock by using demographics that are very well researched and there are very good reasons why Prince falls into those demographics and you don't."

Chris would have liked to have been more optimistic about his school mate's new bid for pop stardom but felt that there was little point in building up false hopes. There was very little chance of any major account championing the new Otway single, and with no stock in the High Street stores there could be no record in the charts.

It was six months before the release date. Other companies were starting their singles campaigns for release on 30th September 2002 while John's had been going for a year. Other companies knew what the song was going to be and had just started work on making it a hit, Otway knew it was going to be a hit and had just started working on the song.

The Onelist, who were now more regularly referred to as The Hit Squad, had discovered Ingmire Hall, a 16th century stately home in Sedburgh in Cumbria that just happened to be the ancestral home of a Sir John Otway 400 years ago. This seemed just the right sort of place to host an Otway weekend for the most passionately involved fans and to plan the campaign. Nearly all the central characters attended: Patsy Andrews, Alistair McClean, Billy Green, Chris Nuza, Karen Wintle and Xav. Mark Pegg also arrived with a camera crew to document the progress.

The event was like a mini-Dunkerque, with a show in the town on the Saturday night and the rest of the weekend focusing on the task ahead. It essentially took the French trip one stage further: instead of merely travelling with the fans, you actually moved in with them for a few days.

John rented the country house for a couple of days after the weekend, to work with the band on Hit ideas. One promising idea had been e-mailed to him by fan Jane Skellet, who had written some lyrics about the fairy story Rumplestiltskin. "I tend to focus on my own writing, and not pay much attention to anyone else's," says John. "But as I was going through my mail this caught my eye, which I thought was brilliant:

> Gi's the baby
> Gi's the baby
> Just give us the baby!

All that Ingmire Hall weekend I just kept going up to the band saying 'Give us the baby' – I mean it's such a catchy chorus for a punk song."

So the band worked on the Rumplestiltskin idea, together with a song of John's called My American Friend and a musical idea of Murray's which eventually became a song called Pauline.

After the passing of six months before release Cotton started to get worried. He had been working on the campaign for a while, there wasn't that long to go, the record company and distributor were in place and the B-side had been recorded, but no-one had heard any ideas for The Hit itself. As six months before turned to five months before, Cotton's concern turned to panic. But John eventually started to pull the tracks together that would be on the voting CD for the fans to pick The Hit.

Barry Upton had a studio in his house and John spent a day there putting his vocals on *Bunsen Burner* and the disco version of *Beware of The Flowers* and seeing if there was anything else they could do that resembled Hit material. John had fancied doing a new version of the song *We Know What She's Doing (She's In Love)* from the *Premature Adulation* album. Richard Holgarth's production was a powerful rock number with a sharp bite which captured the strong feelings of hurt and betrayal in a relationship poisoned by deceit. Otway felt that there was another way to interpret the lyrics in what he described to Barry as a *poperetta*, where however painful these situations are they are still a combination of the same basic emotions that one finds portrayed in photo-stories in the pages of teenage girl comics. And not surprisingly the Steps producer had exactly the right sort of teen-girl harmony group to add the saccharine to this sweet and sour piece of pop that John was proposing.

John got Jean Paul, who had done the Aylesbury Youth Orchestra arrangements, to have a look at *Poetry and Jazz*. "That's the one I really wanted to be chosen," says John. "It took me years to write that song, and I've always felt it was the best thing I had ever written. Jean Paul did a great arrangement and worked with Barry Upton producing it."

John himself produced a track for the CD – a Seymour arrangement of an old Otway favourite *Too Much Air Not Enough Oxygen*. Richard Holgarth produced *Rumplestiltskin* and a new version of *Josephine* and Murray produced *My American Friend* and *Pauline*. The last of the new tracks was *I'm Cured and I Can't Catch Love* which was put together at the very last session with Barry Upton: Barry played John something he had been writing on the guitar and John showed Barry some lyrics he had just written. They had the basic track sorted out within the hour – an unbelievably short time for an Otway song.

It had been ten years since Otway had worked on a batch of new recordings and with the belief that within a few months one of these new tracks could grace the charts, he felt very excited.

CHAPTER 21

When Cotton had first heard Mad Donna's *The Wheels On The Bus*, he was convinced it was commercial enough to be a hit and secured it for Shifty Disco, the company he was working with. The record secured a substantial amount of radio play and Shifty Disco was able to tie in with a large company who would take the financial risk and get it in the major stores. But by then Richard had left and he was not happy as he watched the discovery he had made rise in the charts and deprive him of the number 17 hit he felt should be his. So for him that was the number to beat: Otway's campaign had the promise to do it, but lacked what a lot of people often think is the most important factor in a chart record, a commercial-sounding song.

If Richard Holgarth had heard Mad Donna's *The Wheels On The Bus*, which was essentially someone singing a nursery rhyme and trying to sound like Madonna, he would not have been excited in the way Richard Cotton had been. In fact it is quite likely that he would not have been able to listen to it all the way through without turning it off. Rather than feeling cheated by not being associated with it, he would have been relieved.

It is therefore not surprising that the two Richards reacted in radically different ways when presented with the Barry Upton productions.

"Bloody amazing, even better than *The Wheels*," was the Cotton reaction on hearing *Bunsen Burner* and the disco *Flowers*. And when he eventually listened to *We Know What She's Doing* and *I'm Cured* he became concerned that there were now too many good commercial tracks for the fans to pick from. "It could split the pop vote and allow a less radio friendly 'credible' track in," he thought.

Richard Holgarth was also concerned: not only did he have to listen to these tracks all the way through, he was also expected to play on them. With a degree of trepidation he added his guitar part to *Bunsen Burner* and the disco *Flowers*. But when he listened to *We Know What She's Doing* he refused point blank to play along with it.

"It's complete crap," he told Otway. "There was a chord progression that made the song interesting that has been replaced by a three chord piece of cheese. It's just horrible." It got worse. When he eventually heard the finished version, the cheese had been caramelised with the layer of sweet teen harmonies that John had suggested when he first came up with the idea of turning this rock song into a *poperetta*. "I was quite miffed," says Richard Holgarth. "I had spent so much time writing that material with Otway and I thought we came up with some pretty good tracks, and then he goes and does that to one of them."

It wasn't just Holgarth, Seymour was upset too. On the disco *Flowers*, the bass notes in the song had been reduced to ones that could be played on one finger and counted on two. It was his favourite Otway song, the one he enjoyed playing the most and the song he felt defined the front man as a punk with a degree of attitude.

"If that gets voted as the single, I'm leaving the band," he announced, and he meant it.

As the tracks came in, divisions hardened on what ought to be The Hit – they basically fell into two main camps and a tent. There were those who felt the pop material had the most potential and should be the way forward, those who wanted "a good record and not a pile of poo", and there was John who reckoned that "there's a quiet majority that would like the good ballads like *Poetry and Jazz* or *Geneve*."

"I couldn't believe it," says Adam the drummer. "We were having this heated debate about what should and shouldn't be chosen, and when I asked John what he thought he said that he really wanted *Poetry and Jazz*. I cracked up laughing, and when he didn't join in, I suddenly realised the guy was serious. Thank goodness he wasn't choosing it."

"Thank goodness Cotton isn't choosing it," was Seymour and Holgarth's strong feeling. "Thank goodness the band aren't," was Cotton's.

And there was suspicion all round that the record chosen wouldn't be based on the fans' vote at all. Some assumed the vote was just a bit of publicity, and the band worried that Cotton might be tempted to fix the result. He was aware of this, and so didn't want to be responsible for counting the votes.

John had noticed that when the PRS (a not-for-profit membership organisation for songwriters and publishers) sent out the ballot papers for the election of board members, the return address on the envelope was to an organisation called The Electoral Reform Society, so he suggested that Cotton should check if they would do it.

And in fact the Electoral Reform Society were delighted to. Most of their work was for unions and large corporations, overseeing their elections and giving confidence to all involved that the process was fair. Fans voting for a hit was fun and more exotic than they usually dealt with, but it still fell perfectly into their remit. If it attracted a bit of publicity then that could only be good for everyone. It was particularly good for the fans, who were more aware than anyone just how much a ballot could be skewed. Doing it this way meant that it really was their choice. Which was just as well, given that one track on the voting CD was the big orchestral version of Geneve – all these years after he had ruined his career with that recording, John still thought it was a potential Hit and could be given another chance.

"What do we do about using the hook from *Disco Inferno* if the fans pick *Bunsen Burner*?" John had asked Cotton when they were collating the tracks. "How is the publishing sorted out with the composers?" Cotton reassured John that you simply agreed a deal with the publishing company who owned the rights to the bits you were using. "It takes about three days," he told John. "It's done all the time, and there's no difficulty because it's an easy way for them to make money. Let's see how the voting goes and if that one looks likely to win I'll get it sorted."

The voting idea was very popular, and nearly everyone on John's mailing list wanted to be involved and help pick Otway the second hit of his career. Over two thousand people ordered both a voting pack and a ticket for The Hit Announcement Concert at the Astoria where the winning song would be revealed.

The Electoral Reform Society had given John and Cotton the option of knowing how it was going as they received the votes – an option they readily took up. The band on the other hand preferred to wait until the big announcement and find out at the same time as the fans. By the first week in July – under three months before release – Otway and Cotton got the first indication of what The Hit was going to be. And it was pretty obvious that the fans were going for pop. *Beware Of The Flowers* was in the lead followed closely by *Bunsen Burner*. A few days later, with the next update, these two songs were well ahead of the others but had changed places, with *Bunsen Burner* now the front runner.

Around this time John and Richard Holgarth played a party at a conference in Bounemouth. After them there was a disco and as an experiment John got the DJ to put on his *Bunsen Burner* track. And an astonishing thing happened – instead of leaving the dance floor people stayed there and continued to dance. "I couldn't believe my eyes," said John. "Quite honestly that had never happened before. Loads of times you would be somewhere where people were dancing and quite often someone would get the DJ to play one of my songs, and it was invariably embarrassing when they did. The dance floor emptied leaving only a few people looking awkward trying to keep the evening going. But I'm sure the number of dancers increased with this song. It was getting very, very exciting."

"I'd better sort out the publishing," said Cotton.

Peer Music looked after the publishing of the Trammps *Disco Inferno* in the UK and were the people that Cotton would have to obtain a licence from, in order to use the parts of the song Barry Upton had inserted into John Otway's *Bunsen Burner*. Unfortunately, Cotton's prediction of three days was wildly optimistic – when he called Peer Music, they told him it would take three months to organise.

Cotton explained that they would have to sort it out quicker than that because the record would have been released by then. No it won't, they responded, because you can't release it until you have a licence and that will take three months. An explanation that Otway's fiftieth birthday was sooner than that and the London Palladium was booked to celebrate the song being in the charts did not help. Cotton was told politely but firmly that they needed permission from the copyright holders in America, who were a big organisation – they would get onto it and let him know when it had been sorted, sometime towards the end of the year.

Cotton called Otway to discuss the options. If they had not involved the Electoral Reform Society they could fudge the vote and choose a song that they were allowed to release to be The Hit, but they themselves had made that an impossibility. They could go back to Barry Upton and get him to take out all the *Disco Inferno* bits, but that would make it a completely different song, one without hooks and not the one the fans had voted for. Or Cotton could get back on to Peer Music and persuade them that they would just have to pull their fingers out and get that licence sorted.

There comes a point when someone ringing up and asking the same question repeatedly and then insisting on talking to someone else in the office to ask the same question becomes an irritation – Cotton passed that point. There comes a point when the people working in the offices of Peer Music wonder when someone will understand the meaning of the word "no", not appreciating that this person, though having some understanding of it, is simply not allowed to accept it as an answer. By the time tempers were raised and loud voices used, the chance of understanding the word "no" had long since past. The only understanding from both parties was that future communication was pointless.

And *Bunsen Burner* remained stubbornly a few votes ahead of *Beware Of The Flowers*.

At the same time as this communication breakdown there was an important meeting. Otway, Cotton, the two Andys and Nigel Reveler met with Judd Lander of Fleming Connolly Lander. Judd was a plugger, "And you are going to need one of those," Nigel Reveler told them. "If you want me to try and get the major accounts to take some stock, the first thing they will want to know is what plans you have for radio and TV. If you haven't got one of the heavyweight companies plugging your product then they will assume that you're really not that serious."

"If we wanted them to assume we were very, very serious then who should we tell them our plugger is?" John asked. And so, surrounded by innumerable numbers of gold, platinum and silver discs that Fleming Connolly Lander had cajoled the nation's media to feature in their programmes, they discussed their campaign.

"I've listened to the voting CD and personally I hope it's *Bunsen Burner*," was Judd's first comment. And apart from Otway and Cotton, who seemed remarkably quiet, there was general agreement.

"I don't remember too much about that meeting," says John. "It's all a bit of a horrid blur. It just seems that every few seconds, someone would say something like 'I think *Bunsen Burner* would be good for Radio 2' and 'well that wouldn't be a problem if they all voted for *Bunsen Burner*' and, I'm not making this up, towards the end of the meeting Judd said in jest 'Of course you've sorted out the publishing.' And everyone laughed, everyone except me and Cotton."

The two of them went to the aptly-named World's End pub afterwards, but neither of them had any ideas about what to do. They had booked the people from the Electoral Reform Society to announce the result and didn't want to get up on stage at the Astoria and announce that they couldn't release the song chosen to be the next Hit, so we'd all have to settle for what was voted second. Cotton saying, 'It'll make a good chapter in your next book,' was the most optimistic thing either of them could think of.

Luckily for Otway there are people who will not take no for an answer, and will go to the most extraordinary lengths to find an alternative. Usually if there is a big problem that keeps one awake at night, there is nothing to do until the morning and so one lays awake fretting. However, whilst people without problems in Great Britain are falling asleep and those with are lying on their beds trying to, there are people in other parts of the world wide awake cheerfully going about their business. Like, for instance, the writers of *Disco Inferno* and their original publisher in the United States of America. That night, having given up lying on his bed trying to sleep, Cotton with his computer and telephone started to put together the *Disco Inferno* publishing history from first principles. Written in 1977 by Philadelphia duo Tyrone Kersey and Leroy Green, *Disco Inferno* by The Trammps soared to No.1 in the American charts when it was included on the soundtrack to *Saturday Night Fever*. Both the writers had sold their rights to Golden Fleece Music and Six Strings Music the same year it was written. And a number of phone calls later Cotton was actually talking to the American lawyer who had subsequently sold their rights to the major American media company DreamWorks. He even supplied the name of the woman who had done the deal there.

"Just one other thing," Cotton asked. "In the publishing deal you did, do the writers themselves have to give their consent to any licence?

This was crucial: if the original writers needed to be contacted for their approval then the whole thing would take more time than they had.

"No."

Now this was a "no" that Cotton didn't mind hearing. DreamWorks had all the rights they needed without having to ask anyone's permission to grant a licence. They were, Cotton had now discovered, the only barrier preventing *Bunsen Burner* becoming Otway's next hit.

"I think I might be able to do it," he told Otway the next morning.

The lady at DreamWorks was Molly Kaye. One of Cotton's New York business friends knew her and had given him the number of her secretary on the West Coast. Molly was indeed the person who would be able to give the go ahead, but was about to leave for a three-month vacation aboard an ocean-going yacht. Cotton had forty-eight hours.

"I've found out what flowers she likes, sourced one of the best florists in LA, and in five hours time when she arrives at work the office is going to be filled with nearly a thousand dollars' worth of them," Cotton confessed.

Molly Kaye had not heard the Otway song *Beware of the Flowers* – neither the old classic version or the new disco one – but she was amused by the extravagant gesture of the crazy guy with an English accent who told her that his life would be saved if she could just sort out a licence for him before she went on holiday. Cotton charmed and flirted, faxes were sent backwards and forwards and a copy of the *Bunsen Burner* track was downloaded and danced to in an office in Los Angeles.

"Have you done it yet?" John asked eagerly six hours before the deadline.

"No, not yet. They've agreed to let you use the track but I'm still negotiating, I reckon I can get you a better percentage."

"We've got it, we've bloody got it. Can't you just accept whatever they offer, then I can breathe a little easier?" said John. Even now he can't understand why, after facing complete defeat, going behind Peer Music's back and taking on DreamWorks, Cotton didn't just say yes immediately.

CHAPTER 22

Otnews, the fans' website, had just reached the milestone of half a million hits, and whilst Otway was facing the incredible hurdles that stood between him and a real hit record, many a fan was facing other incredible hurdles trying to get Otway a virtual one. Xav had created the game Otopoly on the Otnews site. In this game the fan got to play the part of John Otway as he tries to get a hit, pressing up as many CDs as possible and usually running up a huge virtual overdraft keeping their popularity and publicity positive.

In many ways it was like the real Otway. Over thousands of attempts the fans achieved a mere 332 top tens and 5,801 complete flops. More ominously, in getting the results the fans earned a whopping minus £469 million, a huge huge overdraft. But like the real Otway, undaunted they kept coming back trying to have hits.

Up until the voting CD, recording the B-side and getting a good score on Otopoly were all that the fans had been able to do to help. But when they received their voting packs they were heavily involved moved on to do what many regarded as the most important decision in the music business, choosing The Hit itself.

John sent out an A5 brochure with the CD, listing the tracks and telling his electorate:

I won't try to advise you on how to make your decision – with my track record I'm hardly qualified to. One thing I can tell you is that even the people involved can't agree between us which one it should be.

Just before the voting CDs had been sent out, Cotton had readily accepted a ten pound bet from Otway that the fans would pick *Poetry and Jazz* as The Hit. And although John had said that he would not try and influence the voting, when Johnny Walker had him on his Radio 2 show to talk about the vote, John requested that this was one of the tracks he played. The unusual method of single selection attracted other radio interest too, with Jonathan Ross playing *I'm Cured (And I Can't Catch Love)* on his Saturday morning show.

John had asked for a fiver for the voting CD, to cover the cost of pressings and to pay for hiring the Astoria for the announcement gig, but so many fans wanted to vote that there was a reasonable surplus. "Let's spend it on fireworks." said Cotton, "As soon as we announce what The Hit is, have the finest pyrotechnic display a surplus will buy." Since he had just finally nailed the publishing deal, John reckoned that he had earned a few flashes and bangs.

The Electoral Reform Society had enjoyed the whole process greatly. "I should think so too," says John, "it was their first hit." They had agreed to send some representatives down to the Astoria for The Hit announcement, and John's original plan was for the band to play each song and then have one of the invigilators announce how many votes it had managed. "That's a really rubbish idea," said Richard Holgarth. "What happens if one of the first numbers we play gets a huge number of votes, then the audience will have to sit through all the rest knowing what had won, where's the excitement in that?" John, who by now had seen what the votes were like and had a strong idea of what the results were going to be, could only agree.

So the evening worked out like this.

After The Big Band had played *Really Free* to give the fans a taste of a hit, Steve Frost came on to tell the packed venue that they were now about to do some pop-picking in earnest. He then introduced the independent scrutineer and returning officer from the Electoral Reform Society, Nick Stylianou. If the song was in the bottom six, Nick was to announce the number of votes it had received and declare it a flop. In this case a young lady Miss Miss "we can't call her Miss Flop, because it's rude" would take the card bearing the name of the particular Flop and place it on the board stage right reserved for the songs that in the view of the electorate did not stand the greatest chance of chart success. If, however, the song was one of the top five, Nick would point out that the audience had just heard a potential Hit and another young lady Miss Hit would take that song's card to a board stage left.

First up was *I'm Cured (And I Can't Catch Love)*. The band played it, then Nick walked on stage and read the score. "Eighty-nine votes I'm afraid it is a flop," and the *I'm Cured* card was handed to Miss Miss.

So far so good, but things were about to turn scary for Richard Holgarth. Next up was *We Know What She's Doing*, with teenagers Natalie, Sophie and Danni supplying the sweet harmonies that had destroyed the song he and Otway had laboured over all those years before. And after Richard Holgarth had played the simplified arrangement, i.e. the one without the classic chord structure and the blistering solo he had refused to add to the track when it was recorded, Nick came on stage to announce that it was a "potential Hit". A card with its title written in capital letters was carried stage right by the other Miss, as to Holgarth's horror the fans started to yell the words "hit, hit, hit."

"I knew the results," says Otway. "But Holgarth and the band had opted for not finding out until the announcement at the end of the night, so that can't have been easy."

It did not get better. After *Josephine* – one of the tracks that Holgarth had produced – Nick told the audience "twelve votes". No yells of "hit, hit" and its card was taken to the opposite side of the stage to be placed on the bottom of the Flops board. As an election night, for lifelong labour supporter Holgarth it was like watching the Thatcher government getting back into power with an increased majority and the Conservatives taking the constituency of his home town of Harlow.

Things weren't that much better for Seymour. He had agreed to use the second finger of his left hand to play the two notes that Barry had chosen as the only ones needed for his disco *Flowers*. If that track was the one chosen then he would be leaving the band. "Potential Hit," said Nick. "Hit, hit, hit," said the fans, and Seymour wondered if the next forty-five minutes were to be his last working with Otway.

Adam Batterbee was surprised that *Poetry and Jazz* made it to The Hit Board, and even though John knew it hadn't won, he could pretend to Adam that he thought it might as Miss Hit carried its sign across the stage. After *Bunsen Burner* was carried to The Hit board it looked as though the night was a Barry Upton whitewash. And it was, right up until the final track – the punk number *Too Much Air Not Enough Oxygen*.

At the end of the show, when they had played all the songs and the representative from the Electoral Reform Society came on to announce the votes for the five potential hits, Seymour could not hold out any longer. He looked over Nick's shoulder to get a sneak preview of the final result. It was bad, but not quite as bad as he had dreaded. Between them, *Bunsen Burner* and *Beware Of the Flowers* had more votes than all the other songs on the ballot put together. And it was close, very close, with only thirty-three votes separating the two disco songs, the one that Seymour really hated and the one that he could live with. Thirty-three votes that kept him in the band and still in the big campaign for the charts.

In 1855, when Robert Bunsen designed a device to produce a controllable source of combustion for the laboratory at the University of Heidelberg, he would have been surprised at the way his invention was used nearly one hundred and fifty years later to ignite a whole battery of pyrotechnic devices on a stage at the London Astoria. No naked flame was necessary, just the reaction produced when the name of his invention was used in conjunction with the word Hit. Huge flashes and bangs went off around the band, the two thousand fans went ballistic and the track that Otway hoped would end his twenty-five years without chart success pounded out of the Astoria's massive speakers.

This was the third time that John had stood on that stage with the hall completely packed. But this time there was a huge excitement and an energy that looked forward to something as opposed to celebrating something that had just been achieved. "I remember thinking of what Chris France had said, about two thousand avid fans playing havoc with demographics, and here they were, all in one room going mental. I thought then that we had a really good chance of pulling off something spectacular," says John.

Subsequently, as with all elections, there was a good deal of sober analysis of the results, and over many a pint of beer analysis of a more profound nature. Cotton was delighted that the song he thought was the most commercial and had the best chance was chosen, despite having to visit Hell to collect the publishing agreement for it. Barry Upton must have been delighted: he had offered to produce some tracks for John and let the fans judge his work, which exposed his pride to what could have been a bit of a battering. But with these voting results, he was rewarded for this bravery with a welcome boost to the ego. Richard Holgarth wasn't delighted and he still believes that the fans voted for the wrong songs, for the wrong reasons. "I think they all listened to the tracks and just thought, 'what sounds most like what I hear on the radio', and not what is the best recording."

What was, by far, the most important factor, was not which of the eleven tracks the fans picked. It was the fact that they had collectively chosen one. Amongst them there would obviously be many like Richard Holgarth who would have liked something on the other side of the spectrum. But, by having a fair vote and being able to decide themselves what The Hit should be, the fans, along with the band and everyone else involved with the project, got behind *Bunsen Burner* and sang from the same hymn sheet, upon which were written the words "hit, hit, hit".

CHAPTER 23

A quarter of a century and a generation earlier the singles charts were compiled by taking a relatively small number of record shops and giving them each a diary to record every sale. The week's chart would be made up from this sample. Those who study statistics know that a truly random sample of this nature gives a very accurate model of the total sales in all the record shops in the country. However, if the sample is not truly random then the results can be skewed and give an inaccurate picture of what's happening. If, back in 1977, those studying statistics were given an examination asking them to name two ways in which bias can influence a sample survey, they would have got good marks for the following answer:

1) When the rep for Polydor, EMI or WEA records goes into a record store and notices a sales diary supplied to them by the British Market Research Bureau and asks the sales staff for a few extra ticks in that diary in return for free copies of a best-selling LP.

2) When someone who wants a hit single employs a team of people known as a "strike force" to drive around the chart return shops buying up copies of the single.

If in this examination they were then asked how to reduce bias in the survey, they could have suggested using a census instead of a sample survey. A census is a survey where every sale of every record is recorded in every shop.

There had for many years been a cat and mouse game between the chart compilers and the record companies, with the compilers aiming to get their charts more accurate and the companies trying to influence them, and over the years the game had become more and more sophisticated. By the time Otway was gearing up for his second hit, what would have been seen as just a hypothetical answer to a statistical problem in *Really Free* days could in effect become a reality in *Bunsen Burner* ones. The sample survey had come to resemble a census.

Each single had a barcode which was read at the checkout in a record shop: as well as telling the cashier how much to charge, it also told the manager what he had sold for his accounting and stock re-ordering. This information could also be used by the chart compilers and by 2002 the company Millward Brown, who were supplying the chart to the BBC, had around ninety percent of all retailers giving them pretty much real-time information on record sales.

But that information was only about what shops were selling, which was not the same as information about what people wanted to buy. And it was the correlation between these two bits of information that the record companies tried to affect.

"The power wielded by the buyers who bought for Woolworth and the supermarkets was awesome," says one industry insider. "If they didn't take any stock from you, you could say goodbye to that big hit or that *Top Of The Pops* appearance. There must have been a great deal of temptation put their way to influence their decisions and it certainly allowed them to demand large discounts for the sale-or-return stock they ordered."

However, even if there were offers of beautiful girls, trips on luxury yachts and lots of brown envelopes stuffed with used fifty pound notes in return for them taking tens of thousands of free CDs, this was not how the major buyers did the majority of their business. For this they used sound business principles built on the demographics that Chris France had told Otway about. It is quite simple to have a stab at how they might derive those demographics. Is the single related to a popular music-based television show? What chart position did the last single get to? How many Radio One plays has the single had in the last week? Does this single appeal to the core market, which is between the ages of sixteen to twenty-four?

The problem for Otway and anyone else hoping for a surprise or unusual hit, was that the largest supplier of singles had a buying formula, and only singles that adhered to that formula could get into the top end of the charts.

"And that's not fair," thought an act who did not particularly appeal to teenage girls, was unlikely to be played on Radio One, whose last single did not chart and who was not a Pop Idol. By the time John Otway knew that his next hit was to be *Bunsen Burner*, EUK (the largest supplier of singles) knew what was going to be number one. Will Young and Gareth Gates (who scored really well demographically) were putting out an Elvis song and it had been pre-ordered in such quantities that both Will and Gareth would have to commit a terrible abhorrent crime and have been taken to the tabloids for them to be wrong.

Nigel Reveler had been abroad for The Hit announcement gig, but his daughter, Pollyanna, who worked for his company had been there, and had given a glowing account.

"If you've got that many avid fans," he told Otway and Cotton, "I might well be able to get you a top thirty. It's still tough though."

"Neither of us could tell him that we wanted to get a Top Ten," says Otway, "because he would have told us that we were being unrealistic and naïve. But I kept doing the arithmetic and thought there must be a way of managing it."

It was easy for John to see a conspiracy in the situation: the buyers for the main stores looked to what the radio stations were playing and the radio producers looked at what the main accounts were buying because they were going to be the hits they should be playing. It was a huge industry and there was a lot of money at stake. "They've got it stitched up," he thought and although he knew this was a simplification of the way it worked, whichever way it worked appeared to disenfranchise *Rock and Roll's Greatest Failure* from getting a hit for his fiftieth birthday.

Otway and Cotton found a way to convey this complex situation to the fans in a few simple words: "Retail is our enemy. They will do everything they can to stop us from having a hit."

"Neither of us could tell Nigel that it was a war," says Otway. "His company's best and biggest customers were the very people we were trying to bring to their knees. We had different agendas: he wanted a livelihood and we wanted a hit."

With a different distributor there could have been no war and not even a little skirmish: only a few independent stores would have the record in their shops and when fans asked for the record in any of the High Street retailers, they would simply be told that they did not have the single in stock. Nigel had nearly thirty years of experience and many friends in the industry, and was in the position to ask a few favours. Most of the buyers at HMV would not have been interested at all in *Bunsen Burner* as they were young and knew the current trends, but there were a few higher up in the corporation that remembered the mad Otway, the man who injured himself most painfully astride Wild Willy's amplifier live on *The Old Grey Whistle Test* – an event that had possibly brightened their teenage years.

"John's fans would like to buy his new single for his birthday present. Could HMV put it on their computer system?"

HMV had a particularly efficient computer system which allowed customers to order CDs and pre-order certain titles before they were released. This enabled the shops to sell a greater range of product and give the company an indication of likely demand.

If a single was on this system it could be paid for in advance at the record shop and the CD would be there to collect when it was available. Asking to include the single on the system was not asking the impossible, this was not asking HMV to take thousands and thousands of copies of an un-proven product (that would come later). It was just a favour for an old punk rocker for his birthday that would take someone working in the IT department five minutes.

"They've put it on the system," Nigel announced at one of the now regular meetings that he had with Otway, Cotton and the two Andys. The Virgin shops had an ordering system, but it worked differently, and more significantly, they did not usually take pre-orders for singles. However, they had liked the idea and Nigel had got them to agree that if anyone wanted to pre-order that single they could. He had done very well with some of the smaller chains too, "Even Our Price said they would help."

But all the shops (like Woolworths and Tesco) supplied by EUK did not do any pre-orders, ever. Instead, around three weeks before release their buyers looked at things like air play, press and pre-orders and would then inform the distributors how they would like to scale out to their stores. It was time to summon the troops and let the battle commence. "You must order the single in advance before September 6th," the fans were told. "It is then that the buyers for the major record shops order stock for their entire chain of shops for the following weeks. This will be based on the number of 'pre-orders' that there have been for the single: too few pre-orders means not enough stock and a flop, loads of pre-orders means we will have a chance of a hit." They marched to their local HMV and Virgin stores in their thousands.

No act had ever put a single campaign together in this way. The more common tack was to get your fans to treat your record shop as your friend, talk nicely to them and ask if they would have the next single in, and trust that if enough people did this then news that there was demand on the street would filter up the chain of command. Of course it didn't work like this. Usually by the time the fans were asking for the single the buyers had already decided whether their chain was stocking that single and in what quantity (or as Otway cynically put it, what chart position it was going to have). But these were not fans in the traditional sense of the word. They were on the record, they had chosen it and some had backgrounds in marketing, press, media and IT. Of course, being Otway fans they all had a sense of humour.

The HMV system worked smoothly and the orders started coming in, but the Virgin one didn't work at all well. The head office had felt it unnecessary to inform staff in all the stores that an agreement had been made and there was one single – John Otway's *Bunsen Burner* – that unlike any other single they sold could now be pre-ordered. So when a fan was told by the shop assistant "We don't know if we're going to be stocking that, come back a couple of weeks before release and we'll let you know," that fan did not go away happy. They had been warned of such skullduggery and the subsequent reaction meant that, in this case, the demand on the street did filter up the chain of command.

"Can you please get those fans off our back," Nigel's friends at Virgin Head Office asked him.

"It wasn't just what was happening in the shops," recalls Cotton. "Around that time, if you googled Virgin Retail, amongst the top hits were complaints about their sales staff from our fans, some of them very funny. Well, we found them amusing."

It wasn't just Nigel who was unaware there was a war going on, Virgin Retail had no idea either. When they were presented with a list of ultimatums and conditions they just saw them as good sensible suggestions and did not fight back.

A letter from Virgin's Head Office that the fans could download, print out and take to the stores when ordering was "a really good idea that should remove any confusion" and "of course John should come to some of our stores and sign his single on the week of release."

Back in the days when the chart was a sample, sales at events like signings would have been discounted, because they introduced bias in the sample. But now with most stores supplying data all the sales counted. You did however have to let the chart company know that you were doing them, so they could differentiate between a large number of fans queuing up to buy one record (which was allowed) and a record company employee arriving with a wheel-barrow buying a large number of one record (which was not).

By four weeks before the release date a good number of orders had been taken. There was a long way to go, but John already had a hit in the bag, albeit a very tiny one.

CHAPTER
24

Any recent material John had written up to this point had been put onto the voting CD in case it was a hit, but now this had been decided it was time to start thinking about B-sides.

Things had changed since the days of 1977, when a trendy teenager placed a 7-inch diameter piece of black vinyl upon a turntable rotating at 45 revolutions-per-minute and a diamond needle following a groove pressed into this piece of plastic was made to vibrate in such a way that when the microscopic movements of this sharp fragment of precious stone were amplified, the sound of someone yelling *"Cor Baby, That's Really Free"* could clearly be heard. A few years later the creators of dance music discovered that the needle could be made to vibrate more violently if the groove had more room and the luxury of a 12 inch piece of vinyl. Those responsible for the singles chart agreed that this format should be eligible. Then there were cassettes and CDs, and by the time John had got around to his follow-up there was a plethora of different formats and different mixes allowed.

Otway, the Andys and Cotton plumped for 3 CDs with a different mix of *Bunsen Burner* and two other tracks on each. One of the other tracks on the CD with "The Hit Mix" of *Bunsen Burner* would be *House Of The Rising Sun*, which meant that in total there was room for five other tracks. As all the fans had already got *Bunsen Burner* on their voting CD, it would make release day so much more exciting if these tracks were brand new Otway numbers. But it would mean the recording artist who had taken two and a half years writing the lyrics for *Premature Adulation* had four weeks at the most to write and record these.

John was very keen to get these five tracks sorted, and Barry was up for helping. And such was the enthusiasm at the time that after a bit of singing down the phone to Barry and a couple of trips to his studio John had all the necessary tracks recorded in time for the cutting of the three CDs ready for release.

It was an exciting time to be an Otway fan, and it was infectious. The War Cabinet (Patsy, Ali, Chris, Billy and the more active members of The Hit Squad) had now split the country into regional areas, so posters and stickers were spread evenly across the land without missing out any big bits. And a variety of people found other gaps in the campaign which needed filling. John Padget's wife Jan, for instance, spotted that no-one had yet come up with a dance to go with *Bunsen Burner*. It was a strange omission seeing as Barry Upton's biggest hit *5-6-7-8* was all about a dance (hence the band's name, Steps). But four weeks before the release date no-one had given any attention or put work into this important area.

"So she just worked one out, got me and Holgarth together at a duo gig and made us go through the choreography," says John. "I really didn't think Richard Holgarth would do any disco dancing, but he did and he could do the John Travolta-like moves better than I could. I was quite shocked."

"Knowing Otway's co-ordination, nobody else was," is Holgarth's reply.

So they had the A-side, the B-sides, the beer, the poster, the dance, what else?

The video. It's not that it hadn't occurred to anyone that a video would be a desirable addition to the promotional package, but all involved just thought it would be impossible. For a start it wasn't until the very end of July that everyone knew what the song was going to be and anyway the budget for one is usually huge, often more than the record itself. Steve Barker, John's friend who had been at the gig when Maurice Bacon had suggested The Hit idea, offered to make one. He was in the ideal position to, as he worked at APTN (Associated Press Television News) and had access to their studios at Camden Lock. Being a news organisation the studios were not large but Studio One was large enough to build a big chemistry set for John to play with, and had an area for the band to pose in and somewhere for Jan to do the *Bunsen Burner* dance.

When most people are asked to envisage a chemistry set, they tend to remember Christmases past when their parents, trying to encourage them to play with more educational toys, bought them a cardboard box with items that looked plastic and pathetic and that you instinctively knew would never produce any impressive bangs or smells. If you work in film or television and you want a chemistry set, you can get something that gives entirely the opposite impression, as you simply hire a Frankenstein laboratory kit from a props company. And if you drop a small chunk of dry ice into a conical flask containing water and a few drops of food colouring, it looks like unstable compounds are reacting in a manner that might worry those who have a concern for health and safety. And where did the small chunks of dry ice come from? They came from the car-load of the stuff Cotton had bought from an industrial unit in Acton.

Watching the video, Otway looks as one would expect him to – pleased with himself that he is in front of cameras miming along to the song with the confidence of someone who had already sung along to it a few thousand times. Adam and Murray looked cool, even in lab coats doing a disco number. Richard Holgarth looked like a lead guitarist from a rock band. Barry Upton looked like a member of a pop group. The only surprise was Seymour, the bass player. Seymour, if you remember, was the only member of the band who felt his credibility so important that he was prepared to leave the Otway band had they gone and released "That god awful *Disco Flowers*." After John had sung behind his chemistry set, and headed to the pub to recover, Seymour was the next member of the band to be placed in front of the cameras.

Steve Barker, who was directing the *Bunsen Burner* video, used a technique to make the musical instruments look like they were on fire. This would mean, for the video, that Seymour would not be using his state-of-the-art Musicman Sterling bass but instead would be issued with a bright blue guitar-shaped piece of cardboard upon which was stapled some bright blue pieces of cotton fabric. "What I would like you to do," explained Steve Barker, "is bounce up and down going from one side of the set to the other, but at the same time swing the cardboard around so that the bits of material flap around."

Murray was shocked. "You can't ask Seymour to do something like that," he thought. But Steve had asked, and to everyone's amazement Seymour just went for it. And it was amazing. "Seymour's done his bit and it's hysterical," Murray told Otway when he returned. And when Steve Barker used the words "it's a wrap", Seymour's performance really was the most outstanding of the day – apart from possibly that of the remaining large blocks of dry ice. Rather than take them home to melt gently in the car, they were unloaded and thrown into a fountain in Oxford. "I was told it would look pretty impressive and it did," says Cotton. "People just stared as all this water suddenly looked as though it had spontaneously started boiling and clouds of dioxide billowed forth into the surrounding environment leaving behind this huge carbon footprint."

It wasn't just fans like Steve Barker who worked for TV companies and Graham King who had his own PR company and could help with the press, there were other fans who found ways to help. What if you worked for Chiltern Railways? Well obviously you could name a train the 'Otway Hit Express' and take the star on part of the journey to the charts. And if you were a roofing surveyor who was in love? Then you offered to "propose to your sweetheart and tell her that you would marry her if John Otway had another hit record" in front of as many cameras and news organisations as possible.

There were smaller, less extravagant, ways to help – you could be a pain in the bum and put a few stickers on every bus shelter and phone box you passed. Or not be and put a poster in your window. You could become the Team Leader for the one-member Northern Ireland Hit Squad (which is what Alastair Dickson did) or just pester your local radio station to play the track.

The best chance that John would have in securing his Top Ten Hit Record was for the BBC producers to playlist his single on Radio 1 or Radio 2. Radio 1 was not going to happen as John had made everyone aware that he was fast approaching fifty and the apparent cut off age for the Radio 1 playlist was closer to twenty-four. Radio 2 had more listeners and the playlist on that station had produced big hits in the past. Johnny Walker had been inspired by the campaign from the start and had played *Bunsen Burner* a number of times on his show. But in the early weeks of September when John needed to be put on the playlist to secure the several plays a day, he was unsuccessful.

"I'm sorry it's not going to be a hit," one of Judd's pluggers told John when he got the news. John did not understand the plugger, because hits were based on what went through the shops and he had enough advance sales already to squeeze him into the top thirty.

"Of course it's going to be a hit," John replied. The plugger did not understand, because he was unaware of anyone getting into the charts without the support of the BBC or Woolies, and preferably you would want both.

However, the week before release, *Bunsen Burner* surprisingly made the Radio 2 playlist. There are a number of possible reasons: John's argument that it was going to be a hit anyway swayed the BBC's producers; it could have been ground roots pressure from the fans; maybe it was the BBC's birthday present to *Rock and Roll's Greatest Failure*. But he was on it for the first time since *Really Free*.

So would EUK take any copies now? No, they had a good commercial reason that John had not heard before. Although the Otway single might sell on the week of release, the following weeks it would not sell at all well because the fans were buying it for his birthday. Something like the Holly Valance single would have a longer "shelf life" and therefore be a more cost-effective stock item.

So on October 6th every other single that would be in the top twenty would be available in any outlet that sold records, but *Bunsen Burner* would be in only a minority of them, and even then not that easy to find as the major companies often had deals with the shops for all the best display areas. During the following week many fans would be told off for rearranging the shop displays and putting Otway CDs in the best spots. "I know they want him to have a hit, but these people don't realise that we get paid a lot of money by the record companies to put their records in the front row," shop managers complained.

Nigel Reveler gave Andy Payne the stock orders and between them they worked out the logistics of the distribution. Nigel was happy and upbeat; the way things were going he should be able to deliver them the top thirty hit he had told the U-Vibe team might be possible. Otway and Cotton were worried, their ambition went further and they wanted to make the numbers work and get the Top Ten that they had told themselves might be possible. In six days they had to sell between fifteen and twenty thousand records through the shops.

Apart from WH Smith and EUK-supplied Woolworths and supermarkets, Nigel had done a remarkably good job in getting the single into the other record shops and they had agreed to take as many copies as they would any other potential hit. But, because these outlets totalled less than half the market, theoretically the Top Ten was impossible.

Being a pop star in 2002 was so much easier if you were an Avril Lavigne than if you were John Otway, as your age, your looks and your talent would fit you into the right demographics and your major record label would make sure that there was plenty of highly visible stock in places where people bought singles, groceries and pick'n'mix sweets. If there were enough people prepared to pick a copy up and carry it to the check-out then "there you were on *Top Of The Pops*".

John, Cotton and the Andys did their arithmetic:

1) They had five thousand pre-orders.
2) There were the signings and events in the stores which were an essential part of the battle plan. If the shop had not taken enough stock, they could be topped up with stock that Cotton would carry with him and add significantly to the total sales.

3) If the fans could be persuaded to buy their copies on the Monday, the shops would have time to re-order for the weekend.

And the secret weapon:

4) Although Amazon online sales did not count for the charts the new HMV online sales did. The Hit Squad knew how to "do" things online, a few thousand valuable sales there could make the difference.

It was possible they agreed, just.

It was to be a battle between the big companies who were going for things like an Elvis song performed by Will Young and Gareth Gates and a little independent company going for a disco chemistry song performed by John Otway. The Goliath and David struggle was summed up on one of The Hit's B-sides that John had written with Barry Upton.

In the red corner with One Hit
that soared to number 27 in 1977 – Mr John Otway
In the blue corner with 27 hits
who soared to heaven in 1977 – Mr Elvis Presley
Who's them guys stepping into the ring?
One's a punk and the other's the king
It's from earth below and from heavens above
It's Bunsen Burner versus Burning Love!

On 29th September John Padget drove the John Otway Band from Northallerton to Sheffield. It was the day before the release of the single, and there was definitely an air of anticipation. Hambleton Community Centre the night before had been a sell-out show and tonight was the opening salvo in the main theatre of the chart war.

A deal had been struck with the local HMV to open at midnight; the Otway band would finish their show at the Sheffield Boardwalk and John would lead the whole audience out of the venue the one hundred yards to the record shop. These would be the first fans to buy The Hit and, to commemorate the occasion, John and the band would sign the CDs. They could also, if they wanted, get a "first day cover" stamp. Because the biggest fans were at the front of the stage, it was only fair that they should be able to get the first copies. So in the final minutes of that Sunday night, when the last notes of the final encore of another sell-out show had died away, John parted the audience so there was a space down the centre of venue.

"You know how they leave the church at weddings," Otway told the audience. "Well the band are going to leave through the aisle first and starting with the front row, then the second follow us and we'll lead you up to the shop. At fifteen minutes past midnight we are going to be number one in the charts because no-one else will have sold any records yet. Let's see how long we can stay there." John found out later that this wasn't strictly true, because Sunday sales counted for records that had been released on previous weeks, but it sounded fantastic and everyone was inspired by the idea.

The crocodile of three hundred fans who snaked their way up to the shop delighted the store's manager by buying nearly all of the copies of *Bunsen Burner* he had in his store by

0:45am on Monday 30th September. He'll be getting some more, thought John.

The next morning, John was in the HMV store in Aylesbury to sign copies in his home town. A great crowd awaited John at the Aylesbury HMV and even his mum queued up and let John sign and stamp her first day cover of her son's next hit. As hoped the shop had completely underestimated the demand for the single and lots and lots of fresh stock had to be fetched from Cotton's car. Local TV was there doing a piece and so were a reporter and photographer from The Guardian newspaper to cover both the signing and the subsequent trip from Aylesbury Town to London's Marylebone train station aboard the Otway Hit Express. Otway sang some songs, performed some acrobatics and did his interview on the hour-long journey to the capital. Then on arrival, as he made his way through the barriers, he could hear the tannoy echoing through the station. "Marylebone station would like to announce the arrival of the John Otway Hit Express bringing John Otway to London and *Bunsen Burner* to the charts."

It was just like pop stardom should be. There were reporters from other papers and two, yes two television crews: one from Steve Barker's company APTN and another from ITV's *London Tonight*. Looking over to his right as he entered the station concourse, Otway could see Billy Green on one knee proposing to his girlfriend Catherine in front of the gathered media.

"Could you lead your fans out of the station for our last shot?" the *London Tonight* crew asked John after the interview with him. If asked, John will explain that somersaults whilst playing guitar are always a bit painful because you can't use your hands to break your fall, and you land on one shoulder. If you are doing it on solid concrete it hurts more. But as John explains further, if there is a film crew capturing the somersault and there is a chance it will be shown on that night's news it's probably worth it. And a very good somersault it was too – the crew were just expecting Otway to walk out of the station with his fans behind him, so the cameraman was a bit surprised that the main focus of his shot suddenly rotated three hundred and sixty degrees. But the footage he captured looked very funny and would make a good finale to the piece they had just filmed.

After the station there was a performance and signing at the Virgin Megastore in London's Oxford Street. The fans had been working on this one for a few weeks and The Hit Squad had tried to get as many Abbey Road choir members together as possible to sing the B-side. It was packed and after John and Richard Holgarth's set it took nearly two hours to sign and stamp all the singles.

Delighted and exhausted the team and a bunch of fans headed to the pub round the corner. Nearly three pints of beer later John noticed that the picture on the television just over Cotton's left shoulder changed from Trevor McDonald's talking head in the studio to Otway's somersaulting body in Marylebone station. "Look, look it's *News at Ten*," yelled John. "We've just been on *News at Ten*.

It was a brilliant end to a great day. There was a belief that in that first day of battle, the Otway fans had won a great victory.

Confirmation of that victory came the next day from the official chart company – *Bunsen Burner* was currently number eight in the charts. As exciting as it was, everyone was aware that this position was unsustainable. The fans had been encouraged to get their pre-orders and buy the record on that first day, and the biggest in-store events had been on that day too. Then there was the Saturday effect – sales of singles surged on Saturday when kids between the ages of nine and sixteen went out with their pocket money to buy the latest offering from their favourite act, which was unlikely to be John Otway. "Keep it up and we should stay in the Top Twenty," was Nigel's advice.

Tuesday had another busy performance and signing in Bristol followed by a signing in Oxford. Not the great crowds John had achieved on the Monday, but the fans were there and still buying records. And everyone just hoped they had done enough to stay in the Top Ten for the important mid-week chart that was published on Wednesday. Whatever the fans were doing they were doing it remarkably well because the following day, which was actually John's fiftieth birthday, he had retained his position at number eight.

It was to be a pretty good birthday. There was the traditional Coventry gig, The Guardian published its feature with a big photo of John singing on The Hit Express, Johnny Walker did a live phone interview on Radio 2 and as things stood chart-wise John was on top of Atomic Kitten.

Meanwhile, whilst John was going about his pop star business, Cotton had gathered as many friends as he could find to stuff envelopes and post the following note to all four thousand addresses on John's mailing list:

JOHN OTWAY: –
'BIRTHDAY BOY' STOP PRESS:
Great News – BUNSEN BURNER!!!

Hi everyone – Richard Cotton here from Otway's office. We have just found out some fantastic news! It's John's 50th Birthday today, and Paul (the Palladium Promoter) and I, have clubbed together to let you all know about it:

GET THIS! – BUNSEN BURNER is in today's UK Chart 'mid-week', officially at No.8 in the charts!

PLUS: We have been told if we stay in the Top Ten Otway should get Top Of The Pops next week! The only problem is that we asked everyone to buy at the start of the week. Of course all the kids buy the pop stuff at the weekend – so we will probably drop a fair few places.

Look, John doesn't know about this mailout (he would probably kill me) but can I just ask you all? PLEASE, PLEASE – just for John? Can you please just all give it one more little push to keep us in contention? We are so close... To come so far and slip to No.11 would be just tragic. Imagine Otway in the Top Ten! And on Top Of The Pops! If we all buy just one more copy – I reckon we CAN do it. I know stocks are patchy in some areas, but remember: if you can't find the single you can get it at HMV online. HMV sales (unlike Amazon) DO COUNT for this week's chart right up until Saturday midnight – I hope you can help! Thanks everyone, see you Sunday – Cheers, Richard Cotton

p.s. Paul Clerehugh says (despite rumours to the contrary) there are still a few Palladium tickets left.

John had thought the Palladium would have easily sold out by now as it was not much bigger than the Astoria, but for the last few months it had remained stubbornly at around two thirds full. "The fans were very fond of Otway, and loved his mad schemes," says Cotton. "But a lot of them could not bear to go to a gig and watch Otway walk on stage announcing after all this work he had produced another flop. They thought it was going to be a wake. As soon as they saw the mid-week chart and realised that he was going to beat *Really Free*'s twenty-seven place, it sold out."

It wasn't just these fans who were skeptical. Apart from The Guardian the national press had not covered the story, but with the release of the mid-week chart John had a call from The Sun newspaper. "We've known about this story for ages," they told him, "we just didn't think it was going to happen."

The most surprised though were the team from Millward Brown, the official chart company. A team of them arrived at the birthday gig headed by chart director Bob Barnes. "How the hell did you do it?" was his first question. "Every year there's a few people who try to get their fans to get them a hit, and the best any of them ever manage is the bottom end of the top thirty. You are the first one to ever get into the top twenty, never mind the Top Ten," he said.

And he could see that Otway was not cheating as the company had some pretty sophisticated software that could spot those who did. "It's like an alarm that goes off when there are unusual buying patterns." He also told Otway some wonderful tales of attempted chart rigging. One of the most common apparently was a large sale of a single in one shop followed by another twenty minutes later just ten miles away and "you would just wait about seven or eight minutes and the next shop five miles further on would get a big sale too. You can tell it's somebody driving round just buying up copies of the record."

"Did my single set off any alarms?" asked John.

"About every three or four minutes," he replied. "But you could tell that it was fans because it would be Southampton, then Manchester, then Cardiff – all over the place. It was obviously a fan thing."

"We discussed the problems with getting the stock in the shops and the difficulty we had," says John. "What surprised me was the sympathy he had for the retailers. He was telling me how tough it was for them and how much effort they put in, while I had only thought of them as 'the bastards who are trying to stop me from getting a hit.' He did understand the difficulties we faced, and knew the shops might be out of stock by the weekend. He told me that on the figures we had done so far we wouldn't fall below about fourteen in the charts. 'Give me a call if you want any information,' he said handing me his business card."

If Bob had been at all doubtful about the fervour of the fans, he had no doubts by the end of the night. Johnny Walker had told the nation exactly where *Bunsen Burner* was currently in the charts and the Coventry audience knew that the show they were watching was going to be Otway's last as a one-hit wonder. And when the band played *Bunsen Burner*, it was pretty obvious that not only did they know the words, they knew the dance too.

Thursday saw more signings in record stores – still at number eight – and Friday was the last day of active campaigning. It was the last day Otway could do personal appearances in the shops, and, unbelievably, the fans had maintained Otway's position at number eight above Atomic Kitten. But stocks in the stores were terribly low and the Otway team was about to be dealt a blow that would almost certainly ruin any chances of remaining in the Top Ten.

The big secret weapon that Otway and Cotton were relying on was the HMV online sales. The pair had thought that the Internet-savvy Otway fans could order the extra few thousand singles from their computers and keep abreast of the Saturday sales that the teenagers were racking up for the likes of Busted and Atomic Kitten when they went out shopping with their pocket money. Cotton, though, had just discovered that sales at HMV online only counted for the charts after the items had been dispatched, and not when the orders came in. And the online department was only ordering a few hundred and not the few thousand that they needed them to.

The online shop was a new venture by HMV, doing a fraction of the sales of their stores. They had no idea that the Otway team was relying on it to sell a huge quantity of records and were about to be inundated with orders. And what would have been regarded as a fair and realistic size order from this new small HMV department by most people (including Nigel Reveler) was seen as sabotage by Otway and Cotton. They smelled a rat, and saw it as the method the retail trade and the big record companies were now going to use to keep the small guy out of the Top Ten.

"Tell HMV that unless they order the amount you tell them we'll get Radio 2 and the press and everyone who'll darned well listen and let them know that HMV deliberately ruined our chances of a hit," Cotton yelled at Nigel.

"You can't do that," replied Nigel. "These guys have been the ones that have helped us the most and have done us the most favours. I told you it was possible to get top thirty and we've achieved an incredible top twenty. What do you keep going on about the Top Ten for?"

There is a limit to the number of decibels an earpiece of one telephone can emit, even when yelling into the mouthpiece of another. Both Nigel's and Cotton's respective mouthpieces and earpieces reached this limit many times on the morning of October 4th 2002.

The brief relief of Nigel's call saying that HMV online had increased their order was shattered by the later call saying that the lorry had been unable to leave the warehouse in time to deliver the stock. All the HMV online orders would now be counted for the following week's chart. "Tell Cotton I've gone home," Nigel told his office staff and he did. He really had done all he could.

Otway and Cotton were devastated. They had been so close, they knew how many records were out there in the shops and they knew how many they would need to sell. The rule of thumb in retail was that you could sell about one third of the stock you had spread across the outlets around the country at any one time, and yet they would need to sell almost every remaining CD in every shop that had any left to stay where they were in the charts.

Karen got caught up in the excitement and spent that Friday helping. She phoned around the record stores to find out which ones still had copies of *Bunsen Burner*. Then, whilst her partner headed for his last signing in Swindon, Johnny Walker called. After playing the record every day that week and seeing the mid-week position, he was unaware of any problems until Karen told him that because the shops were refusing to take copies of his record, John would not make the Top Ten.

"Johnny was marvellous." she says. "He said he would say something about it on his programme and offered to come to the London Palladium and read the chart rundown to the audience."

That afternoon Johnny told the nation that there were problems with getting the new hit, but the Otway fans were a resourceful bunch and they would know what to do.

John's last day as a one hit wonder was one of lows and highs. He knew as soon as he woke up that the following day he would have another hit record, and one that would be much higher than the number twenty-seven he had reached twenty-five years before.

When Maurice first mentioned the idea eighteen months earlier a top twenty hit would have seemed like the huge achievement it was. He knew that he would have to walk on to the Palladium stage and tell the fans that they had won and got that second hit, bigger than *Really Free*'s twenty-seven, when part of him felt that he had let them down. They had been willing to give him a Top Ten, but he had been unable to let them. He could picture a young teenage girl casually tossing a copy of Busted's *That's What I Go To School For* into her mum's Tesco trolley as they did their weekly shop, whilst the Otway fan was unable to find a single copy of *Bunsen Burner* in any of the record shops.

Spirits were about to lift a little though. Those in the media did not know about the stock crisis, so a piece for television was being filmed a few hours later, and meanwhile Cat Deeley was presenting CD UK on ITV. "I just turned it on to see if the single might get a mention," says John. "To my astonishment, *Bunsen Burner* was announced at number eight." Many people would remark over the following years that the most surprising thing about the whole campaign was not John having a hit, but Cat Deeley introducing Seymour dancing on a Saturday morning children's television programme.

"Well a lot of fans would have seen that," thought John on his way to the filming at the Half Moon in Putney. There he met up with Billy Green and his fiancée Catherine, a couple of other fans, the crew from Channel 4 and Mark Pegg's documentary crew, here to catch the last days of the campaign. The piece for TV was a spoof of the TV programme *Pop Idol* with Otway doing a spot of performing and the fans judging it. Afterwards, everyone left John as Mark went with Billy and the fans to film them buying records in Oxford Street

That afternoon, after re-playing Cat Deeley and Seymour several times on his video machine, John paced the living room of his house feeling impotent. There was nothing he could do now. Karen and Amy had gone to Kingston to buy their copies of *Bunsen Burner*, as a phone call had told her that there were some copies in HMV there. So he was alone in the house.

"I just turned my laptop on to see what was happening with the Onelist, and The Hit Squad had been very busy," says John. The first postings were before 8:00 am.

It's Saturday morning and my pocket money is burning a hole in my pocket, me thinks a visit to browse a few different record stores is in order. Is it really true that Mr. Otway has a new single out – must remember to buy a copy or two!

and

If you find somewhere with a few spare copies post the shop's location here so someone else in your area can hopefully get there and buy another copy by the end of today.

And before 10:00 am Ali was posting:

Just bought a further 15 copies in various Newcastle establishments but there are very few left on the shelves and lots of kids drooling over Holly Valance (and some big kids too if I'm perfectly honest).

A typical example of one of the many postings before 11:00am

HMV Edinburgh – plenty stock – BUY THEM TODAY!!!
St James Centre (0131 556 1236 to confirm)
Princes St (0131 225 7008 to confirm)
They'll lay them aside for you to collect too. 'These things are flying out the door' 'Just got another batch a wee while ago'

Every few minutes, someone was posting details of where the stock was available and in what quantity and an hour or so later someone else would e-mail in to say it had been cleared. By the time John was catching up with it all, Billy had reached Oxford Street.

FOUR copies (of mix 3) under 'O' in the racks. Would have bought them, but some bald geezer beat me to it!

It now became apparent that the Saturday effect, where sales soared "because that's when people could get out and buy singles" was actually helping, rather than ruining *Bunsen Burner*'s chances.

The fans who had been working all week spent that day simply driving around the country and literally stripping the stores of any copies they could find, and if they couldn't get them all, posted the details and someone else would finish the job. Otway just paced around his living room floor watching the last battle being played out on his Apple laptop and his spirits lifted. There was still a chance, a very small one, but a chance that the fans had done enough. That night he went to bed and slept just a little easier than the night before.

The greatest day in John's career had a wonderful start. The way a pop star's day ought to start.

"I had a radio interview early the next morning," says John. "So the alarm woke me up and I went down to make coffee, opened the curtains and there parked outside the front of my house was a BBC outside broadcast unit. How fabulous was that? I was going to be able to stroll the ten yards from my front door and talk live to the nation about my hit." According to Otway, having an outside broadcast van parked by your house is a pretty neat achievement. He had been to the BBC many times over his career, but this was the first time ever that the BBC had come to him.

Over the years John had managed very easily to shield his daughter from the trappings of pop stardom, but this was too much of a temptation. "Amy, Amy, come outside and look at this," he yelled to his daughter after the interview. Amy sat where her dad had just been, on what the engineer described as "a seat that has supported the bottoms of almost every very famous star and politician there has been in the United Kingdom."

It was only 8:30 when John and Amy said goodbye to their visitors, but already there was a piece of paper that was burning a hole in his pocket. Someone somewhere knew what position he had reached in the charts and their phone number was on the card that Bob Barnes had given him on his birthday in Coventry. John called Millward Brown, the official chart company at 8:32. There was no reply, and John realised he would have to wait a little longer for the results. When he called again at 8:35, someone did answer the phone. "Ah, we were told we might get a call from you," said the voice on the other end, when John said who he was. "You're in the Top Ten with one to spare."

"Does that mean what I think it does?" ventured the nervous pop star.

"Yes, Top Ten with one to spare. Be careful who you tell, because we haven't officially announced it yet, we have to run the computer again, but don't worry it won't change."

Otway thanked him very, very much.

"It was strange," remembers John vividly. "I didn't immediately go bananas. There was this knot in my stomach that had been there for so long that I had taken it for granted, but as he repeated the news it just disappeared and I relaxed for the first time in what seemed like months. It was great telling Karen, her reaction was far less cool. Cotton, when I rang him, just said, 'Can I tell the band? Go on let me'."

By 9:00am Paul Clerehugh had arrived at the pop star's house and they thought it would be good to get a cab into town together. On that journey to the Palladium, Nigel Reveler called as he was on his way to the airport to fly to America and would miss the celebrations, but would eventually be pleased that he missed some of the fireworks that was to follow them. The band heard from Cotton that they were now a number nine hit act. They, like Otway, had thought that it would not stay in the Top Ten and Murray had bet Cotton a tenner that it wouldn't. It was to be paid on stage that night.

"Willy completely surprised me," says John. "I thought he'd be furious at me for having a hit on my own, but he was completely the opposite. When I first asked Paul Clerehugh if we could do the Palladium on The Hit Day, I thought it would be great to start the evening with the first hit, and finish with the second. I never thought Willy would join in, but shortly after I arrived at the Palladium he did as well. Not only that but we actually spoke to each other."

The official chart was announced on a three-hour BBC radio programme presented by Mark Goodier which started at 4:00pm and finished at 7:00pm. It was perfect timing as the Palladium show was due to begin at 7:30pm, so the fans would have had just enough time to absorb the result and be ready to celebrate. The Argyll Arms pub is just about one hundred yards from the entrance to the Palladium and that was where several hundred fans congregated to listen to the rundown of the charts. Not that they could hear it very well, as there was only one small transistor radio placed on top of a beer barrel outside the pub. There was a great deal of excitement as no-one there knew where *Bunsen Burner* had got to.

John thought it would be good fun to join the fans for the announcement, so he got someone to keep an ear on the radio, and when they got to number twelve he started walking up to the pub. Suddenly a huge cheer went up from the crowd outside the Argyll. "I was a bit bemused," says John. "I knew they couldn't have got to number nine. Then someone told me that they had just announced that *Life Goes On* by LeAnn Rimes was at number eleven, so everyone knew I must have made the Top Ten." They were ecstatic.

Standing on the barrel ten minutes later waving the transistor radio around and singing *Bunsen Burner* is probably John's favourite moment in his career.

At that moment a taxi bringing Cotton to the Palladium pulled up outside the Argyll. "I won't drop you here," said the cab driver. "It looks as if there is a riot going on." "That's what I've come for," replied Cotton as he watched Otway do the now familiar *Bunsen* disco dance above the heads of the gathered rioting throng who were screaming "Burn Baby Burn" at the tops of their voices.

Then it was back to the Palladium for a live television interview for a programme called *Liquid Gold*. John loved it, and so did Seymour, for each of these television pieces chose to play a bit of the video, and the bit everyone wanted to use was the funny chap dancing with the flaming bass.

The atmosphere when John's old friend Paul Bradley walked on to introduce Johnny Walker was incredible – there had been no other show like it before in that theatre. After eighteen months' work, the audience had discovered less than an hour before that their efforts had paid off. "And half the audience were the choir featured on the record," says John.

Johnny Walker had come to do the chart run-down, but unfortunately in the excitement no-one had got a copy of the chart. Everyone knew what was number nine, but that was all. "I have here the top twenty," he told the audience. "At number twenty, a pile of old bollocks, at number nineteen a complete load of crap, at eighteen someone you've never heard of..." And the reaction built and built until "and at number nine" the predictable happened and the Palladium roof was raised.

Then Otway and the Band were able to start the show the way they had hoped, with Wild Willy Barrett and the first Hit, *Cor Baby, That's Really Free.*

The night holds a Palladium record: the bar completely sold out of drink. There was not a drop left. The show running at the theatre at that time was *Chitty Chitty Bang Bang,* and when the figures were calculated the Otway audience consumed over thirty times the amount of beer, spirits and wine than the audience did on a night when that other very popular show was on.

The Palladium roof was raised several other times: when the band played the current number nine hit; when the audience yelled 'Who's a prat?' during the performance of the B-side of the current number nine hit; and during the finale when the DJ played the only disco single in the Top Ten that week and everyone came on stage and danced to it.

CHAPTER
27

It is not surprising that John had a bit of a hangover the next day: after the show Paul Clerehugh had organised a surprise after show party and the celebrations had gone on into the early hours. So for the first time ever John turned down a major piece of television. TVAM wanted to have the pop star on first thing the following morning, but even Otway knew that it was not wise and he would not look his best.

There was one piece of television that Otway did not want to turn down, one that would make all the effort of The Hit worthwhile, and they had got it. One of Cotton's favourite phone calls was the one he made to the band to tell them this news, and one of John's favourites was the call he made to Richard's Hairdressing in Southfields to ask the question "Can you fit me in? I need my hair done for *Top Of The Pops*."

Getting back on that programme was as important to Otway as the chart position. The question "Have you been on *Top Of The Pops*?" was the one that the majority of the population would use to decide whether or not you really were a pop star, and the answer to the question "How long ago?" was the one they used to work out whether they should have heard of you. Two years previously John could not work out how he would ever get back onto the programme, and for people younger than forty to know who he was. The band, whatever Otway had told them about "going on to great things", could not have envisaged it either. But here they all were at the studio.

John was worried that the new generation of stars wouldn't know who he was, but he worried needlessly. As soon as he arrived, Damian Gough aka Badly Drawn Boy yelled "Hi Otway," across to him, and later the two bands managed several pints in the BBC bar. Richard Holgarth got 'high fived' by Shaggy, Murray got close to, but completely ignored by, Christina Aguilera, and Barry Upton failed to recognise Justin Timberlake.

"Has this guy got fans or what," was Otway's introduction. "They chose the record, marketed it and got it to number nine in the charts. After twenty-five years since *Really Free*, welcome back, John Otway."

Everybody else who recorded that day looked cool. Otway just looked happy. It was everything he could have possibly wanted.

Top Of The Pops was filmed on the Thursday and was due to be broadcast the following day, which for Otway was another day with a bit of a hangover. However, the star's timetable was quite relaxed that day: John Padget would be taking him to do a radio interview and then later John would catch the train to Harlow and watch *Top Of The Pops* with the band at their local pub, The Willow. However, things had happened to make John's day a lot more complicated than that.

Cotton had been dining out on the difference between a Top Ten hit like *Bunsen Burner* and a top twenty hit like *The Wheels On the Bus*. As he pointed out, because of its position in the lower end of the chart the latter was not even considered for *Top Of The Pops*. He was therefore a little put out when told by a young lady that she had been into Woolworth's and that John's single wasn't at number nine. In fact wasn't even in the top twenty at all.

"It was just so unfair," he says. "We had done all this work to get into the Top Ten and Woolies just disqualified us. It's not as if there was a sign pointing out that this is just a Woolworth's chart and not the official one: you walk in and it just says the top twenty, and on the record racks they've just put someone else at number nine. I was furious."

Otway had always urged caution, as he felt that complaining was negative and unlikely to have any beneficial effect. "We've got the proper number nine and we're on *Top Of The Pops*, so why complain?" would have been his view. But it wasn't Cotton's. This was John's birthday present and someone was trying to steal it, so he rang the reporters at The Guardian. They had done the Otway Express feature and followed it up with a congratulatory piece when the chart was released. The reporter did not believe Cotton that the biggest retailer of singles would just leave a record out of their chart simply because they had chosen not to stock it, until he checked it out for himself. But sure enough, John's hard work for his number nine position had simply been filled by another act with better demographics. And so a piece appeared in The Guardian with the headline 'Cor Baby, That's Not Fair'.

Mr Pop
Barry Upton.
(Upton Archives)

Mr Rock
Richard Holgarth.
(John Haxby – Art Surgery)

One of The Choirs at Abbey Road Studios. *(Craig's Photos)*

The video shoot for the B-Side. *(top: Craig's Photos / below: Steve Barker)*

Nick Stylianou of the Electoral Reform Society with the Ballot Box. *(Otway Archives)*

Murray on rhythm guitar & Seymour on bass. Adam on drums. *(John Haxby – Art Surgery)*

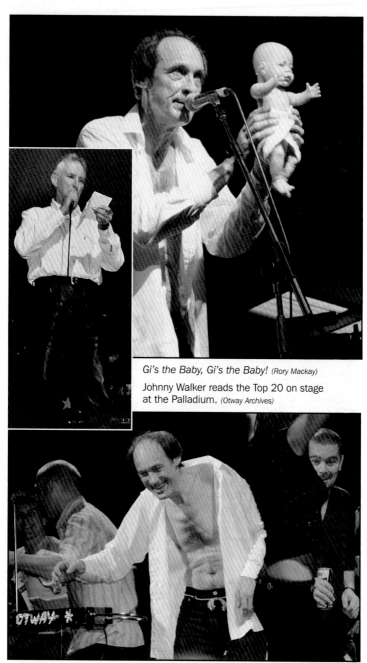

Gi's the Baby, Gi's the Baby! (Rory Mackay)

Johnny Walker reads the Top 20 on stage at the Palladium. (Otway Archives)

Palladium celebrations. (John Haxby – Art Surgery)

It's a HIT! Otway and fans listen to the Chart run-down. *(Glen Stanley)*

Top Of The Pops. *(Courtesy of the BBC)*

Mad, Bad & Dangerous Tour
with Slim from The Hamsters and Wilko Johnson. *(Andy Billups)*

Backstage after the *Anniversary of The Hit Gig* – Aylesbury
left to right: Karen, Robbie Gladwell, Otway, Steve Harley, Wild Willy. *(Otway Archives)*

Richard Cotton with his 'Ot-Air Crew'. *(John Haxby – Art Surgery)*

Aylesbury *Hobble on the Cobbles* –
promoting the World Tour.
above: Rainbow George
right: Chris France
(John Haxby – Art Surgery)

The Band – Aylesbury *Hobble on the Cobbles*. *(Bucks Herald)*

John launches Ot-Air – model made by Alan & Pam Ireland. *(Judy Totton)*

While John was drinking the first coffee of the morning to try and clear his head, there was a call from BBC TV News, asking if they could do an interview that morning. "I had no idea at first, I just thought that it was a bit late to be doing something on The Hit because that was a few days ago. Yesterday's news, literally. Then they asked if I had seen the piece in The Guardian that morning and I knew instantly: Cotton."

The BBC were to meet John near Chesham, where he was to do an interview with the British Forces Radio. As they were halfway there Karen called. "You'd better ask John Padget if he wouldn't mind staying with you today and driving you around. I've just spoken to Cotton and you've now got ITV News, Channel 4 News, and PM on Radio 4." This was big, and John realised immediately that there would be no-one else in that week's Top Ten that would be getting that much attention. Plus it was going to make the evening's television viewing at The Willow in Harlow a lot more fun, because now as well as *Top Of The Pops* there was also the news. The news, of course, meant another excuse for the major television channels in Great Britain to show the disco dancing Seymour with the flaming guitar.

So before they watched *Top Of The Pops*, Otway and the band and all their friends from Harlow gathered with pints of ale in hand in front of the pub's television to watch the news. Just before the end of the programme the newsreader said:

"Finally, earlier this week we reported on the return of cult music hero John Otway to the charts after twenty-five years in the wilderness."

Big cheers from the crowd in The Willow.

"Well today the success was soured when he discovered that having a Top Ten record did not necessarily mean that all shops would stock it. They say he's not cool enough."

"Boo" went the crowd in the pub.

Then came the flaming guitar disco dancing clip from the video. "Hurray! Hurray!" they yelled.

"*Bunsen Burner* has shocked the industry by reaching number nine. But walk into Woolies or W H Smiths or Asda, and it's not their number nine. They refuse to stock a joke single from a bald fifty-year old."

And when they cut to Woolworth's spokesperson Nicole Lander, the following explanation was almost drowned out in true pantomime tradition. "Our core customers are eleven- and twelve-year old girls, who love Gareth Gates. They love Will, they love Robbie Williams, but I'm afraid that they don't have a particular keenness for John's single, and this is going on past buying experience."

Basically EUK had been kicked in the demographics by the "few thousand avid fans causing havoc in the marketplace" that Chris France had told Otway about. "Even so, it should not have been able to happen" Chris explains. "EUK had such a dominant role and had such a large market share that if I was in their position I would have been confident that if I chose not to stock an item it could not have made the Top Ten. Furthermore, if you are a small record company, you are most unlikely to go to the media and complain that the biggest buyer of records is smelly, and should be booed and heckled in a pub because they tried to spoil someone's birthday."

If it was a battle and retail was the enemy, Otway knew he had won when a few weeks later he noticed the following announcement:

Woolworths is to sponsor Capital Radio's Hit 40 UK chart, which replaces the Network Chart, in a deal worth £8m, making it the biggest in UK radio history. The Hit 40 UK chart will be broadcast on Sundays between 4pm and 7pm from February 2 and will be called 'Woolworths Hit 40 UK'. It is hosted by long-time Capital Radio DJ and former 'Pop Idol' judge Neil Fox. It is broadcast on 96 national radio stations and targeted specifically at 15-to 24-year-olds.

"Spending eight million just to keep people like me out of the charts is a bit expensive," John thought.

And what were the spoils of war for the victor? They were the important three words "around for years" now added to the end of his old title "has been".

CHAPTER 28

There now followed a period of relative calm. Usually a Hit record is followed by a Hit tour and a follow-up single, but John had done a huge hit tour before it and he felt that both he and his fans were too exhausted to go back to battle – if they attempted another hit straight away they might lose. "I liked being able to say that my last single was in the Top Ten," says Otway, "And by the clever technique of not releasing any more, I still can."

John was now able to release a record he had not been able to before, John Otway's *Greatest Hits*. As Richard Holgarth pointed out, "It was the first time the letter 's' has been on the right side of the word Hit."

There were other benefits too. Because of his new notoriety, he was back on *Never Mind The Buzzcocks*, as the first person in the history of the show to go from the "Where are they now" line-up into the panel of "current stars and celebrities". During the 'Guess The Lyric' part of the show, Mark Lamarr read out some of the words from *Really Free*. "It's my hit, it's my hit." yelled Otway, glad to have won his team some points. "Sorry, wrong," said Mark. "It's *one* of your hits."

The family suffered no adverse effects from the notoriety. "I was worried that Amy might be embarrassed by what I did, and get a hard time at school," says John. "But no, it turned out that it was cool to have your dad on *Top Of The Pops*." And the young teens who hang around the street corners in the Southfields area would start singing "Burn Baby Burn" when John walked by on his way to the shops. When Karen won a national award for her glass, presented by the Lord Mayor Of London, her partner was recognised instantly as "The man who beat the system," even though he was dressed in a dinner suit and didn't look like a pop star.

So what was John going to do as his next project? Roslyn Collett, a friend of John's from the War Cabinet, had given him a DV camera, and Cotton discovered that it was possible to buy satellite time so that anyone with a Sky box could pick up the programmes. So as encouragement he bought John four fifteen-minute slots and told him to go and make some shows, which is how Otway got his own series on Sky – all made in his house at great expense to the harmony within.

When it was transmitted, *The Cube* actually did pretty well as this excerpt from a piece in The Guardian entitled 'Tailor-made television' shows:

Open Access will allow everyone with a credit card and an idea to have their programmes shown on the box.

That an email-based publicity strategy can be effective has been proven by veteran musician John Otway, who has used Open Access as a vanity broadcaster to screen The Cube, a tongue-in-cheek series of four 15-minute episodes which he produced "to give something back to the music industry and to share the knowledge he has gained from his 25 years as a chart act". Otway promoted the show by posting information about it on his website and emailing everyone subscribed to his mailing list. As a result an estimated 20,000 Otway fans tuned in to the first episode.

It would probably have been the direction Otway continued to move in, but a new studio would be required for the second series, and before this was found John re-discovered another project that would literally "take over everything."

First though, John was to do a big gig in the Civic Centre Aylesbury to celebrate the first anniversary of the second Hit. It was a large venue and one that John would have struggled to fill on his own, but because it was a show to celebrate the recent success it would be great if it was crammed. So John and Cotton, who had offered to promote the show, discussed some ideas for special guests.

"I had seen this TV programme about number one hit records," remembers John. "They had all these acts on playing their big hits. Most of them looked past their best and bored with playing something they had played thousands of times, and then Steve Harley came on and did *Come Up And See Me* and I just thought 'he can still do it.' He was really going for it. So I got Cotton to contact him and it turned out that he was a bit of a fan, and particularly liked my song *Josephine*. Because he couldn't do the show officially he was prepared to come and do a guest spot for nothing. Not only that, he would do a duet with me on *Josephine* and if I wanted to we could do his biggest hit together too."

So although none of the advertising for the show could mention Steve Harley he was quite happy with the Otway website containing enigmatic clues like "A special number one guest who's coming to see us to make us smile," he even played a couple of Otway tracks on his Radio 2 show, dropping a big hint about where he was going to be in a couple of nights' time.

The result was a fabulous home town gig and more brownie points for John, as Karen was a fan of Steve's and had been to his shows as a teenager. John made a promise to himself that if he was ever in the position to return the favour and do something special for Steve Harley, he would.

A number of people had been asking Otway what he was going to do next, now that he had gone from down and out to the Albert Hall and on to *Top Of The Pops*. He was now fifty-one, and had always believed that he was special and that stardom was his destiny. He also felt that there should be a follow up to his *Rock and Roll's Greatest Failure* book with a *Rock and Roll's Greatest Success* one. "I had a sequel in mind when I wrote the first book," he says. The problem for him was that however big the achievement of The Hit was, it didn't resonate with the word "greatest" and he needed something that could fall into that category.

Early one morning he had an idea that he thought would resonate both with the word "greatest" and the words "rock and roll". That he felt that he might well be able to pull it off.

Years ago when Amy was just a baby, John had come remarkably close to selling an idea he had for a television documentary. The concept for *Around the World in 18 Days* involved buying an around the world airline ticket and at each stop around the globe playing a gig. And for a considerable time, when asked Otway could legitimately say, "I'm working with Channel 4 on a new project". Of course eventually he had to say the same thing illegitimately.

The episode had planted a seed and he had often re-visited the idea of doing a world tour, but a combination of cost and young daughter had made the idea impractical. Amy was growing up and within a year would be doing her GCSE exams, so John guessed he would soon have more freedom to do a few more extravagant things. And that morning he put an embellishment on his World Tour that was so inspiring that he just lay there smiling at the sheer magic of it.

There must be fans who would be prepared to do the tour with him so why not take their own plane around the world?

That was the ultimate Rock and Roll thing to do. "Go Johnny, Go, Go, Go." No-one had ever done that before.

He arranged a meeting at his local pub with Cotton, Ali McClean (who as well as being a fan and war cabinet member ran a travel agency) and Steve Barker, who could film this occasion for whatever form the inevitable documentary of the tour might take. Watching the footage of this meeting now, you can see how quickly everyone is seduced by the idea. The tape is an hour long, and during those sixty minutes the foundations of the last great Otway project are laid.

It starts with John taking a globe that he found in his daughter's room out of his bag and explaining. "Last year with *Bunsen Burner*, we cracked the UK. We are now going to crack the rest of the world." It takes only a couple of minutes for the whole concept to be fully appreciated and long before the first pint of beer is consumed the four of them are acting like kids in a rock and roll sweet shop. "The great thing," says John, "is that if we've got our own plane, we can pretty much go where we want."

The globe is passed around the table and each of them takes turns in saying where they would like to go. "What about Rio de Janeiro?" says one. "We ought to do a gig in each continent," says another. First the globe is held in the right hand and rotated clockwise, with the Ali index finger stabbing it seven or eight times, and then Cotton turns it anti-clockwise stabbing it one less. "If you go round this way, you lose a day, but the jet lag is less severe."

Many other ideas that would be a feature of the campaign are discussed, like the fact that you could have both winter sun in somewhere like the Alps and summer sun in somewhere like Hawaii. During that meeting Ali becomes the first person to ask the question that will be repeated by almost everyone who becomes involved in the project. "Have you thought of asking Richard Branson?"

As the video tape of that meeting comes to an end, and the third pint of beer is brought to the table, Otway is looking most pleased with himself and everyone else is looking inspired and excited. Over the next few days, Ali used his travel agency to look into chartering the plane, and John put the refinements to his tour in his head. And John's head was a very exciting place to be during those days. He kept finding out things like you need your own check-in desks at the airport, and that they would call the John Otway World Tour over the tannoy. And on the web he found a picture of the plane used for the Led Zeppelin tour, with the band's name in big letters on the side.

It was during these heady days that it was brought to John's attention that the Sydney Opera House had a couple of small studio theatres, along with the suggestion he could do one of those. If you had to put your finger on where it all started to go wrong for Otway, it could be when he climbed the stairs to his office in his house saying to himself, "If the Carnegie Hall has a small theatre too, then that's it, whatever it takes, we're going."

A quick internet search was all that was needed to discover that the Carnegie Hall had three stages: The Isaac Stern Auditorium – 2,804 seats; The Judy and Arthur Zankel Hall – 599 seats; and the Joan and Sanford I Weill Recital Hall – 268 seats. Or, as John later described it, ten jet loads, two jet loads and one jet load.

It is then that he fired off the e-mail to Cotton that starts this book.

A couple of days later Ali McClean came back with the fruits of his labour, but they were not the fruits John wanted. Ali had received several quotes with details of various options for planes capable of doing the tour, but they were all well above a realistic budget. "I'm sorry, but we're not going to be able to do it in our own plane," was his message. This was not too much of a setback for Otway: it was just like Maurice Bacon or Nigel Reveler saying you're not going to have a Top Ten. The idea was just "too bloody brilliant," and Ali would just have to "try a little bit harder."

And Ali did try a bit harder and the quotes got a bit better, but still far and away from the figures necessary to make this a feasible reality. And whilst Cotton did what most people had suggested and contacted Richard Branson, John went looking for a jet himself. Ali had explained that jets were ridiculously expensive and to keep air fares as low as possible operators kept them working all the time doing as many flights as possible each day. To do what Otway wanted to do and tie up an aircraft for two weeks for just six or seven flights was extremely uneconomical.

However, John had seen a photo in one of the papers that showed loads of passenger jets parked up in the Nevada desert because there wasn't enough work for them. "I just thought, what about one of those? And if we were going out of season, I reckoned there had to be some bargains about."

John did not get very far trying to get an aeroplane on Google, so he caught the tube into Wimbledon and searched the magazine section of W H Smith. Amongst the plane spotter monthlies were a couple of industry periodicals, and in the classified section at the back of one of these were a couple of charter companies. He then got Cotton to chase them up and consequently two executives from Air Partners headed to Oxford for a meeting with the Otway World Tour manager, and within a few days had supplied a quote.

"I don't know where Cotton can get a 747 for that price," said Ali (the travel agent) to Otway (the pop star). "I've checked out about a dozen operators and they've all come up with the same sort of figure." John thought it prudent not to point out that a trip to a local newsagent was all that was necessary.

With the new and better price for the airliner Otway and Cotton were now able to move ahead with plans for the tour. As this was going to be the ultimate Rock and Roll dream, they decided that it might be best to give themselves a bit of extra time and do the tour in 2006. This would give them a whole extra year to make it work.

The actual date for the tour was finalised after John had a lively discussion about astronomy at a Viz party in Newcastle and discovered there was a total eclipse of the sun in Turkey in March 2006. To someone who believed in destiny, this was like saying "there's a small venue in Sydney Opera House," and discovering there was one in the Carnegie Hall as well. The revelation that a tour combining these two great venues might include something as spectacular as a solar eclipse was just perfect.

"The idea that at a certain point of the tour one straight line could be drawn between the centres of the sun, moon, earth and my seat on the jet was wonderful," he said.

It was easy to get details of the path of the 2006 eclipse on the internet. Would the path of totality cross an international airport upon which the Otway Jet could land? Yes – Antalya airport was slap bang in the middle. And if there are clouds? "No problem," thought John. "We'll just get back in the plane and fly above them to make sure we get a good view."

The itinerary was then quite easy to work out. They would need to be in Antalya Airport on March 9th, so you just worked backwards and forwards from there. The decision had been made in favour of losing the day and not having the jet lag, so they would leave the UK and keep heading west.

Otway was "T-shirt led" meaning that if something looked good on the T-shirt and tour jacket, then that's what you should try and do. The John Otway World Tour would have the ultimate venues in the world, so John wanted to add the Royal Albert Hall to the tour. He asked Paul Clerehugh to find out if it was available for the 2nd April 2006, and although it was, Paul had a big problem with the idea. "Otway's idea was amazing and spectacular, but it had the effect of excluding most of his fans," explains Paul. "It was great if you could take the time off and had the money to go on the plane, but if you couldn't would you really want to go to the Albert Hall and clap and cheer all those fans who had a holiday that you would have loved to go on?"

So John suggested 1,500 capacity The Globe, Shakespeare's theatre, as that would look good on the World Tour T-shirt too, but eventually reason prevailed and the much smaller Cavern in Liverpool was chosen for the UK date on the World Tour. If the tour started there you could fly out of John Lennon airport, and Otway did like being able to say "We start at the Cavern, fly out of John Lennon airport, land at JFK and play Carnegie Hall." He said it to himself only twice before memorising it perfectly as a single soundbite.

John even found a way to get around the exclusivity and to include the fans with the idea of the Geneva Convention. After the eclipse the jet was to fly to Switzerland and after dropping off the circumnavigators would fly back to the UK where it would pick up a jet load and fly them back to the Alps for the final weekend of the tour. During the weekend a tour boat with Otway fans would sail across the lake from Montreux and as they reached the city harbour, with the snow-covered peaks of the mountains behind them, John accompanied by the band and a string quartet would sing *Geneve*. What fan would want to miss that?

After a cabaret Vegas show and a pub gig in Dubai had been added, the following itinerary was proposed to the fans.

March 16th	**Liverpool**	The Cavern
18th	**New York**	Carnegie Hall
20th	**Las Vegas**	Caesar's Palace
22nd	**Tahiti**	Beach Party
25th	**Sydney**	Opera House
28th	**Dubai**	Red Lion
29th	**Turkey**	Total Eclipse Of The Sun
April 1st	The **Geneva**	Convention

Steve Barker found library footage at APTV and put together a short promo video with a voice-over from John. He had the cities, the venues and a previous eclipse and used his editing software to put "OT-AIR" on the tail of a 747. Otway instantly adopted it as the title for the tour, as he loved being able to say that the fans were flying on OT-AIR.

Otway wrote to the newsgroup and sent an e-mail letter out with a survey to judge the reaction to the proposed tour, and the results looked positive enough to launch the idea to the whole fan base.

CHAPTER 29

John's 52nd birthday fell on a Saturday, which meant he could do a big gig like the Mean Fiddler and launch the world tour properly.

Six weeks before this launch he had an idea that would complement it: there had not been a new Otway album since *Premature Adulation* ten years before, why not do an *OT-AIR Album – The Album To Launch The World Tour?* If he did that, no fan would fail to be aware of exactly what he was up to.

"As I had managed to do the five B-sides with Barry in a couple of weeks, I thought I should see if we could get an album together. I was passionate enough about what I was doing, so I spoke to Barry, and he was up for giving it a go. It was very tight though, two weeks to write it, two weeks to record it and two weeks manufacturing. If we could do it then it would make the launch a lot more than just a band gig."

John was doing a solo show at the Edinburgh Festival for the first of those six weeks and spent nearly all the time he was not on stage writing lyrics for the album. The enthusiasm he had can be seen in some of the lines that he wrote for the title track *OT-AIR*:

Rock and Roll dream, Rock and Roll heaven
I've got my very own 747
I'm doing it cool, I'm doing it large
Got my name on the fuselage
I'm going crazy, going mental, I'm going intercontinental
I'm going to hyperventilate
I'm going to circumnavigate

Another song, *The International Dateline*, was inspired by the idea of Richard Holgarth playing the longest guitar solo in the world, starting two minutes before they crossed the international dateline and ending two minutes after. A quick check of the clock would show that twenty-four hours and four minutes had elapsed between the first and last notes. Barry thought they could attempt to write a rock anthem, "Something like *We Will, We Will Rock You*," he had suggested. So John subtracted the words *We Will, Will You* from the title and came up with, *We Rock*.

By the time Otway was back in England to meet up with Barry there were firm foundations from which Barry could start to build half an album. Building the other half, however involved...

"Scraping the bottom of the barrel," says Murray Torkildsen from the band. "There are five or six really good songs on *OT-AIR* – one of them mine, may I add – and then there's some complete rubbish. *Three Kinds Of Magic*, how bad is that?"

Murray wasn't alone in thinking this particular song was not one of John's better pieces of writing, the rest of the band thought it as well. But they had two problems. One, since *Bunsen Burner* John "would not listen," and two, Barry's other job at the time was producing a female duo called the Cheeky Girls.

To try and resolve the problem with John, the members of his band would take it in turns to sing the chorus to him.

There's only three kinds of magic
And one of them would be making love to you

They hoped that the penny would drop and he'd suddenly realise "that it was crap."

They found the Barry problem harder. "How do you tell someone who has just had a hit with *The Cheeky Flamenco*, and has a band called Hot Pants a Go Go, that this piece of cheesy pop is unacceptable?" says Richard Holgarth. "The problem is, you can't."

But with a promise of a trip around the world the band recorded the songs... apart from *The Old Fiddler*, a Benny Hill track. "I knew the band were getting a bit sensitive about the direction Barry and I were taking," says Otway. "But I had this idea to do a Benny Hill poem I learnt when I was a kid, so Barry and I just did it and I sneaked it on the album when we cut it, two weeks before the launch gig."

It was not the only thing to be sneaked upon the album. If you listen carefully to *The International Dateline* a Cheeky Girl can be heard to say "Hi I'm Gabriela from Romania and I'm waiting for you."

John Haxby, who had produced the Albert Hall images, took some pictures of a shirtless Otway holding a large disk. He then superimposed the western hemisphere of the earth and managed the almost impossible task of getting Otway to resemble Atlas in the few days he had to design the cover.

It was always going to be a bit tight trying to get back copies of the new album only fourteen days after sending it to the manufacturer. John had got his old friend and roadie Peter Bullick's company Sound Discs to arrange getting the new John Otway album *OT-AIR* made and delivered, but come the morning of the launch they had not arrived. The album was a crucial piece of the strategy and a lot of fans were turning up that night to get a copy of the first new Otway album in a decade. Not having it would spoil the whole event: the fans might well think if he can't get the album together on time, how is he going to manage with the rest of the project.

But John panicked less than he would have a few years before. Hadn't Cotton sorted the *Bunsen Burner* publishing at the last minute? Hadn't the fans saved The Hit on the final day when all was lost? Hadn't he been able to get the songs together with Barry and hadn't he been able to record them in time? Yes. It was to John as if these things were supposed to happen. The hit was a great idea and it had worked; if this was, as John believed, a truly beautiful idea then this would work too and they would have the CDs for the evening. And, sure enough, five minutes before he had to leave for the show they arrived: the printed parts, cases and CDs were all separate, but enough bits arrived to furnish the fans and launch the big tour.

It was a great birthday. The performance of the new song *We Rock* was received as John had hoped and became a permanent part of the Otway band show.

Most people John spoke to that evening told him the World Tour was something they would love to be a part of, even if they might not have the £2,880 for the ticket or might not be able to take the time off: "I only get one holiday a year, and my wife expects me to spend it with her and our kids" was a common excuse. But it was still something they would think about a lot. Out of the ten thousand fans John reckoned he had, only three hundred were needed to make it work in a 767 and less than double that number for a 747 Jumbo Jet.

Because it is illegal to take money for flights without the necessary travel agent's license, Cotton set up a trust account to put the tour deposits in, and the World Tour went on sale.

By Christmas the feeling was that the project was on course: around seventy fans had either sent in a substantial deposit or set up a standing order into the trust account. It was three months since the launch, fifteen months from take off, and a third of the way to the 240 minimum people needed to make the tour viable.

During this period of relative euphoria a college in Worcester invited John to give a lecture to students interested in going into music. John was delighted if a little daunted at the prospect of talking to an audience of teenagers about how to make a career out of the industry: it was, he felt, a way of "giving something back."

Amy taught her dad the rudiments of Powerpoint and her father had learnt very quickly how to put Otway pictures, Otway videos, Otway articles and Otway songs into a seamless presentation. John loved talking about himself and Powerpoint was a wonderful aid because it allowed him to illustrate how he became *Rock and Roll's Greatest Failure* with moving images, music and graphs that showed exactly why he became so unsuccessful. When they had taken that in, John was then able to explain with other moving images, music and graphs how with perseverance he fought his way back into the charts, and was now able to do something no Rock and Roll act had ever done.

It worked very well and was very funny. It was unlike any lecture the students had ever had before, and they all got the message: if Otway can do it anyone can. All you needed to do was work hard, keep faith and something would happen.

With spring 2005 came the 'World Tour Pub Crawl', an Otway-inspired World Tour sales drive. His idea was to visit pubs around the country and invite fans to come and join him for a drink. "We'll chat about the world tour and sign them up for it." If John thought that fans would travel miles to have a drink with him in a pub, in the same way they did to see him do a gig, he was wrong. Otway and Cotton would turn up to pubs and lay out their globes, travel guides and Airfix model 767 *OT-AIR* plane. There would always be four or five fans, but they were invariably ones already booked to go.

Barry Upton brought cameraman Andy Sutton to one of these meetings and he and John discussed the TV options for the tour. "From the interest Channel 4 had expressed in *Around the World in 18 Days* fifteen years before, I knew that there would be a good television programme in the World Tour," says John. "But I thought this time what we were doing was a lot bigger than just a one-off TV documentary. This was flying around the world in your own jet playing the greatest venues so it deserved a series, but I felt that we wouldn't be given one by any of the major channels. If you didn't have a series, then you couldn't build an audience: a one-off documentary would come and go and be largely forgotten within a year."

It was Andy who came up with the solution to that problem when he suggested doing it as a movie. "The new high definition cameras blow up beautifully," he said. "It's perfect for all the film festivals, if it goes down a storm in them you get a theatrical release, if not you just sell it to television anyway." This was a brilliant idea, and more and more pieces seemed to fit together. The World Tour would make a spectacular background to *Otway The Movie*, and as destiny would have it a few days later John received an e-mail from Hollywood. Not only was its geographical point of origin exciting, a click on the link at the bottom of the note revealed a film company that had recently been nominated for an Oscar for one of their documentaries.

It was all thanks to Chris France, who due to a series of successful business deals had moved to semi-retirement in the south of France with his wife Isabel and their two children. Chris made a point of playing golf with others who had made a series of successful business deals, and one such entrepreneurial character was Australian Larry Smith. As well as entertaining him by regularly getting around the eighteen holes with considerably less ball hitting, Chris would enthral him with stories of his pop star friend from school days who was about to fly to Sydney Opera House in a jet with his fans. Larry had business dealings with some film people in LA and that had led to John's e-mail from Tinsel Town.

It had been a long time since John had flown business class, but Chris France agreed with Otway that this was the best way for them to fly to the west coast of America. The cost of the trip, which he put on his card, could be reclaimed against expenses when everything got sorted out. "It's not often you get to fly to Hollywood to negotiate a movie deal," they both thought. At this point, the people John and Chris were flying around the world to see were not aware that this was what they were negotiating, they had simply expressed an interest in making a television documentary. "They just need to be shown that what we are doing is a lot bigger than that," John told Chris, which would account for another item on Chris' new black American Express card: a stay in the Georgian Hotel in Santa Monica, overlooking the Pacific Ocean.

The Trans-Atlantic "strike while the iron's hot" trip had to be fitted in between John's live shows: he would only be out of the country for 48 hours, which gave them just over 24 to make the pitch. John discovered that the lecture he had prepared for a bunch of sixteen- and seventeen-year-olds looking to go into the music business worked equally well to a gathering of film producers in Hollywood. They liked the adventures of the Aylesbury dustman with two hits who was flying his fans around the globe. They loved his mum telling them that he couldn't sing, the crushing of the testicles on the *Whistle Test* programme made them all laugh and so did the video where all his fans yelled "Who's a Prat" at him. "They really are not that much different to the Brits," John thought after they asked him about asking Richard Branson.

They would consider making the piece with a view to showing it at film festivals and possible theatrical release before it went to television. And so in the cab on the way back to Los Angeles Airport John was able to text Cotton the two words "done it." Back in the UK John was now able to say that there was a film being made and those who came on the trip would not only get to make Rock and Roll history with their star, they would also feature in a Hollywood movie with him.

Exactly one year before take-off, the Otway band took off on the twinning tour. "I thought it would be fun to twin venues with the ones we would be playing in exactly one year's time," says Otway. "So The 12 Bar in Preston was twinned with Carnegie Hall, The Robin 2 in Wolverhampton was twinned with Sydney Opera House and The New Roscoe in Leeds was more closely related to a Beach Bar in Tahiti than is usually imagined."

It was a great time. Deposits were coming in, and on that tour you could go to the merchandising stall and for £10 get the *OT-AIR* CD, for £12 buy the *OT-AIR* T-shirt and for £2,880 get an *OT-AIR* ticket for the tour itself.

Hollywood film producer Greg Coote was flying over from LA with his wife and Otway had set up a meeting with them and a possible director for the movie, Geoff Wonfor, who had recently directed The Beatles' *Anthology*. He was friends with the Viz team who had suggested that he might be a good choice.

John had also been contacted by another director, David Battcock, who was attracted to the World Tour idea: he had spoken to a commissioning editor from BBC3 and secured an agreement and a budget for the documentary.

Neither of these directors worked however. Geoff Wonfor was ruled out because there had been a mix up with the meeting and John, to Greg's astonishment declared, "that's it, he's not taking us seriously enough." And David Battcock "because he had an agreement to make a television programme and not a movie." "Sometimes," says Chris France, "I have to accept that the words 'with hindsight', simply do not do justice to the decisions made. The words 'who's a prat' work a lot better for me."

Cotton had told John when they embarked on the project that the cut-off point should be six months before take off: either they had enough people to make it work and they arranged to pay for the plane with a suitable licensed operator, or they refunded everyone informing them that despite the best endeavours, the tour was not viable. Coming up to this point, there were not quite enough. They had done well – a quarter of a million pounds sat in the trust account and almost two hundred people were committed to go – but they were about thirty to forty short of the minimum number necessary.

"But as soon as they see the gigs on the gig list and the hotels are up on the web site, we'll get that money no problem," Otway had insisted.

It was Chris France who solved that problem by finding a company of underwriters who would, for a fee, take the risk and guarantee the whole project. "They just need exact numbers for passengers, the precise cost of the plane and the price of the hotels," he said.

And then disaster struck, literally. In August 2005 Hurricane Katrina caused havoc in America, and up went the price of oil. When Cotton went back to Air Partners to get a firm quote on the cost of the plane, the price had soared. The quote that he and John had been so delighted with and had based their costs on was for a 2005 tour: in the new climate the quote for the dates they were looking at was even higher than Ali McClean's quotes eighteen months earlier. "You have no choice but to write and tell them that it is off," Cotton told Otway. "Great idea, but it doesn't work."

And so, two hundred letters were written and posted to those who had booked on the trip, and that should have been the end of it.

CHAPTER 30

Otway could simply not bring himself to do it – the idea was so seductive. As he looked out of his front room window seeing planes fly low as they made their approach to Heathrow, John could easily read the name of the airline on them and imagined others looking out of their windows and seeing the *OT-AIR* logo on the tail. Someone had even e-mailed him and told him they worked for a company who would do the decals for nothing. In his letter he had left himself manoeuvring room should he want to continue, by saying he was looking for alternatives. However, Cotton had made it plain that this was as far as he was prepared to go, he could not see how it could now make money and did not want to be involved in any resurrection of the tour.

After a flurry of helpful e-mails from fans John followed their suggestions and re-doubled his efforts to ask Richard Branson. Branson had by now been asked many times – mainly because there were so many people who knew someone who knew him – and each time John discovered one of these people, a message was sent and he would be asked. So far, the most information had been a message from a Virgin airline employee who got back to say that as far as he was aware they did not have any spare planes at the moment.

John was also about to lose his Hollywood movie. "No jet, no film," Greg had pointed out. This stating of the obvious was taken by Otway as a lack of faith. He determined that he would do the tour somehow – whatever it took – and there was no room for doubters.

Over the years John had found Peter Bullick a resourceful character. Otway's one-time roadie was now living with Debbie Bonham and playing guitar in her band, and John knew that the trick of "find me a jet and you can play support on the World

Tour" might produce some interesting results. Which it did. A couple of days later John was in Tunbridge Wells at the offices of C T Travel talking to director Mark Kempster. It was certainly an unusual meeting, the young company director with the pop star he had never heard of who had an impressive number of passengers and an interesting idea. Mark promised that he would do his best to help him out.

"If this works," John had told him, "we can have OT-AIR as a brand and do a tour each year. We can do an American tour the year after and an Australian one the next. Then there's Europe. It doesn't have to be the whole world each time."

One of the difficulties posed by the current tour was crossing the Pacific Ocean. There was a minimum size of aircraft you could use, preferably one with more than two engines, which was why they couldn't just get a two-hundred seater and do the tour with the number of passengers they had. Otway knew all this, he had been over and over the various configurations of aircraft many times. He was therefore surprised, delighted and over the moon when Mark Kempster came up with an older aircraft, one that had been round the world many times, one with three engines. A Lockheed Tristar.

There was a way. John e-mailed the World Tour passengers with an image of the plane, told them to hang on, there would be a readjustment in terms of the cost, but the World Tour lives.

The next thing to get back on track was Otway The Movie. John went back to Andy Sutton who first suggested the feature film idea and asked him if he fancied doing it. Andy was involved in a production company called Athena Films, whose main work at the time was producing Monkey World, a programme about the lives of primates in an ape and monkey sanctuary. It was, in retrospect, a fitting choice. It was agreed that Athena would make the Movie and start shooting the build-up to the tour immediately.

By the time Otway had put together the first meeting for the Athena crew to film, several decisions had been made. The World Tour would be postponed until the autumn of 2006. The total budget was now a staggering £1.1 million and the ticket price would be closer to £4,000 – a large increase. The fans had been told, and although some of them couldn't make the new date or it was now too expensive for them, around thirty-five had agreed immediately and the rest had not responded and so were presumably undecided.

It was not a wonderful start, but the cameras were coming and John had arranged a private room in a pub in London's West End for all the interested parties. These included Chris

France, who had flown over from Cannes, Peter Bullick and Mark Kempster, who had brought along an airline broker called Chris Clapham. Chris (the jet) Clapham told the group that instead of the Tristar, for the same price he could get a modern Airbus 340 from Air Tahiti. This would mean a deposit of £60,000 with staged payments before the trip itself. Peter Bullick pointed out that £60,000 divided by five was £12,000 – he would guarantee twelve thousand and went around the room followed by the cameras collecting enough twelves for the deposit, to be called in if the tour was cancelled.

Otway felt that one of the reasons they did not make up the numbers previously was because the only people who knew about the tour were on his mailing list. If the deposit was paid on the jet and the date fixed, it could be advertised more widely "and we only need three hundred people," he had said.

There were good reasons to be optimistic. Johnny Walker had recently had John on his Radio 2 show again and the two of them had discussed the project on air, and that autumn John and Richard Holgarth were doing The *Mad Bad & Dangerous* Tour with Wilko Johnson and The Hamsters – a long tour in front of a lot of people many who were fascinated by the trip around the world. They said things like "I would really love to do something like that" so often that John was convinced it would not be too difficult to get enough people to go on the plane if they knew about it.

MIDEM is the world's largest music industry trade fair, held each January at the Palais des Festivals in Cannes. John had been there in 1978 and Chris France had been there most subsequent years. The two of them thought it would be good to start the 2006 World Tour year with Otway giving his lecture there on "How he beat the music industry at its own game and how the victory has enabled him to move onto bigger and bolder projects." There would be big players flying from all corners of the globe for the event, and being Cannes there were many iconic locations, so it made sense for Andy to come and interview John and Chris there as well as filming him talking to the industry about his plans.

It was not a good omen that Andy, John and Chris between them made up one third of the people in the lecture theatre. But one of the others was Judy Totton, who enjoyed what she saw and gave Otway her card. Chris France was impressed, as Judy was a particularly successful PR agent who was careful about what she took on. Chris had used her company before and had been delighted with the results.

Back in London a week or so later, she met with John and discussed his plans for the tour. She felt she could get him some press on his idea – and she wasn't wrong. The day after she issued a press release, Otway faced a grilling on the lunchtime edition of *London Today*. There were radio interviews, The Independent, The Daily Telegraph, the Metro and numerous other papers started printing articles, and *The Word* had the Otway Tour included on the cover high on the list of contents with one of John Haxby's photos of John holding up the world.

John's press cuttings scrapbook, which had not filled up much since *Bunsen Burner*, was now getting pages added almost daily.

Before John could book the venues, take on a tour manager, hire equipment, advertise the shows and do all the myriad things that would need to be done to make the World Tour work smoothly, one simple thing needed to happen. Two hundred and thirty people needed to book to go on the tour. When that happened the whole trip became viable and there would be enough money to pay for the plane, the hotels and the venues. At this point, those who had agreed to guarantee the jet deposit could be assured that they would not be called upon for any money, as CT Travel would be able to release the ticket money and all expenses including jet payments would be covered. But up until the magic 230 was reached the tour was not yet viable and the ticket money could not be used because it may need to be refunded.

There is (and possibly will be) another book's-worth of stories about the following six months and how the Otway World Tour kept going, and why the plug was not pulled, but the principles are easy to grasp.

Every time a jet payment was due, unless there were the 230 passengers then the tour would be cancelled, unless the money could be found elsewhere. Over this time the passenger numbers never crossed that line, though they were increasing and John was confident that they soon would. So on each occasion the team working on the tour had to go hunting for investors (the team now included fan Peter Cook who invested a large amount of money, city broker Mark Horne as well as Otway, France, Mark the Travel agent and Chris The Jet). And each time they managed it through a combination of meetings, phone calls, e-mails, air miles, road miles, approaching sponsors and losing sleep trying to hang on to the jet.

Meanwhile John also had to piece together the rest of his tour – so far he only had the Liverpool Cavern booked. It gives an idea of how far he had started to become detached from reality, that when someone in jest had told him "you can't play in the Cavern unless you have practiced in Hamburg first" (referring to The Beatles' early residency at the Star Club). He did some research. On discovering that there was a 48-hour return trip between Southampton and Hamburg on the Cunard ship the QM2, he got really excited and said that this could be a trip for those fans with families who wanted to be involved. They could come on the World Tour Practice trip and be on what would be a fabulous addition to the movie. The idea was quietly dropped when CT Travel put it up on the web site and had sold only a single ticket in a month.

Sydney Opera House had e-mailed John back regarding his request for a date.

Our indoor venues, Opera Theatre (1547), Drama Theatre (544) Playhouse (398), all have scheduled performances or production activity on both 05 & 06 November. The Concert Hall (cap 2679) does have a session available on Monday 06 November.

Pure common sense should have told John that taking on a venue the size of The Royal Albert Hall and trying to promote the show from the other side of the planet was not the wisest course of action, especially with only six months to go. But for Otway to make his tour live up to its claim of the Greatest Rock and Roll World Tour ever, it had to have the most famous venues. But there was also the question of the ten-thousand dollar deposit to secure the date.

That spring, Dominic Sylvester had booked John to play at his company's annual party. Dominic was an old fan who'd gone to many shows in the seventies and early eighties, but the two had not seen each other in years. In that time Dominic had become very successful and was now living in the Bahamas. So John spoke to Dominic to try to get him involved, and a couple of weeks later received a message: Because John had played Dominic's sister's birthday party for the hefty fee of two sausage rolls thirty years ago when he was broke, Dominic would now donate $10,000 to help Otway get his World Tour off the ground.

Was it another case of serendipity? Was it fate? "I suppose it just depends how close the American dollar is to the Australian one," thought John. They were eerily close. So two e-mails later – one to The Sydney Opera House saying "Yes, we'll take it, the money is coming from the Bahamas" and one to Dominic to tell him – that was it: he could now tell everyone that The Sydney Opera House was booked.

But as much as John Otway might have felt that fate and the heavens were behind him in his circumnavigation of the earth, even he knew that he could not skew the laws of physics to move the date of the total eclipse of the sun by six months in order to fit in with his new timetable. So he needed something exciting to replace it and was inspired by the suggestion of one of his sponsors, Carlsbro Amplification, about doing a gig in China where their sound equipment was manufactured. The country was opening up, but so far no western rock act had played the huge Chinese city of Ningbo. The Chinese were also building a massive new airport there, and the OT-AIR jet could be the first foreign plane to land at Ningbo International. That was a very exciting concept indeed and the opportunities for sponsorship huge.

The New York leg of the tour was not proving straightforward to sort out. Cotton had tried the year before to book the act formerly known as *Rock and Roll's Greatest Failure* into America's most prestigious venue but the lady responsible for making the bookings was having none of it. From what Cotton had explained, she felt the Otway World Tour was an inappropriate show for the venue to host. Cotton must have made a strong impression because when Otway contacted her direct about playing there the response was both immediate and emphatic: "no, no, no!"

John wanted something good to put on the T-shirt for his New York show, so persevered for a while with Carnegie Hall who persevered with saying no. It was Adam Batterbee, recently returned from a trip to the Big Apple, who came up with the next suggestion, something Otway felt would look almost as good. "There are a couple of bars and restaurants in Central Park you can book for private events," he suggested.

John checked and there were. He checked the dates, they were available, and then rang Wild Willy. "Will you do The Otway and Barrett Re-union in Central Park?" To which the answer was "No, I don't like New York, I'll do Australia or Tahiti." It was very frustrating. Madison Square Garden sometimes booked out the foyer for corporate events, but John wasn't getting far with that either, CBGBs another famous New York club was approached, but they were closing down the weekend before the tour was due to start. Finally Judy Totton pulled a big favour and got the World Tour into a classy New York Bar called B B King's.

Whilst the battles were going on to keep the jet, John had to also look after the more creative elements. None of these was more important than the decals, getting the OT-AIR logo in big letters on the tail of the plane. John had found a company that was prepared to do them for nothing, they just needed the plane for twelve hours before the tour in a hangar. "It was difficult for me," says John. "I wanted to tell Chris Clapham, the jet broker, to arrange to have the jet early when we were behind with payments. The problem was, he would have just been cross and said 'that's the last thing I should worry about,' and I would have got cross and said it was the first thing I thought of, so I just kept my mouth shut and decided that it would all work out in the fullness of time."

Similar to his approach to his Royal Albert Hall show, John was eager that this was known as The John Otway World Tour, and not have the publicity hijacked by other pop stars, but he was also aware that the addition of other acts could make the movie look good and sell some extra seats. He also was well aware that some serious work would have to be put into selling the 2,679 seats in the Sydney Opera House. John felt this was an opportunity to repay Steve Harley for his generosity – would Steve like to join them on the jet and play Sydney Opera House?

The tour had come to yet another crunch point: the next jet deposit was overdue and Chris The Jet had warned that time was nearly up. John resigned himself to the fact that the passenger numbers, although rising, had not hit the magic number and to find fifty thousand pounds in a few days would need a miracle. "If something happens now, I know that it is supposed to happen and that I'm just destined to do this. That's my only hope," John thought.

And as if to prove that miracles do happen, into the story comes the almost mystical figure of Rainbow George. His Wikipedia biography states:

Rainbow George Weiss (born 1940) son of a diamond merchant, is a fringe UK politician who stood in 13 constituencies at the 2005 General Election.

He founded his own parties from the proceeds of the sale of a house in Hampstead, North London which he moved into in 1969 but stopped paying rent on in 1984; remaining there as a squatter. He made a profit of £710,000 on the sale of the house in 2004 after HM Land Registry awarded him ownership of the property.

In July 2006, Weiss disclosed on the Clive Bull radio show that he had about £50,000 remaining from the windfall.

Rainbow George had often employed Peter Bullick's Sound Disks company to manufacture CDs for the Rainbow Revolution Party and Peter had told George about the Otway tour. George felt that the World Tour was a good way to spread the Rainbow message around the globe.

"Pete took me to meet Rainbow George in about July 2006," recalls Otway. "And there was this very sweet idealist who was prepared to invest in the project. I didn't know whether to accept it but if I turned it down, the tour and everyone else's investment would be wasted. This kind old chap was offering to keep the show on the road with a cheque for fifty thousand pounds, which he would get back from the ticket money as soon as the tour was viable and he would also get a share in the profits from the movie. I decided after some thought the best thing to do was accept the money and just work harder and make sure the damn thing happens."

Working harder meant new ideas like allowing people to do part of the tour if they didn't have the time to do the whole thing. You could now do OT-LEGS. John told the fans that it was now a three-legged tour. "I've been staring at these legs for ages now, and I think you will agree that they are very sexy," said John. "You can do the American Leg, The Circumnavigational Leg, or the Eastern Exotic Leg.

Judy Totton worked hard too – whilst in Edinburgh doing the lecture at the festival, he got a call from her saying that he had been booked as special guest on the Saturday Morning Jonathan Ross show on Radio 2. Jonathan was away, and the replacement presenters were Mark Lamarr and Dale Winton. It was to be one of the best sales pitches of the project, not because John was good at it, but because Dale Winton was superb. He got excited about the venues, he was shocked at how cheap it was, he simply adored the idea of the jet and was just mortified that he couldn't go himself.

It worked. For weeks, John had been trying to get Glenn Tilbrook to do some dates and within hours of the interview received a call from his manager Suzanne: the Squeeze singer/songwriter would be able to do the first few dates. Then finally, after the interview tickets started selling faster than they had for months.

Then Judy arranged for a large feature in the Independent on Sunday. The interview took place over two days, with one of them in Aylesbury, so that feature writer Robert Chalmers could interview Wild Willy Barrett and John's mum. When it appeared the piece took five whole pages of the magazine, and the cover was completely filled with a picture of Otway holding up Amy's Globe – the one that he had shown Cotton, Ali and Steve Barker when he first presented the plan two and a half years previously.

The cover of that Sunday magazine was possibly the most prestigious piece of press he had ever had. Suddenly everyone seemed to be aware of John's tour plans. And there was one big gig to come: John and the band had been booked to play in the Market Square of his home town Aylesbury. The last time he played the Market Square had been in 1978 right after his

Hit, with the whole town turning out to see the town's new star and the gig being filmed by ATV for a documentary *Stardustman*. It was another piece of wonderful synchronicity. Before he took on the world he would play Aylesbury Market Square with a film crew to capture the event, and in editing they could cut between the young star just after his first hit about to go for his second and the old star just after the second about to go for the World.

It was truly a great day. Karen and Amy made huge *OT-AIR* signs, new Haxby-designed flyers had been printed with the special guests on and Mark Kempster came down with the staff of C T Travel to distribute them. The fans turned out in force and many a veteran of Dunkerque, Abbey Road and *Bunsen Burner* were there, as were investors Peter Cook and Rainbow George. Chris France flew in from Cannes too.

"It was an electric Otway performance," says Maurice Bacon. "He was on fire and no-one doubted the man when he announced to the ten thousand at the show that he was about to do what no Rock and Roll act had ever done before."

But a couple of weeks later the problems were back with a vengeance. A call to Chris the Jet to make tentative enquiries about getting *OT-AIR* on the tail was hijacked by the more sober and pressing fact that the rest of the payment for the plane was due. The balance between costs and ticket sales had not still reached the point where the tour became viable. If Air Tahiti did not receive the next sum due under the contract, they would have to cancel so they could place the aircraft somewhere else. This was not the tens of thousands of the earlier deposits, this was the hundreds of thousands necessary to put the logistics of the tour together for the airline operator.

Other pressures were coming into place too. The travellers needed to start applying for visas and arranging immunisations from various tropical diseases and malaria. Deposits needed to be put down on hotels and the band needed work permits. Steve Harley had been in touch as he had been offered some shows in South Africa and wanted John to confirm one hundred percent that the show was going ahead. It was crunch time again.

They had done well over the last few weeks with the publicity and sales, in fact they were only between thirty and forty passengers short of what was required to make the tour work, and which would allow Mark Kempster to release the ticket money he was holding to pay for everything. John did the arithmetic: total tickets plus the original sixty thousand guarantee (obviously those who had offered to pay twelve each if the tour didn't go ahead would pay the money to make sure it did) plus the six first class seats the film company would need. All that minus the costs of the tour. The shortfall was a massive £146,000. Otway started facing up to the reality. This was such a huge sum that, heartbreaking and painful as it might be, this surely was the end of the road.

"Let me contact Dominic again," said Chris France. "He remembers Issy my wife from when she was doing your merchandising, I'll just tell him the situation you're in and see if he is up for helping out." Unbelievably, John's gig for two sausage rolls thirty years before was about to pay huge dividends. A mere twenty-four hours before the Air Tahiti deadline, Dominic replied saying if Chris could come up with some deal he would see if he could help out.

Chris had an idea he felt Dominic might just entertain: if Dominic lent the World Tour fund the £146,000 necessary for the tour to take off, he would be repaid first as soon as any money came in from any source. Any further ticket sales, any sponsorship and any profit from the movie would go first to pay off Dominic's investment, and then he could also share in any profits down the line. As Chris pointed out, a large number of people had said they fancied going, and even if they didn't quite make the thirty or forty needed to pay back the whole amount, there was a great deal of interest in *Otway the Movie*. John had been approached by over twenty production companies wanting to make the film of the World Tour since the Radio 2 show and The Independent feature. "We could fill up the plane with those," John had joked to Andy Sutton.

A few hours before the deadline, when the tour was about to fold, Dominic came back and said he would do it. He didn't want any profit, just the money back when they had got it. The deal was signed and the money transferred to CT Travel.

"That was bloody close," thought Otway.

"It was very nerve wracking," says John. "Everything had been last minute, starting with the *OT-AIR* album, all the jet deposits and now the final finance within hours of collapse. But this was the last one. It was scary too when I thought about how much everyone else had now put into the project, with the total coming to over £300,000."

But John was at last able to tell Steve Harley with confidence that the tour was going ahead, and the band could be told to start practicing the songs they would be backing him on at the Sydney Opera House. The fans could be told to sort out their visas for China and get their inoculations and malaria tablets and John could phone up Cotton, tell him we had finally got it sorted and ask him if he would come back and sort out all the bits and pieces.

The main problem Otway now had was how to broach the subject of the decals to Chris The Jet. As far as the airline broker was concerned, getting *OT-AIR* on the tail was the least of his worries, as far as the star was concerned it was now one of his biggest. John would have to find a way to explain just how important the shot of the *OT-AIR* jet taking off from John Lennon Airport was – it was a defining scene in *Otway The Movie*.

CHAPTER
31

Less than two months before take off Cotton was shocked at how little had been sorted out for the tour. The entertainment had been budgeted into the ticket costs, none of which had been available in case it needed to be refunded. When asked the simple question "How much is Sydney Opera House going to cost to do?" Otway simply had no idea. Everything, simply everything, was dwarfed by the cost of the plane: the gig costs were possibly ten to twenty thousand while the jet was close to a million.

But Cotton got to work and surprisingly quickly things started to make more sense. He discovered Sydney Opera House to be remarkably helpful and after a couple of midnight phone calls he had changed the Otway World Tour venue from the huge auditorium to the more sensibly sized Playhouse.

Ningbo was coming together too. The Chinese authorities had asked to have a look at what the performers on the World Tour would be doing, and while the Steve Harley performance was fine, a change would have to be made to John's act, as a very embarrassed translator explained. Her English was very good, but she couldn't find the right word to explain the problem. She got more and more flustered and started pointing to her breasts. This behaviour continued far too long for anyone's comfort until finally it dawned upon the Europeans from Carlsbro Amplification that the word she was searching for was "nipples". Understandably, the Chinese did not like the manner in which Otway ripped his shirt open and exposed his naked torso to the audience.

To give the shows a bit more variety John thought it would be fun to let Richard Holgarth be the musical director for the New York show, and Barry Upton could arrange the 'Otway Plays

Vegas' cabaret show. To make the shows different Barry had managed to get the Cheeky Girls to agree to join the band for a few numbers, but only John, Barry and the film crew knew. "I was certain it would look great in the movie," says John. "But I reckoned that Holgarth and the rest of the band would have thought it was taking some of the Rock and Roll out of the tour. I don't know if Glen Tillbrook or Steve Harley would have approved either, so we just kept it as a surprise. They never found out."

John discovered another way to spice up the movie. In 2006, according to the 'Ask Jeeves' search engine on the internet, the best hotel in the world is the Burj Al Arab Hotel in Dubai. Obviously not everyone could stay there, but it could be an added extra, and Otway could be filmed staying there whilst the band stayed in the local Dubai bed and breakfast. And it would add the world's greatest hotel as well as the venues on the T-shirt.

Before the final payment could be handed over to Air Tahiti and Cotton given the money for the venues and payment made to the hotels, Mark Kempster at the travel company had to carefully go through the finances and make sure that they had absolutely all the money necessary to do the whole tour before he could allow the ticket money to be used. And he started finding holes in the hastily calculated Otway arithmetic. John had assumed that the original group who guaranteed the first jet payment in case the tour didn't go ahead would be quite happy to put the money in to make sure it did. John himself was very happy that his twelve thousand would see the jet take off, some of the others were not. And in one case the paperwork hadn't been done so there was no real guarantee anyway.

Chris France had done his sums like this. "I'm putting in twelve thousand: if the tour goes ahead then that is three tickets, and if it doesn't I lose the money." John had done his sums like this. "Chris France guarantees twelve thousand plus three tickets that's twenty four thousand."

"Bloody Hell Otway, with our Hollywood trip that's over thirty grand! There is a limit," was the France response to the Otway calculations.

John had also assumed that the film crew had the money needed to buy the six first class seats they needed, which was more optimistic Otway accounting. Any one of these holes could possibly be patched with another bit of optimistic accounting, but not all of them put together, not another sixty thousand pounds and as any incoming money from any source had to go to pay back Dominic's massive loan first, this shortfall presented a huge problem.

And there was another deadline looming, one that was final, and could not be moved if the Otway World Tour was to stay on the right side of the law. The Civil Aviation authority, the CAA, have rules, one of them being that if you have a problem with your trip you must make your passengers aware not less than four weeks before take off. And that was now perilously close.

After clearing all the hurdles and sprinting as fast as he could towards the finish line, Otway could not believe he would run into a brick wall. The lessons he had learnt from life were that if you believed, worked hard and kept faith something would happen – there would be a miracle. Forty eight hours before the deadline John looked like a nervous wreck. He knew it had to work out, the tour would just have to undergo amputation and lose a leg. Each time a change was made Chris The Jet had to contact Air Tahiti in the opposite time zone and each time, twenty-four hours later, they were back and saying the saving would not be enough to save the trip.

John went to Tunbridge Wells to sort out with Mark Kempster what they should do. The situation was dire and had to be faced. If more of the tour was curtailed or down-graded the chances of selling any more tickets was zero and Dominic would never get his money back. Even though there was no personal guarantee, John would spend the rest of his life feeling that he owed the hundred and sixty thousand pounds. John could not think of a way to save the tour, and the fans would have to be told the following day. Mark needed John to tell him if it was now cancelled.

Otway went to the pub on his own for a pint of beer and tried to make one of the hardest decisions he had ever made. But nothing he could think of would make it work. When he returned he simply said, "If you don't get a call from me by eleven tomorrow saying it's happening, then it's cancelled."

It allowed eighteen hours for another of those miracles to happen. John would not have to actually give the death sentence if a miracle did not happen in time, it would just die.

Karen was worried about John when he returned home – he was in a mess. He had been so sure that the tour would happen that when faced with a hurdle instead of thinking "this will make the tour more difficult to achieve" he had thought "this makes the tour more likely to happen" after a way around it had been found. But he was now very worried. For the first time the concerns about how OT-AIR was going to get on the tail of his jet had been replaced with an admission that there might not even be a jet, and that he had probably lost the movie. He was frightened and exhausted. He took Karen's offer of managing the phones, went to bed and had nightmares.

But he still couldn't let go of it. Surely something would happen. And surely it did. Mark, Chris The Jet and Karen worked with Air Tahiti on a plan that would involve taking the *OT-AIR* jet to Sydney, missing out Ningbo and everyone returning by scheduled airlines, and Chris France arranged a new deal with Dominic which involved taking less of his money now that further passengers were unlikely. It was not the wonderful tour John had originally envisaged, but they would go around the world and the finances worked out.

The following morning Mark started phoning around the fans to see if they still wanted to go. They were right up against the deadline, so far they all did. Karen woke John up to tell him that there was still a World Tour and a slightly refreshed pop star went upstairs with her to the office. There was suddenly a great deal to do.

And then within three minutes it was all over. In the haste to re-organise the jet costs, the expense of returning the plane from Sydney to its point of origin had been missed so there was an extra thirty thousand pounds needed. By law the passengers would have to be told there was a problem and if five or six pulled out there would be a further twenty or thirty thousand pound hole. It was obvious to all, even Otway, that this was the end.

"Cotton and I will deal with everything," Karen suggested, "you are in no fit state to. Go back to bed."

CHAPTER 32

For one who had only ever had to cancel two gigs in his 3,000 gig career, pulling a whole world tour was incredibly painful. Two hundred of Otway's greatest fans had been saving up for two years for the trip of a lifetime and had only recently had their jabs to protect them from the tropical diseases they were now very unlikely to come into contact with. The two couples who had planned to get married as they went round the world would not now have a star as their best man – a name John now felt was inappropriate anyhow.

The one hundred and twenty thousand pounds given to Air Tahiti to secure the jet was now lost, as was the ten thousand dollar deposit on the Sydney Opera House. As well as his own money he had persuaded others to part with huge sums as an investment, on the promise of the capital back from the tickets and a share of the profits from the movie of the tour. As well as no tour there was now no film of it. These people were unlikely to be very happy when they heard the news.

Others who were unlikely to be happy on hearing of the collapse would be the special guests Steve Harley and Glen Tilbrook – much bigger stars than Otway. John had only spoken to Steve Harley a few days before and assured him all was well and he would be well advised to turn down the lucrative South African tour he had just been offered as he would never forgive himself if he missed out on the great opportunity John was offering him.

Otway was reeling from the scale of the failure. He had been so utterly convinced that the wonderful project would happen that he never really contemplated what the consequences would be if it didn't.

The media had taken a keen interest in John's big plans, with radio, TV and most of the major national newspapers covering the story. The Sunday Independent had gone further than most with its five magazine pages and John on the cover with what was now an apt headline 'What Planet Is He On?' The milliner who was designing the hats for the stewardesses would now be told they would not be needed and so would the designer of the huge Otway World Tour decal that was to cover the fuselage of John's jet airliner. The hugely influential mayor of Ningbo in China would have to cancel the civic reception, with his new International airport now not seeing the *OT-AIR* jet land and its people not seeing the Otway chest, clothed or otherwise. The President of Tahiti, who had been intrigued by his country's inclusion on this British pop star's world tour, would not now get to meet the band.

The John Otway World Tour of 2006 was not a disaster, but it was a failure. In order to be successful it would have needed to be a little longer, but now the whole tour could be counted on one line of a T-shirt. It was not a disaster because the one date that John had salvaged from the ruins was a great gig. It got off to a good start as John was arriving at Liverpool Lime Street Station, when Radio 2 wished the Otway band and fans well on their travels... unaware that the tour now both started and ended in the place where The Beatles started and carried on.

And when he arrived at the venue, nearly everyone who would have been on the jet had turned up. Rainbow George, who had put in his remaining fortune was there, as was Mark Kempster, Chris The Jet and the two couples who had arranged to get married on the trip. Some of the fans were leaving shortly afterwards having spent their refunds on a two-week trip to South America or Australia to see the cancelled posters at the Sydney Opera House. "We just decided to get a new kitchen," another couple told John, even though they, like a great many people in that Liverpool venue, had had their injections for tropical diseases.

Surprisingly the gig was a sell out and the audience was in what could almost be described as a celebratory mood. There was a great deal of sympathy towards the star of the show, even when he started the evening with a new version of John Lennon's *Imagine*.

Imagine there's no World Tour
I wonder if you can.

And Glen Tilbrook, the special guest on this leg of the tour/ gig, marked the occasion by starting his set with *Leaving on a Jet Plane*.

In some way, the fans were getting the Otway they loved back. Didn't they originally make him a star after he made the impossible leap onto an amplifier only to land painfully upon his testicles? And now he had attempted an even more impossible leap only to land painfully from a much greater height.

At the end of the night, after the band's three encores, the impoverished star of the show was looking the best he had for weeks and went to pay Glenn Tilbrook his gig money.

"Just give me the train fare," the successful star said to the failed one. "You need that more than I do."

Which was probably true, as it kept Otway afloat the following week as he started to get his career back together.

A little while later Otway was approached by the major record company Sanctuary. John had not been approached by a major record company for decades. "We want to put out an album," they said. "We can pay a good advance on sales and we even have a good title for it: *John Otway – Patron Saint Of Losers*."

APPENDIX

Cor Baby, That's Really Me rejuvenated my career and gave me many fans I would not otherwise have had – those who did not like the sound of my singing, but found the story of my unsuccessful career very funny. Not to spoil a winning formula I have continued to write my life story in the third person.

I was told that quite a bit of what I had composed did not help the narrative flow – some of this was corrected by the addition or subtraction of various punctuation marks, but other large swathes of text had to be removed. However, I have been allowed to place them in the following appendix. As a mark of respect to any readers who dip into this collection of bits and pieces, Nick has had a quick glance at the writing and the spelling and John Haxby has kindly added a few pictures to make it more interesting.

APPENDIX

SHURE MICROPHONES

One costly area of John's life was his microphone bill, which could on occasion account for 25% of his income. John had discovered a remarkable quality of the Shure SM58 microphone, it was incredibly robust: he had tried swinging them around 'Roger Daltrey style' and they still worked; he dropped them on the stage and banged them together and his voice would sound just as 'melodic' as it had before; he batted them across the stage with the back of his Gibson SG Junior guitar and the SG Junior suffered the most.

At the time there was a fashionable toy called 'Clackers', two balls on strings which you could repeatedly bounce together above and below your hand, a feat that John achieved with two microphones with no noticeable adverse affect on sound quality. One memorable October gig, John and Willy had a seasonal game of conkers with two of these hardy mics, a game which ended not because one of the microphones won, but because Willy's knuckles were swelling due to Otway's occasional misses.

Eventually though after a long rally, a few aces or a good conkering, the round grille at the top of the microphone would become so distorted that either it would hit the internal capsule and break it, or the grille would have very sharp edges on the top. When this happened Otway did not like to do the song *Headbutts*, because it involved banging his head against precisely this part of the microphone.

Peter Bullick, mindful of John's desire to be more thrifty, thought correctly that a spot of sponsorship on the microphone front would be a big help, so he contacted HW International, the distributors of SM58 microphones. Andy Wood was their man in charge of sponsorship and Peter persuaded him to come to a gig.

"I knew they were strong, but because people tend to look after microphones and put them away carefully in foam rubber boxes, you never knew what they could put up with. I always told people that if you bought one of these it would last you a lifetime. I mean most people wouldn't even blow into a microphone because it wasn't good for them," said Andy. "John told me that he had tried a few other makes, but they didn't manage to last a single song in his show. I decided that it was a pretty good advertisement for our product, so we did a deal and supplied him with them. Both John and Peter were fun too and we became good friends."

However, this new friendship was about to be put to the test. Shure Microphones were about to bring their new Beta 58 microphone to the market, and HW International were having a big press launch at the legendary Ronnie Scott's club in the heart of London's West End. It was a prestigious occasion, with the music press, the trade magazines for the music industry, buyers from the UK music shops and studios all there along with a good sprinkling of stars. Andy knew that Otway was both entertaining and great at showing how strong Shure microphones were and invited him to perform.

Roger Daltry appeared first and through one of the first Beta 58s to arrive in the UK told the assorted throng about how he had always used Shure microphones. Then Kenny Ball and his Jazzmen played the first music that an audience in this country had heard using this brand new microphone. Otway was the climax. He sang the song *Middle of Winter*, which has a verse that goes:

Who's the boyfriend what's he like,
His car's outside your house all night.
And I don't know what's happening,
And it makes me feel like hitting him!

At which point, for dramatic effect, John would thwack the microphone as hard as he could across the mic stand. On this occasion the thwack resulted in the brand new Beta 58 splitting into two halves. The top half, the bit with the grille that you sing into, went flying into the audience – the music press, all the trade magazines for the music industry, buyers from the UK music shops and studios as well as a good sprinkling of stars. The bottom half, which looked like a grey metallic tube with two bare wires sticking out of the top, remained in John's left hand. He was confused. This had never happened with a Shure microphone before. He stopped and stared at it, doing what one is supposed to do when promoting a product by making the microphone the focus of attention. Sadly for HW International, it was only half the product that the prestigious audience was paying attention to.

"It must be a duff one," John heard someone say, as the half microphone in his hand was replaced by one of the few remaining Betas in the country. "Try this one."

And I don't know what's happening,
And it makes me feel like hitting him!

The audience cracked up as Otway was left holding another half a Beta. Unbelievably, another two of these microphones were sacrificed at their UK launch.

"I've never been to a product launch like that," says a veteran of thousands of these types of affairs. "You know you just go for the free drink and someone gets up and talks for ages about how fab their new thing is. Having someone breaking it up in front of you is quite unusual."

You would have thought that this would be the end of our star's relationship with the Shure brand but if you did, you would have thought wrong. Incredibly, Andy Wood explained to Shure that their sponsored artistes had complained that the new Beta 58s were not as robust as the old SM58s. To the great credit of the Shure microphone company, they re-tooled the machinery used to make these microphones at the cost of over a million pounds. It's another example of Otway costing the industry dear. But it does mean that if you buy one of these microphones for the purposes of contact sports or conkers instead of singing, it will do the job.

OTOPOLY – AN INTERACTIVE GAME

Otopoloy was an otnews.net interactive game, in which the player got to play the part of John Otway attempting to have a Top 40 (and preferably a No.1) hit. All they had to do was try to keep the coffers full (in order to pay for the pressing of the CDs), whilst keeping their popularity up and their publicity positive. The game started on Otway's 49th birthday, and came with the warning. "Please remember that this is just a game. Success in Otopoly does not, in any way, indicate that you should actually try to become a record company impresario."

This was just as well because 7,066 games of Otopoly were played and only 332 games resulted in a top 10 single. The total number of virtual CDs sold over all the games of Otopoly was 38,274,397. That figure sounds pretty good, until you realise that the total amount of money earned in the game was –£469,548,873 (yes, MINUS £469 million!)

At one point a bug was introduced into the game that allowed people to cheat when betting on the outcome of the events in the game. There was code in place to prevent them betting too much, but some enterprising players discovered that if they bet a large negative amount, and deliberately lost, they would "lose" that negative amount from their bank account – in other words they would gain huge amounts of money. This led to some incredibly high scores one month and a number of games were forfeited.

For the record:
– The highest score overall was earned by 'SteveBob' with a #1 single, sales of 323,367 CDs, but owing £15,124 to the bank.
– The lowest score overall was earned by "Insect" who managed a flop with no CD sales, and debts of £3,376,072

And for all of you who never got the chance to play the game, here's a taste of what it was like, with the three possible outcomes if you happened to land on an 'Ingmire Hall' event:

1) It is the weekend of the Ingmire Hall event. Everybody seems to be enjoying themselves, and today's events have proven to be very popular. You even manage to get a little interest from the localpress.

2) It is the weekend of the Ingmire Hall event. Unfortunately a discussion between some of the attendees, about whether or not 'Parma Violets' taste better when eaten north of Watford, has turned sour. Fists and furniture fly freely. The mini-riot spoils an otherwise great weekend, and although the damage is paid for by the wrong-doers, your reputation suffers a blow when the local press get hold of the story.

3) It is the weekend of the Ingmire Hall event. As you settle down to bed for the night, you are visited by the ghost of one of your ancestors. At first you assume it to be a dream, brought about by bedding down before your chicken kiev has been fully digested. But the apparition persists. For a few minutes you convince yourself that it is due to inhaling a toxic combination

of chemicals from Richard's haircare products. But yet again the phantom beckons you. You decide to follow the spirit guide as he leads you to the main hall at Ingmire. He extends a bony finger towards a slightly miscoloured brick in the surround of the fireplace, then passes directly through the chimney breast as though it wasn't there.

With trepidation you begin to examine the brick. Your hands trace its outline, as you half expect it to recede beneath them and expose a hidden chamber. But no matter how hard you press against it, the stone refuses to move. In a final act of desperation you lean against it with your full weight. Both hands are pressed against it, and your feet are slightly spread, for stability. You lean into it with all your might, head bowed in order to arch your back for the maximum transfer of effort into the wall.

It is whilst you are in this position that you open your eyes, looking down at your feet, and notice two slightly discoloured paving slabs set into the floor, and partially obscured by a fine rug. You shuffle your feet forwards, one onto each slab, and in doing so hear a barely perceptible click from the wall. You press against the discoloured brick once more, and find that it moves easily inwards, releasing a mechanism which slides away the rear wall of the fireplace to reveal a hidden chamber within.

In the chamber you find the Otway family fortune. Plates of gold, statues of marble, and the finest pearls and rubies from the Empire lay tumbling from vast treasure chests. Lost masterpieces lines the walls. Jewellery and ceremonial weapons lay scattered across the floor.

Your discovery makes the national press, doing wonders for your publicity. You are also given a share of the treasure trove, amounting to a cool £170,000 for the campaign fund.

TOURING

The story of this book covers a period in which John Otway played around 2,500 shows. Jon Padget calculated that just during his stint as a roadie he drove about 450,000 miles so Otway must have done over a million between pages (1) and (181) of this book.

The miles might have all seemed the same, but the shows themselves came in all shapes and sizes. John would refer to himself as a "jobbing gigger" and would happily do a solo birthday party in a living room one day, and a festival with the band the next. Occasionally though, this "gigs of all sorts" would change into a run of similar sized venues and sensible routing around the country. This happened when Otway got booked on

to someone else's tour and went on the road with one of Rock and Roll's successes. Maybe the reason that these tours do not fill the pages of this book proper is because they were like the '60s (if you could remember them you weren't there).

What they did, and what John really enjoyed about them, was to give him a whole new audience to play to – people who would never otherwise have come to see his show. In 1989 Fish invited John and his guitarist Ronnie to do his UK tour, then in 1995, John and Richard played the Alexei Sayle tour, a wonderful trip around the larger theatres with nights in the better hotels in between.

By far the most substantial of the tours though were the Two *Naughty Rhythms* Tours and *The Mad Bad and Dangerous* Tour. The Hamsters and Dr Feelgood were putting a package together, and both groups felt that the show John and Richard Holgarth were doing would work well in a compere role gluing the show together. The Hamsters were legendary for the size of their mailing list and the phenomenal administration machine with which they promoted themselves. They were one of the few acts that worked consistently much harder than Otway: they had already overtaken the 2,000 gig mark and had been doing considerably more than the 120 or so per year that John was doing. By putting together a good package, they hoped to fill the more desirable theatres and civic centres and away from the pub circuit. The final line-up would be The Hamsters, Dr Feelgood, Eddie and The Hot Rods and John Otway.

Both Otway and Holgarth loved the idea. Not only were they both confident that this idea would work but it was also a good

long tour, which once started would take them up and down the country several times and keep going until Christmas. As they would be playing to around 500 people a night, approximately 40,000 people would get to see Otway live in action, most of them for the first time.

"We're going to start the evening off and do bits throughout the night because I've been told by the other bands that I'm best in small doses," John told the audience. And between the fine music of the other acts Otway would be hitting himself as the human drum kit, ripping his shirt open, waving his arms at the theremin and leaping off ladders and amusing the new audience as he had been entertaining his old one for years.

Murray, the band's guitarist, came to see the show and was most shocked by the finale and what he called later Otway's "shameless exploitation'. "I couldn't believe they'd let him get away with it. The Hamsters had just played really well and done this perfectly executed set and they let Otway on stage."

It had started out as quite an innocuous idea, to make the evening a complete *Naughty Rhythms* show, as opposed to four acts doing separate bits. All the performers would be up on stage for a final number, *Born To Be Wild*. John performed the song by taking its title literally. He tore round the stage grabbing all the microphones and swinging them around in such a manner that they ended up in a huge tangled knot causing complete chaos – turning the stage from a scene of orderly rock and roll to one of complete devastation in precisely two minutes forty-seven seconds. This outrageous behaviour became a popular ending to the show with the audience, so the other bands generously allowed him to carry on.

The following year Dr Feelgood teamed up with the Kursaal Flyers and American band Canned Heat for another *Naughty Rhythms* tour. Although suffering numbers-wise without the Hamsters mailing power, it still played to large audiences, as it came at the beginning of The Hit Campaign and was fortunate timing for Otway: only those who stayed in the bar for the whole of the evening did not hear the news that Otway would soon have two Hits. They would have seen or read the news though, as a significant number of the thousands of hit flyers were generously distributed around each venue.

In 2005 The Hamsters teamed up with Wilko Johnson for a similar tour called *The Mad, Bad and Dangerous*

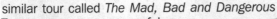

Tour – a very, very successful tour compared to the one that was to come because only those who stayed in the bar for the whole of the evening did not hear the news that Otway would soon be flying around the world in the OT-AIR jet. They would have seen or read the news though, as a significant number of the thousands of OT-AIR flyers were generously distributed around each venue.

CHERYL, A ROCK OPERA

Attila the Stockbroker had supported John at the Marquee Club in London. Both their careers owed much to the punk movement of the late 1970s: John's because punk made the combination of rudimentary guitar skills and being shocking fashionable, and Attila because certain acts, particularly The Clash, had an overtly socialist stance.

Attila's political views were strong and left wing, honed by many hours of fierce argument, even the occasional physical battle with the National Front, and were informed by years of study and travel to places like Albania and East Germany.

"Attila phoned me," recalls John. "He was great, he had a column in The Guardian and wanted to put in a bit about the book. During the conversation the subject came round to the Edinburgh Festival, which both of us had done regularly. I hadn't got a venue that year so Attila offered to share his slot with me and suggested meeting up to work out the feasibility of doing a joint show."

It turned out to be an interesting meeting for both of them.

"I hadn't really thought much about politics, so I was quite fascinated by Attila," says John. "Shortly after we met I remember asking Attila what exactly was wrong with Margaret Thatcher. I got this strange puzzled look which went on for quite a while, which, I believe now, was Mr Stockbroker waiting for the punch-line of a joke. This was followed by a smile at the sudden unexpected realisation that I really did not know exactly what was wrong with Margaret Thatcher.

"He was quite amazing: as soon as he realised it was a serious question he composed himself and launched into this wonderful speech that covered the past and current polices of the current Prime Minister and the subsequent social and economic effects of these policies. It was eloquent, funny and completely off the cuff. I was pretty impressed. 'Well he knows his stuff,' I remember thinking."

Their first Edinburgh Festival together proved to be a success and both the artistes were pleased with the three-week run. They decided to tour their *Headbutts and Halibuts* show, and come back the following year with a completely new and original show.

Cheryl's Going Home had been in John's show since his first whole gig back in his schooldays. The song was written by Bob Lind and was the B-side to his hit single *Elusive Butterfly*; it was one of the first records John's sister Margaret had bought and one of the first songs John had learnt to play on guitar.

The song originally was three verses long, but John had added a middle section, half worked out, half ad-libbed, that he used as a vehicle for the most theatrical part of his show – it was during this song that Otway had leapt astride Willy's amplifier on *The Old Grey Whistle Test*. When John was on form it could last as long as ten minutes. What John was about to suggest to Attila for the next Edinburgh show was quite radical. "Let's make it last an hour."

Yes, Otway's suggestion for Attila and Otway's next Edinburgh show was a performance of just one song.

"It doesn't have to be verse, chorus, verse, chorus it can have different tunes and the tempo can change, but it's just one long piece that lasts the whole of the show. We could do the whole *Cheryl* story, not just when she leaves, but the complete picture. An epic, like a musical *Doctor Zhivago*."

Otway suggested that he would go and write the first part of the song, then pass it on to Attila who would write the next bit and then they would pass it backwards and forwards until they had the complete story. Attila was a prolific writer whose output positively dwarfed the number of songs John wrote, but his poems and songs were observational – he had not written, or felt a great need to write about, matters of the heart. You can only guess what he thought when John presented him with his first piece:

Out of everyone I've ever met I chose her
The one with the deepest eyes and the golden hair
Someone who could cheer you up the moment you felt sad
Someone to whom the more you gave
You felt the more you had

But that ignores the passion and the physical desire
The way that two souls become one great ball of fire
A rhythmical inferno like a new Paul Simon song
Where the sweetest of melodies blend with an African drum
And we made love

"There you go Attila, your turn."

I know this Cheryl – wretched spawn of Hell,
And I know that I must bring myself to tell
this sad, deluded fool her awful story
although 'tis squalid, fetid, hideous and gory –

She was an addict too – cocaine and crack,
Methadone, mandrax, acid, glue and smack –
She took them all, and then came back for more
As she had done for many years before she met this fool
But he had no idea, though to a brain dead sloth,
the truth was clear.
When asked about her varied drug collection
She told him that she had an ear infection,
Though ear infections of which I've heard speak
Don't cost around a thousand pounds a week to medicate

John was not going to give up Cheryl that easily and when
his turn came to write again he vigorously defended the love
of his song.

I bet you've never suffered,
or had to have regular injections
To try and keep the pain at bay
from endless ear infections

Throughout the writing of that song, Attila believed that there
would come a point when John must realise that Cheryl was
not worth it and let her go, and John believed that if you love
someone then you stick with them through thick and thin. The
battle would continue, and after Attila's turns Otway would have
to defend Cheryl as she became a prostitute, a time-share flat
seller and a Satanist vivisectionist speech writer for Kenneth
Clarke the Conservative Cabinet minister.

The piece captured the essence of the two people: Attila the
realist who believes in the reasoning and the persuasiveness of
analytical thought, and John with complete trust in the strong
passionate feelings that transcend all logic. It was an epic
battle between the heads and hearts of the audience.

They both knew that "a one-song show" was not going to
be the best way to sell their new work, so they came up with
Cheryl, A Rock Opera which they felt would work better, as
there were successful precedents for these sort of things, like

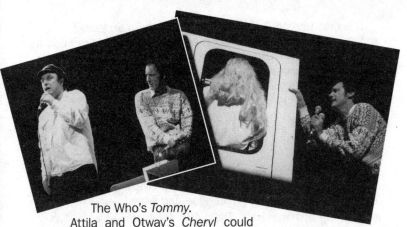

The Who's *Tommy*.

Attila and Otway's *Cheryl* could not really be described as a long song or a rock opera, it was more like a montage of music and verse – Otway's love songs and Attila's poetry (a narrative in rhyming couplets inspired by writers like Hilaire Belloc).

As a live performance piece it had started to come together. The difficult problem of how Cheryl, the central character, was going to appear on stage was solved by John's considerable theatrical experience.

There comes a point in the opera where Cheryl is on a train about to leave for Slough, whilst Otway stands on the platform singing a passionate plea begging her to stay. "One of the things to remember with theatre," says Otway, "is that you don't actually need a whole train and platform to create the illusion. We got around it by making a train door that Attila could strap on his back, and to give the impression that Cheryl was on the train he wore a blonde wig that flowed out of the train door window. He could shuffle on and off the stage sideways, and it was very effective as long as he never faced the audience."

The preview show two weeks before Edinburgh went very well and the sideways-walking Attila wearing the train door got all the laughs Otway insisted it would.

"We ought to record it and put it out as a CD," suggested John. "As we're up in Edinburgh for three weeks why don't we book a studio and record it during the day, and perform it in the evening?" *Cheryl* might have been amazing to watch, but Attila was fully aware that this would not necessarily work on CD. If they were going to record an hour-long song (a good three times longer than epics by bands like Yes) they were going to need someone with a great deal more musical and production skills than he and John had between them, so they took Richard Holgarth with them to play, produce and arrange the recording.

John sat next to Richard Holgarth on the train from London to Edinburgh and played through what Attila and he had worked out together. And Richard Holgarth confirmed Attila's suspicions that this would not work on CD. Yet on that train journey Richard Holgarth devised a creative technique that would serve them brilliantly over many years – he discovered that there were actually some nice melodic ideas disguised by the way John would try and force them to fit over the few chords he was confident playing. As Holgarth says, "I just got him to sing the songs without an instrument and the immediate improvement was quite remarkable."

John singing new songs at Richard Holgarth became a feature of what was to become a long partnership. "If I sang something at him," says John, "he only needed a sniff of a melody and he could weave these wonderful chord structures around it. Sometimes he could elevate a very rudimentary idea into a song ridiculously quickly. I remember by the end of that train journey being really excited about what we were going to do, both the performing and the recording."

What Richard Holgarth achieved over those three weeks in Edinburgh was quite remarkable. These days with digital recording it would be relatively easy to put together an hour-long piece of music, but back then with the old analogue tape it was very difficult, especially as Otway had demanded that there should be no gaps. "Otherwise people might think that it is more than one song and that would spoil it." John had told him.

However, when they came to master the CD, Maurice Bacon, who was releasing it, insisted that the CD should have 'chapters', 'tracks' or 'movements' so that you could access different parts of the "one song" when it was played. So John, Attila and Richard had to divide the piece into suitable sized chunks – some more suitable than others.

Anyone who knows Attila will know that he is a man of many words and the opera finishes with one of them. The last 'track' on *Cheryl, A Rock Opera* is called *The Last Word* – it is a very short track, with a solo Attila simply saying the word "goat".

"We found the CD on a pub juke-box once," says Otway, "and we took turns in putting that track on. It was really funny, because every so often between the songs the juke-box would stop and say 'goat'… we spent a fortune on it that night.

PREMATURE ADULATION

After Gig 2001, Otway and Cotton were keen to keep the star's career moving onward and upward. One obvious way was if the album John and Richard Holgarth were working on had the

same impact on record sales that Gig 2000 had on ticket sales. It had been nearly a decade since the last real John Otway album of original material and John was determined that this one should be (and be seen to be) a package of completely new work.

"I think that both of us saw it as an opportunity," says John, "and I put renewed effort into getting the material together." Whilst Richard could put the arrangements and musical production together efficiently and quickly, John was agonisingly slow with his bit, sometimes taking an age over a couple of lines.

"One of the problems I faced was that the subject matter I could write about had changed so much. A lot of my previous material was concerned with the angst and joy of being in and out of love. These things were not relevant now and inspiration had to be found elsewhere. I had grown up and I felt more maturity was expected in my work."

"*Poetry and Jazz* was the first song that we had for that album," says John." I had the first verse written twenty years earlier and it had haunted me ever since. I probably put more time into writing that then any other song. I still think it's the best thing I've ever written, and it turns out that it's quite a few of the fans' favourite too."

Inspiration came from the unlikeliest of places. Amy had now started school, and standing outside the school gates John was just another dad.

He would smile and wave benignly at the other mums and dads like a good rock star, but not all of them would smile and wave back like good fans. In fact, some of them avoided this scruffy, awkward bloke, who would often sport a scab in the middle of his forehead. One of the mums really got to our star. "I'd say 'Good morning', and she'd blatantly ignore me. We'd all have to wait outside the school gates together, but she just seemed to pretend I wasn't there."

On the way to a gig at Coventry Rugby Club, it occurred to Otway that one solution could be to write a song, and in the length of time it takes an express to travel from Milton Keynes Central to Coventry, he had written the verses, starting with:

The eyes in her head are angled in a way
She can look down her nose at people like me

And the chorus:

> I just want to yell 'Yah Boo Sucks'
> And wave my willy in the air.
> And all my intelligent, sensible friends say
> 'It's you that's got the problem, not her.'

As soon as he arrived at the gig, John showed Richard Holgarth what he had written, and Holgarth, delighted to have a new set of words to work on, said "I've got something that'll go with that". Which he had, and which worked, and the song was finished before they went on stage.

Even though many thousands of people have enjoyed and applauded the song *Willy in the Air*, the mum it was written about never knew she was responsible for the enjoyment of so many, and continued to ignore our star – and this perceived impoliteness now amused rather than bothered him.

This more mature Otway-writing produced some gems, aided greatly by Richard Holgarth as songs like *God's Camera* avoided the trap of sentimentality by the exciting guitar parts and the arrangements and structures he provided. When John had most of the lyrics for a song, he would often call Holgarth at the studio, so that Richard could record John's idea as he sang it over the phone and then work on the backing track without being distracted. Much later when the track was almost complete, Otway would pop into the studio on the way to a gig and add the main vocal.

Slowly but slowly (it took two and a half years) the brand new Otway album was coming together, and plans made for its release.

Otway wanted to call it either *The Saddest Sound Since The Blues* or *The Photograph Album* after the most romantic ballad on it, and it took some persuasion to make him think of something else. The eventual title came from Adam Batterbee. The band had all walked on stage without their star and were ready to start, and as John struggled towards them the audience started to applaud the band without him. "Premature Adulation" quipped Adam.

"As soon as he said it, I knew that should be the title." said John. And all those who were dreading the wimpy 'Photograph Album' title, hastily and unanimously agreed.

By January 1995, the album was at last ready for launch, with a *Premature Adulation* tour, Astoria gig, and newspaper. So why isn't *Premature Adulation* one of the memorable albums of 1995? There were several reasons.

Firstly, the main promotional weapon for a hit album is the single taken from it, and there wasn't one and John was wary about losing money in the same way as on the last 17 singles he had released.

Secondly, to squeeze into the bottom end of the album charts, which was maybe just possible considering John's fan base, he would have needed them all to buy the album through the shops on the week of release. However, each record sold through the shops would have made him two quid, whereas for every one he sold at the Astoria launch gig he would make a tenner. With the numbers expected at the gig, John reckoned he could possibly recoup the recording costs and be on the way to making a profit. Cotton could only watch as the first chance he had to get his label in the charts disappeared.

Finally, there was the newspaper. John's idea was to have a page of album reviews, but where most music papers review a number of albums, this music paper would have writers and other stars reviewing one album. His. But there was a fatal flaw in John's plan: when the reviews came back and were printed in the paper, not all of them were as glowing as John expected.

Chas de Whalley had written for Sounds magazine in the 1970s, and had given John's most popular first album a bit of a slating when it came out.

"What we'll do is print that review of the first album, and get him to do something on Premature Adulation to print underneath it. From that, people will be able to see just how good the album is and how much I've improved." said John.

"Bloody stupid idea that was." said Cotton. "And John didn't want to offend anyone by editing their reviews."

Premature Adulation by **Chas de Whalle**y

So here we are again. Eighteen years on with a new album which has taken nearly a decade to write. And which prompts the same old question. Will THIS be the big one for Otway?

I'm not sure I'm the right person to ask. I got it wrong the first time after all. Despite a slagging in the pages of Sounds, Otway's debut disc coughed up a top 30 hit, *Really Free*, one of the few tracks I didn't single out for special attention.

So what do I know?

Otway has been trading off *Really Free* (and *Beware Of The Flowers* and *Cheryl's Coming Home*) ever since. On stage, screen and in print, he has courageously carved himself a career of mythical proportions as the wild man of pop who has consistently forced the envelope of failure into evermore ridiculous shapes. As a result Otway has become what he always threatened to be. The unrepentant romantic revelling in the fact that he will be forever misunderstood. Which is probably why we love him so much. There can be no other reason!

So *Premature Adulation* offers a set of semi-autobiographical snapshots, by turns wacky and winsome, from the Otway scrapbook. As far as the charts are concerned, they're probably destined for the scrap heap too. Put bluntly, Otway has not developed that much as a songwriter. Or rather he hasn't moved with the times and remains locked in a time-warp.

Ballads like *Photograph* and *Typewriter* still quiver with sensibility and sensitivity. Not to mention sentimentality. But as a composer of potential standards Otway fails to make the grade as spectacularly as ever.

Which means there are no classics here. No *My Way* or *Send In The Clowns*. But then again, Otway is no Sinatra. And no Judy Collins either. He's the secret lemonade drinker. Born to lose. Lagging so far behind the rest of the field there's always the chance he could just be leading them into the next bend and determined to give them a real run for their money!

The 70s cast the longest shadow over *Premature Adulation*. But by the 70s, I don't mean Abba, Gary Glitter or David Bowie. It's names like Little Feat, and Bob Dylan's *Blood On The Tracks* band which are most immediately conjured up by many of the structures and the arrangements here. The immediately post-hippy stuff that nobody listens to any more. And the fact that songs like *We Know What She's Doing* and *Nothing At All* have been liberally smeared with suitably sloppy powerpop guitar riffs comes as further proof that, like his boss, Otway's current lead guitarist and producer Richard Holgarth is not ashamed to let his pub rock roots show either.

In short, this is an album that could do with a good haircut, a clip round the ear and a spell in the army, as Nick Lowe once said of The Damned. And we should rejoice that there are still idiots like Otway around who are prepared to make them.

For *Premature Adulation* boasts moments of breathtaking tragicomic genius. Or should that be moments of breathless jeanlessness as Otway strives to raise his voice above the level of the band on the truly outrageous *Willy (In The Air)*.

As in 'Wave My Willy' not Wild Willy Barrett.

And what will Otway's staunchly supportive army of fans make of that? Much the same as they'll make of *Please Don't Read My Poetry*, I suspect. They'll love it. This raucous and rocking re-creation of what ought to be an Otway showstopper live (and probably is – which tells you when I saw him play last!) is nothing short of a riot of pathos. And then there's *Entertainment (Not)* too, which perfectly evokes every bad pub or festival gig there's ever been. Sung by the man who has probably played more of them than anyone else alive!

But the real heart-stopper here is undoubtedly *The Saddest Sound Since the Blues*. Otway says he was considering *Saddest Sound...* as a possible title for *Premature Adulation*. but then decided otherwise. Perhaps it was for the best because the song, a cautionary tale about a small-town wannabe pop star who blows his one bite at the big time, is about as close to the bone as you can get.

Whether he's singing about himself or a fictionalised character is neither here nor there. As Otway scrapes away at the bottom of the barrel of a music business which deals in dreams but pays dividends in disappointment and depression, he sings for everybody who ever wanted to be on *Top Of The Pops* but failed miserably.

Just get this lyric:
Then he made this crap record which was totally uninspired
Called the saddest sound since the blues.
It was full of aahs and oohs and doo bee doo bee doos
The saddest sound since the blues.

You have to hear it on CD, complete with a full brass section, to catch its true brilliance. *The Saddest Sound Since The Blues* is so awful, it's awesome.

But then that's John Otway for you.

Just the way we like him. Who could ask for more?

THE ABBEY ROAD CHOIR

Crediting all those who featured on the B-side of The Hit, helped sell many copies of the single and as Otway has often stated in his stage introduction to *House Of The Rising Sun*, "this is what made the difference between Top Ten and Top Twenty." It's not going to do any harm to the sales of this book, so for the sake of history and in the cause of getting a best seller:

John Otway *vocals*, Richard Holgarth *guitar*, Murray Torkildsen *guitar*, Seymour *bass*, Adam Batterbee *drums*, Ann Abineri *backing vocals*, Marcus Affleck, Dyan Ainslie, Graham Aldred, Lynda Aldred, Tosh Allard, Dave Allen, Rosemarie Allen, Emilie Allen, Stuart Allen, Mark Allen, Paul "Alleycat" Alleyway, Zo-Bo Alleyway, Dave Allott, Betty Allott, Barry Amos, Patsy Andrews, Beverly Angell, Anne-Marie, Frank Anselmo, Mark Anstice, Ruth Appleton, Jane Armstrong, Eddie Armstrong, Phil Arnold, Ash, Jess Ashman, Peter Ashman, Jack Ashworth, Edna Ashworth, Joy Atkinson, Joey Atkinson, Sally Austen, Lee Austen, Steve Austin, Brenda Austin, Chris Austin, Maurice Bacon, Sally Baggett, Ian Baggett, Ben Baggett, Paul Bailey, Steven Bailey, Lesley Bailey, Rob 'Rock Pig' Baird, Lorraine Baker, Jan Baker, Dave Banbury, Derek Barclay, Michael Barclay, Simon Barfoot, Derek Barker, Steve Barker, Tracy Barker, Peter Barrett, Roger Barrett, Catherine Barrett, Steven Barrett, John Barrett, Karen Barrett, Ron Bartlett, Pete Bartlett, Annettte Bartlett, Robert Bassett, Phil Bateley, Sherrilyn Bateman, Jacqui Bateson, Tom Baxter, Jeannette Baxter, Peter Beasley, Joe Beasley, Kay Beckwith, Frank Bell, Karen Bell, Andy Bennett, Andy "Benno" Bennett, Deirdre Bennett, Louise Bennett, Gary Bennett, Gaynor Bennett, Simon Benoy, Trevor Berry, Tracy Bickerdike, David Bikerdike, Helen Blakey, Michael Blakey, Bert "Grim Reaper" Blandamer, Markus Blease, Mike "The Dog" Bleathman, Claire Blenkiron, Simon Blows, Russ Blurton, Gary Bocking, Katrina Boffey, Steve Boismaison, Pete Bonner, Phil Borrett, John Borrett, Glenn Borrett, Martin Borrill, Julie Botham, Mark Botham, Martyn Bott, Henry Bradley, Michael Bradshaw, Alan Brand, Debbie Brannan, Nick Breakspear, Tim Bridgstock, Helen Brier, Ian Broome, Michael Brown, Marilyn Brown, Tony Brown, Peter Brown, Adrian Brownlee, Roger Bruce, Debra Bruce, Daniel Bruce, Chloe Bruce, Nick Brush, Michael Bryant-Mole, Karen Bryant-Mole, Chris Bryson, Edna Bucket Experience, Frazer Budd Budd, John Bugler, Anne Bugler, Martyn Bullock, Alison Burns, Robin Burrows-Ellis, Janet Burrows-Ellis, Coralie Burrows-Ellis, Tom Busby, Baby Bush, Gary Buss, Barry Butcher, Derek Buster

Butcher, Louise C, Peter Campbell, Graham "Jock" Campbell, Rob Carey, Steve Carter, Sandy Casey, Luke "Hippy" Cater, Stuart "Skunkfoot" Cater, CatCeri, Ben Causley, Janet Cave, Caroline Channing, Sophie Chapman, John Chapman, Nigel Chater, Bev Chester, Andy Chivers, Beau Chivers, Martin Choularton, Nicola Choularton, Rich Claphan, Richard Clark, Carl Anthony Clarke, Gina Clarke, Paul Clerehugh, Elizabeth Clough, Andy Clyde, Robert Cogger, Steve Coglan, Martin Colclough, Nia Colclough, Tim Coles, Roslyn Collett, Nigel Collins, Heather Collins, Sue Connell, Brian Conway-Smith, Jaqui Conway-Smith, Martin "Skunk" Cook, Alan Cook, Chris Cook, Sam Cook, Steve Cooke, Bernadette Cool, Mike Cooney, Richard Cotton, Chris Cowley, Steve Cox, Paul Cox, Peter Cox, Jane Cox and Bump, Carole Craggs, Peter Craggs, Dave Craig, Nick Creasy, John Cripps, Debbie Cripps, Ellie Cripps, Dave Crouch, Crspy, Crusher, Pat Culley, Jess Cully, Tony Cunliffe, Peter Curran, Rick Cwiok, Peter D'Sena, Kevin Dacey, Steve Dando, Stef Dando, Janie Darley, Tony Darley, Robert Davidson, Ann Davies, Ellen Davies, Lee Davies, Martin Davies, Tricia Davies, Geoff Dawson, Paul Day, Fiona Day, Katie Day, Larry Day, James Day, Victoria Delahaye, Geoff (G4E) Delahaye, Woody Delilegg, Paul Dickenson, Gavin Dickie, Julie Dillon, Dave Dingle, Dixie, Chris Dobbs, Phil Doleman, Barry Donnithorne, Dominic Donoghue, Margaret Doran, Terry Doran, Pipa Doubtfire, Phil Doubtfire, Dougal, Mike Doyle, Martyn Drake, Mark Drury, David Duffett, Maeve Dunne, Keith Dunstone, Helen Dunstone, E, James Edge, Julie Ann Edmond, Steve Eggs, Stuart Ellis, Margaret Ellis, Linda "Babe" Ellis, Ian "Flats and Sharps" Ellis, Richard Ellis, Andy Elwell, Mark Embleton, Simon Emms, Jackie Errington, Don Euripides, Ben Evans, Robin Evans, Christopher Evans, Mike "Painterman" Evans, Sue Evans, Avril J. Evitts, Steve Evitts, Princess Apple Blossom Fairy Cake, Helen Farmer, Linda Farrell, Susan Farrelly, Emma Farrow, Festy, Wendy Field, Brian Finlay, GAP fiona, Mog Firth, Bob Fischer, Andy Fisher, Kerry Flaxman, Reg Flaxman, Jimmy Flaxman, Len Fletcher, Linsey Fletcher, Eva Florido, Tony Flower, David Foot, Emma Foot, David Ford, Juan Four, Tony Fowler, Chris France, Isabel France, Charlie France, Jamie France, Bill Francis, John Francis, Simon & Mark – The Franklin Brothers, Keziah Frazer, Bryn Freeman, Perry French, Steve Frost, Peter Fryer, Les Fuller, Stuart Furby, Dave "The Toad" Fussell, Dr Ian J Fussell, Tim Gage, Vinny Gage, Jasper Gammon, Gappy, Katie Garner, Paul Garner, John Garratt, Gill Garratt, Stewart Garrish, Jan Garrish, Claire Gaskin, Fishburn George, Sam George, Sam George, Guy Gibson, Alexandra Gibson, Henry Giles, Michaela Giles, Fred Gill, Wild Gilly Muller, Paul Girling, Giles Godart-Brown, Phil Goode, Steve Goodson, Nigel Gordon, Darren 'Kid Cock' Goulden, Paul Gray, Roslyn M Gray, Andy Gray, Virginia Gray, Lois Gray, John Green, Billy Green, Joe Green, Zee-Zee "Blouse" Greenman, Andrew Grieve, John Griffiths, Martin Griffiths, Colin Grimley, Grimble Gromble, Mark Grout, Peter Groves, Jean Growney, Ed Growney, G. Martin Gulliver, Drew Hadfield, Trudy Hagon-Torkington, Eddie Hall, Tanya Hall, Ann Hall, Roy Hallam, Debbie Hampshire, Steve "Furburger" Hansen, Jason "Punkrockchimp" Hansen, Keith Harbor, Kay Harbor, Johnny Harbott, Tracy Harding, Jane Harper-Otner, Martin Harris, Jimi "Hamster" Harris, Kevin "Crooner" Harris, Brian Harris, Rob Harris, Georgie Harris, David Harris-Edmond, Michael Harris-Edmond, Sophie Harris-Edmond, Adrian Harrison, Rob Harrison, Melanie Harrison-Dyke, Lee Harvey Osmond, Steve Hatcher, Mark Hatfield, Sarah Hatton, Mark Hawkins, Carolyn Hayes, Steve Hayes, Kevin Hayward, Ben Hayward, Joe Hayward, Michelle Hazell, Chris Hazell, Kieran Heaney, Russell Heath, Dave Heath, Mandy Heath, Chris Heath, Gill Heath, Val Hehir, Ian "Curly" Henderson, Roger Herbert, Ian Hey, Brian Hey, Jan Higgs, Stuart Hill, Phil "Up" Hill, Andy Hilling, Hils, Michael Hilsdon, Chris Hircock, Graham "Rocker" Hirst, Jenny Hobbs, Chris Hodgson, Martin Hoff, Steve "Doc" Hogg, Peter Holden, Jack Holgarth, Jody Holgarth, Kariss Holgarth, Andy Holloway, Mark Hooker, Gary Houghton, Daniel Jack Howard, Kate Elizabeth Anne Howard, Steve Howard, Mary Howard-George, Gary Howchen, Lucy Howchen, Steve Howitt, Phil Howlin, James Huff, Master James Huff, Geraint Hughes, Gareth Hughes, Simon Anthony Hughes, Oliver J Hughes, Julian Hunt, Nick Hunt, Bob Hurds, Simon Ingram, Dr & Mrs Ink, Mr. and Mrs. Jabs, Pat Jackson, Steve Jackson, Andrew James, Joanne James, Sarah James, Abigail James, Tom James, Harvey James, Sam James, Alan Jamieson, Kev Jarman, Mandy Jefferies, Tina Jeffery-Heath, Jeff "Plucker" Jenkins, Birry Jenkins, Helen Jenkins, Jessop John, Angela Johnson, Iain Johnson, Malcolm Johnson, Trudi Johnson, Heavy-Trev Johnson, Lyz Jones, Trevor Jones, Russell Jones, Yasmin Jones, John Jones, Russell Jones, #19 TiM Jones, Alan Joseph, Janet Joseph, Simon "Breeze" Josolyne, Billy Jowett, Neil and Kamila, Kevin Kemp, Jenny Kemp, Paul Kendall, Ben Kendall, George Kendall, Tricia Kendall, Dan Kendall, Jack Kendall, Tricia Kendall, Dan Kendall, Dick Kilburn, Robert Kilburn, Stuart Kinsey, Mark Kinton, "Hamster" Dave Kitteridge, Jeff Knight, Barry Knight, Anna Knight, Tina Knight, Jessie Knight, Timothy Knight, Brent Knoll, Chris "The Original Gomez" Knott, Tim Knott, Derek Kosky, Steve Kramer, Dean Kramer, Kelly Kurtz, Chris Lacey, Trevor Frederick Lailey, Anne Valerie Lailey, Anne Marie Lailey, Julie Lake, Simon Lake, Steve Lake, Big Dom Lake, Dee Lal, Glenn "Plod" Lambert, Helen Lambert, Richard Lamming, Chris Lane, Catherine Lane, Amy Lane, Martin Langford, Greg Lawrence, Karen Lawrence, John Laz, Helen Lear, John Lee, Jo Leete, Paul Leeves, Steve "Lazyhand" Leeves, Janet Leeves, Derek Legg, John Leitch, Tim Lewis, Clare Lewis, Phil Lewis, Mike Lillyman, Loopy Lisa, John Littler, Steve Lloyd, David Long, Nick Long, Lizzie Lowes, Joe Lynch, Rob Lynch, Peter Lynn, Lynne "The Chin", The Mabbs Brothers (Steve & Paul), Stuart Macgregor, Tony Machin, Duncan Macinnes, Grant Mackay, Andrew Maclaren, John Maclaren, Rob Main, Maitland, Tony Mander, Pete Manger, Rosie Manise, Adrian "Buzz" Manise, John K Markham, Vince Marklove, Andy Marshall, Sharon (Wilf) Martin, Andy Martin, Linda Martin, Frank Martin, Kim Martin, Barry "Bazzybaz" Martin, Marvyn The Paranoid Manatee, white Mary Anne, Richard Massey, Masson Massive, Bill Masterson, Paul Mauger, Dave Mayes, Mark Maynard,

Damian McAreavey, Craig McArthur, Ruth McCarthy, Steve McCracken, Paul McCready, Steve McFadden, Jim McGlynn, Martin McGowan, Gill McGregor, Laura McGregor, Paul McNamara, Margaret McNeill, Stuart McNeill, Neil & Janice McP, Andy Meagher, June Meagher, Chris Meddleton, Heather Medley, Kieron Meek, Richard Meek, Paul Mellan, Tim Middleton, Trevor Miles, Simon Miles, Sarah Miles, Andy Miles, Michelle Miller, Robert Miller, Eric Miller, Gordon Mills, Simon "Tudor" Mills, Dave Milner, Xena Minos, Zelda Minos, Rita Mitchell, Kevin Mitchell, Joe W Mitchell, Hilary Mitchell, Roger "A" Mody, Suzannah Mody, Alan Monaghan, Chris Moor, Liz Moor, Brian Morgan, Craig "Wedgie" Morlen, Neil Morris, Janey Moss, Liz Mullender, Nigel "Wise Monkey" Mullender, Richard Mulligan, Sam Mumford, Mup, Matt "Mad Dog" Murphy, Colin Murphy, Kaz Murphy, Christopher Murphy Parks, Fionnuala Murphy Parks, Elanor Murphy Parks, Polly Naylor, Tim Neville, David Newberry, Andy Newell, Dennis Newell, Rob Newell, Gill Newell, Charlie Newell, Stevie Newell, Steve Newport, Richard Noble, Noisy Roy, Ronel Noon, Duncan Noons, Martin Norris, Paul Norris, Lizzie Norris, Paul North, Stewart Nutter, Chris Nuza, Caroline O'Brien, Tim O'Callaghan, David O'Connor, Fiona O'Connor, Caitlin O'Connor, Joseph O'Connor, Meghan O'Connor, Mick & Carol O'Doherty, Martin O'Donoghue, Victoria O'Flanagan, Paul O'Flanangan, Steven O'Malley, Honest Joe O'Neil, Kevin O'Rourke, Derek E Odey, Joe Oksien, Tony Oksien, Ian Oliver, Nick Osborn, Philip D A Osborn, Asti Osborn, Kat Osborne, Jumbo Osbourne, Robert Osmond, Donna Osmond, Andy Otner, Amy Otway, John Padget, Jan Padget, Mark Palmer, Chilli Palmer, Duncan Palmer, Helen Palmer, Hwaju Park, Nick Parker, Sue Parker, Malcolm Parker, Dave "Chutney" Parker, Jenny Parker, Roland "The Rat" Parr, Nicky Parsons, Matthew Parsons, Jimbo Partridge, Luke Partridge, Ami Partridge, Elaine Patterson, Chris Payne, Mary Payne, Andy Payne, Nicola Payton, Alex Pearce, Lucie Pearce, Donald James Pearl, Mark Pegg, Mick Pelc, Mark Pennock, Ian Penny, Laura Penny, Ross Penny, Michael Perkin, Gary Perkin, "Puffin" Pete, Richie Piper, Mike Pitfield, Jane Pitfield, Sophie Plater, Jamie Poole, Ian M Pope, Pervy Rob Porter, Julian Porter, Paul Possee, David Pover, Mr John Presland, Alison Preuss, Gareth Price, Sharon Prince, Neil Pritchard, Nick Pyne, Allan Quinney, Rainy, Elise Ralph, Gordon Ranger, Stefan Rapacz, Steve Rawlinson, Misselaineous Rawlinson, David Rayner, Barbara Rayner, Sheila Redhead, Alistair Reed, Mandy Reeves, Tom Reid, Golly Reid, Ann Revill, C. A. Revill, Veronique Reynolds, Doug Rhodes, Norman Rhodes, Abigail Rice, Charles Richards, Melanie Richner, Paul Ridge, Nigel Riley, Mark Roberts, Pete Roberts, Martin Robinson, Elaine Robinson, David Robinson, Amanda Rogers, Jehann Romaya, Andy Rotherham, Dave Rowlett, Neil Rowswell, Glenn Rowswell, Vikki Rowswell, Jenny Royal, Nic Rudd, Andy Rudd, David Rule, Paul Rumbles, Clifford Runagall, Patrick Russell-Mott, Rusty, John Ryan, Jim Ryan, Steve Salvari, Sparky Marky & Sue Sanders, Sandixie In Absentia, Barry Savell, Paul Scarborough, Big Pete Scarff, Bud "Chook" Schneider, Andrew Scull, Martin Seagrove, Anne Seagrove, Andy Seddon, Neil Sedgwick, Diane Selby, Colin Michael Selby, "Wild" Willy Selka, June Shaw, Simon Sheard, Sally-Anne Sheard, Hannah Sheard, Emily Sheard, Ben Shearer, John "Lefty" Shelton, Nic Sheppard, Claire Sherwood, Colette Shirley, Roy Siggins, Dave Simmonds, Pete Simmonds, Lyn Simmonds, Clare Simmonds, Mike Simpson, Patrick Simpson, Andrea Sinfield, Gary Sinfield, Ann Singal, Paul "Skelly" Skelton, Sean Slevin, Dan Smith, Richard Smith, Roy Smith, June Smith, Helen Smith, Ian Smith, Karl Smith, Dan Smith, Peggy Smith, Gemma Smith, Debs Smith, Chris Smith, Josh Smith, Edward Smith, Beth Smith, Ian Smith, Maureen Smith, Robert Smith, Kathryn Smith, Tracey Smith, Fran Solez, Simon Rx Spencer, Claire Spencer, Richard Spencer, Linda "Funky Diva" Spicer, spock_gb, David Sprigg, Neil Stanley, Paul Stanley, Samantha Stanley, Glenn Stanley, Nick Stanning, Lyndsay Stanning, Alasdair Stark, Stuart Stark, Steve Stavrinou, Martin Steel, Paul Steel, Jane Stephens, Jo Stewart, Moira Stewart, Simon Stewart-Piercy, Keith Stockman, Gillian Stockman, Molly Stoker, Theresa Stoker, Kevin Stone, Steve Stone(d), Gideon Stott, Mike "Lemon Jelly" Street, Diane Strobl, Andy Struthers, Charles Stuart, Pete Sullivan, Ellie Surridge, Dave Surridge, Ian Swan, Alison Sweet, Sheldon Tamsett, Nancy Tamsett, Patrick Tarrant, Lewis Tassell, Krow Taton, Philip Tattershall, Martin Tatum, Keith Taylor, Karen Taylor, Graham Taylor, Thelston, Sorcha Thomson, Steve Thorn, Gina Thorn, Jo Thorn, Michael Thorn, Steve Thrift, Ticer, Mike Tiller, Martyn Timmis AKA Pank, Mark Joseph Timson, Alison Tindall, Rhiannon Tindall, Lindsey Tipler, Jill Tisch, Nigel "Neutron" Todhunter, Nigel "Neutron" Todhunter, Maureen Todhunter, Ruth Townsend, Tozer, Colin Trimmer, Anthony Troman, Jo Tucker, Lauren Tucker, D J Tummy, Paul Turner, David Turner, Julian Turner Bell, Roger "Touche" Turtle, Barrie Tykiff, Ruth Tykiff, Dave Tyrer, Anthony Van Cable, Malcolm Van Dyke, Debbie Van Koutrik, Kay Verity, Liz Viggars, Andy Vince, Elaine Wager, Nick Waldcock, Nicole Waldock, Angela Waldock, Steve Waldock, Julia Walker, Dave Walker, Lorraine Walker, Chris Wall, Sheila Wall, Doug Waller, Steve Walsh, Bryan Walsh, Kevin Walsh, Brian Walter, Debbie Walter, Paul Charles Edwin Watkins, Anne Watling, Dave Watson, Gazza Watson, Dr Eric Watts, Way Out To Woop Woop, Keith Waye, Bonnie Mai Webb, Doc Webb, Gail Webdell, Ian "Webby" Webdell, Tori Webdell, Adam "Titch" Webdell, Tony Weber, Chippy Welsh, Chief West, Gambit West, Janice Westbrook, Ian Whale, Wendy Whale, Sam Whale, Ben Whale, Joe Whale, P "Dolly" Wheeler, Fiona White, Kevin White, Stephen White, Tony White, Little Stevie Whitehead, Selene Widenbar, Caroline Wilkinson, Sarah Wilkinson, Brian J Williams, Adam Williams, Damien Williams, Andy "The Voice" Williamson, Irene Wilson, Kevin Winstanley, Karen Wintle, Sandie Winwright, Paul Wixon, Stephanie Wood, Sam Wood, Harry Wood, Lesley Wood, Chris Wood, Andy Wood, Tom Wood, Jack Wood, Mike Wood, Richard Woodbridge, Steve Woolfrey, Miss Sarah Emmie Woolie, Dawn Worsley, Neil Worsley, John Worsley, Dave Wright, Ms Corrinne Wright, Xav, Andy Young, Kev Young, and Sandy Young.

JOHN OTWAY DISCOGRAPHY 1991-2007

UK ALBUMS

CHERYL, A ROCK OPERA
John Otway & Attila the Stockbroker
Strike Back Records, SBR 46CD, 1991

Overture/A Wembley Central Encounter/
The Sensitivity Of The Broken Hearted/
The Sympathetic Response/Cheryl/
The Penny Drops/Our Room/Cheryl's Decline/
A More Romantic View/Cheryl's Going Home/
She's Gone! But Who's This?/
Boy In The Hood (Trainspotter Rap)/
A Misunderstanding/ A Solitary Tune/
Train Information/The Starlight Express/
The Unsympathetic Response/Finale/
Overture Reprise/The Last Word

UNDER THE COVERS AND OVER THE TOP
John Otway
Otway Records, OTWAY 1 CD, 1992

I Am The Walrus/Woodstock/I Will Survive/
Blockbuster/Theresa/Two Little Boys/Honey/
Je T'Aime Chose Savuage (I Love You Wild
Thing)/You Ain't Seen Nothing Yet/
Billy Don't Be A Hero/Space Oddity

LIVE!
John Otway And The Big Band
Amazing Feet Records, OTCD 4001, 1993

In Dreams/Misty Mountain/Cor Baby That's
Really Free/Bluey Green/ Racing Cars/
Beware Of The Flowers/Josephine/
Louisa On A Horse/Baby It's The Real Thing/
Two Little Boys/Best Dream/Frightened And
Scared/Cheryl's Going Home/House Of The
Rising Sun/Geneve

PREMATURE ADULATION
John Otway
Amazing Feet Records, OTCD 4004, 1995

Judgement Day/Poetry & Jazz/Duet/
We Know What She's Doing (She's In Love)/
The Saddest Sound Since The Blues/
Entertainment (Not)/Photograph/Please Don't
Read My Poetry/Nothing At All/God's Camera/
Willy (In The Air)/Typewriter

THE SET REMAINS THE SAME
John Otway And The Big Band
Otway Records, Way 3, 2000

Really Free/Beware Of The Flowers/Delilah/
Middle Of Winter/Body Talk/Too Much Air Not
Enough Oxygen/Bluey Green/Louisa On A
Horse/Poetry & Jazz/Baby, It's The Real Thing/
Best Dream/Cheryl's Going Home/Frightened
And Scared/Geneve/Two Little Boys

OT-AIR
The Album To Launch The World Tour
John Otway
Microstar, OTCD201, 2004

Ot-Air/Lasers Of Love/Only You Can Do That/
We Rock/Enjoy (It Just Won't Last)/
International Dateline/The Dream Makers/
Slack Jack/Three Kinds Of Magic/
Rumplestiltskin (Revisited)/The Old Fiddler
(Benny Hill Tribute)/Airport

BUNSEN BURNER : The Album
John Otway
Microstar, AMZT 4010, 2006

I'm Cured (And I Can't Catch Love)/
Rumplestiltskin/Pauline/We Know What She's
Doing (She's In Love)/My American Friend/
Crazy Horses/Bunsen Burner (The Hit Mix)/
A413 Revisited/Attractive To You/U R Breaking
Up/Deep Blue Water/Bunsen Burner vs
Burning Love/House Of The Rising Sun

COMPILATION ALBUMS

GREATEST HITS
John Otway
U-Vibe, OTWAYHITS02, 2002

Really Free/Beware Of The Flowers/Louisa On
A Horse/Josephine/Cheryl's Going Home/
DK 50-80/Body Talk/Best Dream/Delilah/
Too Much Air Not Enough Oxygen/Middle Of
Winter/God's Camera/Bunsen Burner (The Hit
Mix)/House Of The Rising Sun (Live At Abbey
Road)/Poetry & Jazz/Green Green Grass Of
Home/Headbutts/Geneve

SCRAPS: Curios & Curious
John Otway
As & Bs, demos, outtakes, rarities & live cuts
OTCD 4009, 2003 (3 CD Set)

CD1: Really Free (Polydor Jingle)/The
Highwayman (live)/Landslide (demo)/Misty
Mountain/Lonely Man (demo)/Beware Of The
Flowers/Running From The Law/Geneve (piano
version)/It's A Long Long Time Since I Heard
Homestead On The Farm/Julie, Julie, Julie/
Natasha (demo)/Travelling Show (demo)/
Cry Cry (demo)/Body Talk (demo)/The Man
Who Shot Liberty Valance (demo)/When
Love's In Bloom (demo)/Day After Day–21
Days (demo)/Are You On My Side?/What A
Women/Wednesday Club/Mine Tonight
CD2: Really Free (jingle)/The Turning Point/

Attila & Otway

CHERYL

A Rock Opera

UNDER THE TOP AND OVER THE TOP

john otway

JOHN OTWAY
Premature Adulation

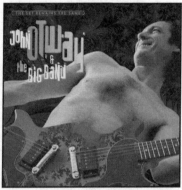

THE SET REMAINS THE SAME

JOHN OTWAY & the BIG BAND

THE ALBUM TO LAUNCH THE WORLD TOUR

OT AIR
John Otway

JOHN OTWAY
insen Burner
The Album

JOHN OTWAY
and the Big Band

Live!

Too Much Air Not Enough Oxygen/You Ain't Seen Nothing Yet/Dreaming Babies (demo)/It Makes Me See Red/Headbutts (jingle)/Headbutts (live)/Racing Cars (jingle)/Best Dream (jingle)/Auld Laing Sammy/Squeeky Bed/The Man I Am/Steely Dan (demo)/The Young And The Free/Fashion/The New Jerusalem/Down In The Flood/Catch The Wind/Whoops Apocalypse!/Bags Of Fun With Buster/Volunteer (demo)/I Believe (demo)/Down The Road (live)/21 Days (live)/American Radio Advert (jingle) CD3: Really Free (Capitol jingle)/Jackpot/Beware Of The Flowers/Too Much Air Not Enough Oxygen/It's Still Hard Breaking Up/I Am A Lion/Tiger's Island Rag/Poetry & Jazz/We Know What She's Doing/Saddest Sound Since The Blues (demo)/Entertainment (Not) (demo)/Tomorrow Never Comes/Eggy & The Chips (demo)/Photograph (demo)/Ever So Blue/Glasgow School Of Art/Hills Of Wales/Crazy Horses/Bunsen Burner (demo)

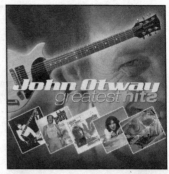

THE ULTIMATE AND THE PEN-ULTIMATE
John Otway
Microstar, AMZT 4009, 2006

CD1: Really Free/Louisa On A Horse/Josephine/Beware Of The Flowers/Poetry & Jazz/Bunsen Burner/We Rock/A413 Revisited/Cheryl's Going Home/Best Dream/God's Camera/Frightened And Scared/Rumplestiltskin/Too Much Air Not Enough Oxygen/Geneve
CD2: DK 50-80/Racing Cars/Bluey Green/Day After Day/Baby, It's The Real Thing/Whoops Apocalypse!/Last Of The Mohicans/Two Little Boys/I Am A Lion/Photograph/Delilah/I'm Cured (And I Can't Catch Love)/You Ain't Seen Nothing Yet/It's Still Hard Breaking Up/Old Fiddler

THE PATRON SAINT OF LOSERS – THE JOHN OTWAY ANTHOLOGY
John Otway
Castle Music, CMEDD 1566, 2007

CD1: Misty Mountain/Gypsy/Murder Man/If I Did/Louisa On A Horse/Bluey Green/Cheryl's Going Home/Racing Cars/Really Free/Beware Of The Flowers/Geneve/It A Long Long Time Since I Heard Homestead On The Farm/Remember The Alamo/Oh My Body Is Making Me/Josephine/Riders In The Sky–Running From The Law–Riders In The Sky/Can't Complain/Baby's In The Club/Frightened And Scared/Makes Good Music/Best Dream/DK 50-80/The Man Who Shot Liberty Valance
CD2: Green Green Grass Of Home/Headbutts/The Turning Point/Too Much Air Not Enough Oxygen/Baby, It's The Real Thing/In Dreams/The New Jerusalem/Whoops Apocalypse!/The Last Of The Mohicans/Blockbuster/You Ain't Seen Nothing Yet/Poetry & Jazz/God's Camera/Photograph/Bunsen Burner (The Hit Mix)/We Rock/Old Fiddler/Enjoy (It Just Won't Last)/I'm Cured (And I Can't Catch Love)/Rumplestiltskin/A413 Revisited/Crazy Horses/Beware Of The Flowers (Country Version)

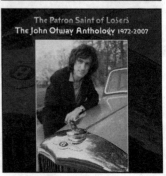

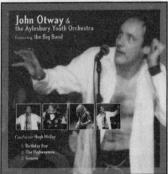

UK CD SINGLES & EPS

CHERYL/BOYS IN THE HOOD
John Otway & Attila the Stockbroker
Strike Back Records, SBR 45, 1991

**TWO LITTLE BOYS/I WILL SURVIVE/
JOSEPHINE/THE HIGHWAYMAN**
John Otway
Otway Records, OTWAY S1, 1992

**The Otway Sings Jones EP:
DELILAH/IT'S NOT UNUSUAL/
GREEN GREEN GRASS OF HOME**
John Otway
Strike Back Records, SBR 43CDS, 1995

**John Otway &
The Aylesbury Youth Orchestra EP:
BIRTHDAY BOY/THE HIGHWAYMAN/GENEVE**
John Otway & The Aylesbury Youth Orchestra
Otway Records, WAY S2, 1999

**BUNSEN BURNER (The Hit Mix)/
HOUSE OF THE RISING SUN/
A413 REVISITED**
John Otway
U-Vibe, OTWAY 02X, 2002

**BUNSEN BURNER (Even Hotter Mix)/
ATTRACTIVE TO YOU/
U R BREAKING UP**
John Otway
U-Vibe, OTWAY 02Y, 2002

**BUNSEN BURNER
(It's Not A Mix, It's A Compound)/
DEEP BLUE WATER/
BUNSEN BURNER Vs BURNING LOVE**
John Otway
U-Vibe, OTWAY 02Z, 2002

NO OFFENCE!
John Otway & Max Splodge
iTunes Download Track, 2007

DVD RELEASES

**BEWARE OF THE FLOWERS –
JOHN OTWAY LIVE**
John Otway
Cherry Red Records, CRDVD57, 2004

Live At The Square 1993
The Really Free Show 1997

**STRUNG TOGETHER –
LIVE AT THE RAM JAM CLUB
KINGSTON-UPON-THAMES**
John Otway & Wild Willy Barrett
Living Beat, LBET 51, 2007

MISCELLANEOUS

BACK FROM THE BIN!
John Otway
Free Promotional CD
for the Albert Hall Concert 1998

Natasha/It's Still Hard Breaking Up/It's A Long Long Time Since I Heard Homestead On The Farm/Best Dream/Travelling Show/Ever So Blue/Whoops Apocalypse!/Bluey Green/Blues Run The Game/In My Time Of Dying/Beware Of The Flowers (Country Version)/America Radio Advert/It Makes Me See Red/21 Days/I Am A Lion/Photograph/Mighty Quinn/Julie, Julie, Julie/Lonely Man/White Christmas/Geneve/Bags Of Fun With Buster

ABBEY ROAD – OTWAY SESSIONS EP
John Otway
Free Promotional CD, ABBEY 1, 2002

Crazy Horses/Country Flowers/Really Free/The Man Who Shot Liberty Valance/Josephine/Day After Day
Bonus Video: House Of The Rising Sun

THE YEAR OF THE HIT –
OFFICIAL HIT VOTING CD
John Otway
Free Voting CD, U-Vibe VOTE 1, 2002

I'm Cured (And I Can't Catch Love)/Rumplestiltskin/Poetry & Jazz/Beware Of The Flowers/Pauline/Geneve/Bunsen Burner/Too Much Air Not Enough Oxygen/Josephine/We Know What She's Doing (She's In Love)/My American Friend

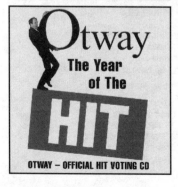

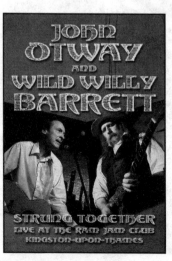

SOME INTERESTING CHARTS

The Viz TOP 10

No 1 BAGS OF FUN WITH BUSTER (Fulchester) £15.05
Johnny Japes & His Jesticles

2 BAGS OF FUN WITH BUSTER (Fulchester) £15.04
Johnny Japes & His Jesticles

3 BAGS OF FUN WITH BUSTER (Fulchester) £15.03
Johnny Japes & His Jesticles

4 BAGS OF FUN WITH BUSTER (Fulchester) £15.02
Johnny Japes & His Jesticles

5 BAGS OF FUN WITH BUSTER (Fulchester) £15.01
Johnny Japes & His Jesticles £15...(P.M...

6 WRAITH £14.83
Lonely (Cooking Vinyl)

7 S. E. ROGIE
Palm Wine Guitar Music (Tuff

8 A BETTER MOUSETRAP
Goodbye World (H...

9 THRILLED SKINNY
A Piece of Plastic

10 ENGINE
Well Oiled

June and beyond

June 6-7 Janet Jackson Wembley Arena, £22.50.

June 6-7 Elton John And Billy Joel Wembley Stadium, £37.50-£25.

June 10-12 Liza Minnelli Royal Albert Hall, £75-£15.

June 10▶ Shirley Bassey Royal Festival Hall, £34.50-£24.50. Also June 12, 13, 14, 16, 17, 18.

Aug 20 The Rolling Stones Wembley Stadium, £37.50, £30. CC 0990 321 321.

Oct 17 Motorhead Brixton Academy, £12.

Oct 30 John Otway Royal Albert Hall, £22.50-£10.95.

Nov 28 Tom Jones Wembley Arena, £23.

▶ Before a day, denotes final date. After a day, denotes subsequent dates.

SINGLES

UKCHARTS · BBC RADIO 1 97-99fm · TOP OF THE POPS

1 (1) THE LONG AND WINDING ROAD/SUSPICIOUS MINDS Will Young & Gareth Gates — s

(2) 2 DOWN BOY Holly Valance — London

3 (3) COMPLICATED Avril Lavigne — Arista

(4) 4 DOWN 4 U Irv Gotti pts Ja Rule, Ashanti, C Baltimore & Vita — Murder Inc/Def Jam

4 (5) JUST LIKE A PILL Pink — Arista

(6) 6 MY VISION Jakatta feat. Seal — Rulin

2 (7) LITTLE BY LITTLE/SHE IS LOVE Oasis — Big Brother

5 (8) THE TIDE IS HIGH (GET THE FEELING) Atomic Kitten — Innocent

(9) 9 BUNSEN BURNER John Otway — U-vibe

7 (10) WHAT I GO TO SCHOOL FOR Busted — Universal

NATION'S FAVOURITE LYRICS

1. Imagine John Lennon
2. Angels Robbie Williams
3. Bohemian Rhapsody Queen
4. I am the Walrus The Beatles
5. Millennium Robbie Williams
6. Yesterday The Beatles
7. Beware of the Flowers John Otway
8. Sit Down James
9. Nights in White Satin Moody Blues
10. Stardust Hoagy Carmichael

"Imagine", John Lennon
Imagine there's no Heaven
It's easy if you try
No Hell below us
Above us only sky
Imagine all the people
living for today ...

"Angels", Robbie W...
And throug...
offers me...
a lot of ...
whe...
w...

Number of ballot papers returned:
Number of papers found to be invalid (blank/spoilt): ... 1
Thus, total number of valid papers to be counted: ... 1,383 / 1,382

Result:-

Bunsen Burner .... THE HIT
Beware of the Flowers 378
We Know What She's Doing 345
Poetry & Jazz 172
Too Much Air and Not Enough Oxygen 112
I'm Cured 98
Rumplestiltskin 89
Geneve 75
Pauline 56
American Friend 28
Josephine 16
 13

205